AF271384

NOV 1 6 2007

MAIN LIBRARY

DEMCO

# HOW THE SOUTH JOINED
# THE GAMBLING NATION

# HOW THE SOUTH JOINED THE GAMBLING NATION

The Politics of State Policy Innovation

**MICHAEL NELSON** AND **JOHN LYMAN MASON**

WITH A FOREWORD BY **THEODORE J. LOWI**

Louisiana State University Press ❧ Baton Rouge

Published by Louisiana State University Press
Copyright © 2007 by Louisiana State University Press
All rights reserved
Manufactured in the United States of America
First printing

Designer:  Barbara Neely Bourgoyne
Typeface:  Adobe Caslon Pro, text; Gotham, display
Printer and binder:  Edwards Brothers, Inc.

Library of Congress Cataloging-in-Publication Data

Nelson, Michael, 1949–
    How the South joined the gambling nation : the politics of
state policy innovation / Michael Nelson and John Lyman Mason ;
with a foreword by Theodore J. Lowi.
        p. cm.
    Includes bibliographical references and index.
    ISBN 978-0-8071-3254-8 (cloth : alk. paper)
    1. Gambling—Southern States.   2. Gambling—Government policy—
Southern States.   I. Mason, John Lyman.   II. Title.
HV6721.S68N45 2007
363.4'2—dc22

                                        2006036557

# CONTENTS

# FOREWORD

On Whose Side—The Angels or the Agents?

In the wake of the influential and controversial investigation of organized crime by Tennessee senator Estes Kefauver in the early 1950s, President Truman, during his many post-presidential campus visits, was frequently asked, "Why no national lottery?" Truman would first refer to Kefauver as "cow fever" and would then let fly against the hypocrisy of "hard-shell" Americans, concluding with his own wager that if we adopted a national lottery we would "wipe out the national debt in no time." Nobody took him up on the wager.

We have come a long way since then—but from what to what? American society has made a number of ethical leaps, which we could say began with the biggest ethical leap of all, the Civil War and the abolition of slavery. The Emancipation did not exactly free the slaves: they only managed to move from slavery to serfdom. But—and this is a big but—no longer could there be any moral defense of treating human beings as chattel.

The spread of legal gambling is one of the more recent ethical leaps. Our authors here report that, in 1960, no state had an authorized lottery. By 1990, thirty-six states had legalized lotteries and, in fact, had to go to the extraordinary trouble of changing their constitutions for the purpose. Four other states allowed casino gambling. Only two of those forty states were southern. But by 2006, all but two of the southern states—Alabama and Arkansas—had made the leap. And that is the story of this book.

It is a political story. And it is a classic story because it involves a struggle between morality and utility—between the angels and the agents. We Americans consider ourselves free of that sort of thing, because we define politics as "the art of the possible" and "the art of compromise" within one grand national consensus. Every American claims to be middle class and middle of the road; we could almost add that, as in Lake Woebegon, all our children are above average. We are thus exempt from the elevated moral struggles of antiquity, as dramatized by Shakespeare and his ilk. Yet, it is worth repeating that the politics of gambling is only one of the more recent American morality plays. America has a history of alternating moments of morality versus utility, sin versus error, principles versus consequences.

A story very much related to the sin of gambling that took place a generation earlier is that of alcohol. To people of strict principle, alcohol and gambling are sins; they are not rated among the seven deadly sins, but too much indulgence in either could surely lead in that direction. These somewhat lesser sins are what social scientists call *countermores*. Harold Lasswell defines these as "culture traits [recognized] as deviations ... and yet are expected to occur ... A certain volume of countermores activities are thus 'normal' (in both a statistical and normative sense), and must be included by the casual observer as part of the culture" (Harold D. Lasswell and Abraham Kaplan, *Power and Society,* 1952, pp. 49–50). Even when prohibited by law and opposed by community opinion, countermores are widespread and knowingly tolerated. And for this reason the alcohol story is a fitting introduction to the gambling story, especially interesting because the prohibition of the production and sale of alcohol is the only constitutional amendment that was an act of legislation. All of the other amendments to the U.S. Constitution were concerned with additions and subtractions in the distribution of power—between the branches, between the nation and the states, and between the nation and citizens. And the prohibition amendment is the only amendment that was eliminated by a succeeding amendment.

The end of national prohibition was the beginning of a new round of moral politics of alcohol in the states, because the erasing of the prohibition freed each state to "stay dry" or "go wet;" and most states outside the south went wet. For a very long time (especially as measured by the thirsty), Mississippi went dry and stayed dry. But all during that epoch, there were signs posted in the windows of innumerable restaurants and highway service stations with the notice: "We pay state liquor tax." This was a case of countermores— the struggle between sin and error, with sin in retreat.

The struggle in Alabama was quite different, but in the same direction. Alabama adopted a constitutional amendment ordaining that the state of

Alabama would "stay dry," *provided however* that each county would have the option to "go wet" by referendum. This was an ingenious resolution of the issue, the invention of a sort of intra-state federalism, avoiding the imposition of a single moral regime by permitting the majority in each county to have its way. The struggle between sin and error, angels and agents, was articulated as "acceptance without embrace," but even so, that is a very large ethical leap from morality policy to instrumental policy. Philosophers might call it "situational ethics."

This ethical transformation in alcohol, with Mississippi and Alabama accepting the countermores in two different ways, cannot be explained as the product of a particular causal force. The superior explanation has to be Darwinian rather than simple causation, because the entire ethical environment had been changing in a manner that was more hospitable than ever before toward the countermores. This development in the environment reaches back at least to the Civil War, if not before. For example, during the second half of the nineteenth century, tort law had become the dominant method of resolving disputes over who was to blame for an injury. The number of injury cases had been growing at an exponential rate as mechanization was incorporated into virtually all manufacturing and transportation. But by that very same development, tort began to decline precipitously as injury cases were too frequent and too complex to rely exclusively on the rule that for every injury there has to be a determination as to who is to blame: "no liability without fault." In addition to the multiplicity of cases, the spread of absentee ownership increased the complexity by an order of magnitude.

Another factor in the turn away from notions of strict liability was the emergence of liability insurance: Give up resort to courts, witnesses, and testimony to determine blame and fault; just hold the defendant/perpetrator blame-free and indemnify the victim. Liability insurance had been considered immoral well into the nineteenth century, because it violated the absolute-morality approach to obligation. As late as the 1370s, the U.S. Supreme Court could still hold that "a common carrier could not contract out of liability for negligence" (Morton Horowitz, *The Transformation of American Law, 1780-1860*, 1977, vol. I, p. 206). Yet, even as the Supreme Court spoke, the industry of "liability insurance" was taking hold and beginning to thrive. Only a moment's reflection is enough to appreciate the distance of the moral leap between, on one side, the tort with blame and fault, and, on the other, liability as an economic good subject to estimation, probablility, bargaining, and contract.

A parallel development, with equal ethical significance, is life insurance, which brings us much closer to an environment hospitable to a utilitarian approach to the gambling industry, as dealt with in this book. During the 1850s, life insurance was showing signs of growth as an industry, but its growth as a "safety net" depended upon the development of two environmental factors. The first was the reconstruction of American values toward the morality of life insurance itself. Throughout the period from the 1840s through the 1870s, the trust side of banking flourished and its cousin, life insurance, floundered; the reason given was that people "regarded it as wicked to insure their lives" (Viviana A. R. Zelizer, *Morals and Markets: The Development of Life Insurance in the United States*, 1979, p. 5). Another observation very much in on point is that "[t]o many . . . the very suggestion of a proposal to insure one's life appears . . . objectionable . . . on moral grounds that it looks like a wager, a bet or[,]. . . appealing to the doctrine of chances, it partakes of the nature of gambling." (Zelizer, p. 68) The second factor is most concisely presented by Nobel economist Douglass North: The successful innovation of life insurance in the United States "awaited the construction of an adequate mortality table" (quoted in Zelizer, p. 13). Nothing could be more utilitarian than that: the science of economics, probability, and the dollar value of risk.

Another spectacularly important contribution to an environment hospitable to a utilitarian over a moral approach to policy was the discovery and validation of the germ theory of the contraction and spread of disease. The mere mention of the story of Typhoid Mary makes it clear that by the end of the nineteenth century there was another step toward a utilitarian definition of obligation. The science of disease implied that we are all murderers and we are all victims. Where once each new communicable disease (or epidemic) was a visitation of God against a sinful humanity, the new response was to search for etiology, treatment, and cure.

While these environmental factors were encouraging Americans to adjust their Calvinist ways to the situation at hand, there were of course moral reactions against every step toward materialism, relativism, and the call to "do what thou wilt." And the moral reaction against gambling as such was expanding by leaps and bounds. Lotteries and other types of organized gambling were being outlawed as "contrary to God's law" under the rationale that gambling separates wealth from work, "the sweat of one's brow." By 1840, twelve of the twenty-six states had made lotteries illegal (Zelizer, p. 67). By the end of the next few years, twenty-four states had legalized lotteries, but by 1860, twenty-one of these twenty-four had banned organized gambling. There was another serious moral movement organized against the expansion of gambling in the 1890s, when lotteries were again legally banned in all of the states, and over twenty of the states were making legalization all the more difficult by banning, through constitutional amendment, all forms of gambling.

Gambling has been only one of the great irritants against the American moral code, but it is a powerful lens through which to observe the rhythm of American politics—or, we could say, the rhythm between politics and its rejection, because, from its origin as a concept in Greek antiquity, politics means talk, talk outside the household (the domain of economics) and in the agora. Moral reaction trumps politics. Principle silences process. Yet, it is impressive how often politics in America prevails, not by corrupting moral discourse but by converting moral commands into policy innovation. "Policy entrepreneur" has become a pejorative term when, in fact, it is a role essential to democracy, more of art than of magic, more akin to Michelangelo than to Machiavelli. Like Michelangelo, the policy entrepreneur takes the shapeless marble of moral principle and chips away the excess rock to reveal the sculpture within.

Nelson and Mason have revived the case study as a method of generating scientific data while maintaining the context of experience and knowledge. Back in the 1950s, the case study was flourishing; it even had it own institution, the Interuniversity Case Program, which sponsored publication of cases, ranging from public administration to policy formulation to civil-military relations to Congress and representation, and so forth. Inevitably, the authors and their critics agreed on a single question: How can we generalize from the case studies? In other words, how can we escape the uniqueness of each story?

Although there is no simple answer to the question, Nelson and Mason have provided an inspiring approach. Their first step was to create not one but a cluster of cases that revolve around the same problem or phenomenon. The second was to formulate a schedule or protocol of questions to pose with rigid observance to each of the stories. Granted, case studies of seven southern states do not produce a "large N." But the repetition of patterns across seven mini-states with known histories and parameters provides an unusually strong basis for the regularities and exceptions that are essential to any science. The cases also incorporate a very large slice of history, a strength that no cross-sectional analysis of large N can improve upon. For example, the authors turn up patterns of policy innovation through "diffusion" across state lines that put substance, orderliness, and specificity to the contention going back as far at least to Brandeis that "states are the laboratories of democracy."

Another less-appreciated contribution of these case studies is their recognition of the *intra*-state federalism: Several states managed, through "policy entrepreneurs," to finesse the polarization between the moralists and the utilitarians over casino gambling by introducing "county option," delegating to each county the decision by referendum. Other states succeeded in a modified approach to gambling by setting up regulatory commissions to license some counties and not others. And those states facing a movement for a state lottery finessed the ethical divide by providing a state referendum to authorize a state referendum on the simple question of yea and nay to lotteries. By such means, many representatives from strong conservative constituencies could maintain their personal opposition to gambling while voting in favor of the right of citizens to vote on the question. This is the way some counties and states at large could make an end run around the power of principle. And finally, although the argument between angels and agents was unremitting, in the end the utilitarian side won in all but two cases by clothing utility in the virtually moral position that the income from sin would be earmarked for education.

If I were writing a review of this book, I would probably criticize the authors for not exploiting the cases as fully as they could have. But from the perspective of writing a foreword, I can say in full confidence that the incomplete exploitation is a measure of the richness of the source. Their prodigious work for the cluster of cases that this book comprises is a genuine service to the profession of political science as well as the craft of democratic politics.

THEODORE J. LOWI

# ACKNOWLEDGMENTS

This book has been seven years in the making. It originated in the friendship of the authors and in the intellectual curiosity that Jay Mason and I shared about how Mississippi, of all states, had become the center of casino gambling in the American heartland and how Georgia had developed the most imitated state lottery in the country. We set out to write an article (and did—thanks, by the way, to *Political Science Quarterly* for permission to draw on "The Politics of Gambling in the South" from the Winter 2004 issue in chapters 1 and 2). We ended up writing this book, which also incorporates the experiences of Alabama, Arkansas, Louisiana, South Carolina, and Tennessee. Between the two of us, Jay and I have lived in a majority of the southern states, and we made research trips to all of the states we chose to include. For family reasons, Jay entered the business world in 2002, and at that point I assumed full responsibility for finishing the research, writing, and editing of the book.

Along the way, Jay and I have drawn on the time, talents, expertise, memories, and in some cases the checkbooks of many in the course of doing the research for and writing of this book. For financial support, we thank Penn Owen III, the Rhodes College Faculty Development Committee, and in my case, the Boyle and Fulmer chairs in political science at Rhodes, both of which I have occupied. For relevant research by Rhodes students doing their own projects, we thank Nathan Ryan (Alabama), Chris Hathorn (Arkansas), Meredith Davis (Louisiana), Chris Ebersole (Mississippi), Dan Calvert (Tennessee), and Katie Frink (Tennessee). For careful and helpful critical readings of the manuscript, we thank Steve Ceccoli of Rhodes College and Wayne Parent of Louisiana State University. For access to helpful information on various aspects of the project, we thank Henry Stokes of the *Memphis Commercial Appeal*, Dean Hestermann of Harrah's, and John Branston of the *Memphis Flyer*. For encouragement at the initial stage of this book, we thank Henry Tom of Johns Hopkins University Press, and for help at every subsequent stage we thank several people at LSU Press: MaryKatherine Callaway, John Easterly, and Julia Smith.

Finally, we thank all those who graciously consented to interviews for this book:

Mississippi: Ray Mabus, Sonny Merideth, Charlie Williams, Gary Burhop, Paul Jones, Wilson Carroll, and Bobby Long

Georgia: Bill Shipp, Jack Black, and William T. Neal

South Carolina: Kevin Geddings, Jim Ritchie, Scott Richardson, Kathy Bigham, and Aaron Sheinen

Alabama: Rick Dent, Milo Dakin, John Rogers, Joe Bob Mizzell, and Jim Cooper

Tennessee: Lamar Alexander, Ned McWherter, Steve Cohen, Matt Kisber, Roy Herron, Tom Humphrey, M. Lee Smith, and John Ryder

Arkansas: Larry Page, Scott Trotter, and Jay Barth

Louisiana: Buddy Roemer, Ken Ward, and Raymond LaLonde

Our deepest thanks go to our families for their patience and support through the long process of researching and writing this book. We dedicate this book to them: Linda, Michael, and Sam Nelson, and Disa, Sarah, John, and Thomas Mason.

MICHAEL NELSON

# HOW THE SOUTH JOINED
# THE GAMBLING NATION

# THE SOUTH JOINS
# THE GAMBLING NATION

The near half-century that has elapsed since 1964 has seen numerous and dramatic transformations in American politics and public policy. The roster of changes is no less impressive for being familiar. Electoral politics has been transformed by the new plebiscitary character of the parties' presidential nominating processes, the increased variety and importance of political media and money, and the ideological polarization of the two major political parties fostered mainly by the shift of the South from solidly Democratic to reliably Republican. In foreign policy, the era has been defined by defeat in the Vietnam War, victory in the Cold War, and a still-unfolding war on terrorism whose outcome remains uncertain. Domestic policy has been dramatically altered by the Great Society, the extension of civil rights protection to a wide range of groups, and the tax-cutting fervor of the Ronald Reagan and George W. Bush administrations.

What all of these transformations have in common is their national character. Many of the most important changes even in state politics and policy that have occurred in this era were initiated in Washington. Congress and a succession of presidents have influenced nearly every activity of state government by offering carrots in the form of federal grants and wielding sticklike federal mandates. Supreme Court decisions concerning legislative reapportionment, abortion, criminal justice, affirmative action, eminent domain, and other vital matters have wrought further massive changes in the states.

Well below the radar screen of the national news media and the Washington-focused scholarly community, however, the American landscape has been transformed in another important way by states acting on their own initiative. State by state, the United States has become a gambling nation. A national map of gambling policy in 1963 would show one state, Nevada, with legalized commercial casino gambling. Today's map shows eleven commercial casino states. The 1963 map would show no states with lotteries. Today's map shows forty-one lottery states plus the District of Columbia. In 1963 forty-nine of the fifty states allowed neither casino nor lottery gambling. Today only six states have neither casinos nor a lottery.

In every instance of gambling legalization, a state government, largely uninfluenced by the federal government in Washington, made a conscious decision to create a lottery, allow commercial casinos, or both. Although these decisions have been influenced by social and economic considerations, each was the result of the state's political process. In many cases, the decisions had the largely unexpected consequence of clearing a legal path for Native American tribes to operate casinos or high-stakes bingo halls on their sovereign lands located within the boundaries of individual states.

Legalized casino and lottery gambling is not a new phenomenon in the American experience, but it has been an episodic one.[1] Scholars refer to the recent spread of lotteries and casinos in the United States as gambling's "third wave." The first wave began during the colonial era. All thirteen colonies licensed private brokers, universities, and even churches to conduct raffle-style lotteries to raise funds for worthy causes, including the construction of buildings at Harvard and Yale, support for American troops during the Revolutionary War, and, after independence was won, internal improvements such as the Erie Canal. Casinos licensed by the city of New Orleans were part of what the United States acquired in the Louisiana Purchase, and riverboat gambling subsequently flourished along the Mississippi River. By the mid-nineteenth century, however, most lotteries had lost their civic purpose and become profit-making (and sometimes corrupt) enterprises. Casinos degenerated in like manner. In 1835, for example, mobs in Vicksburg, Mississippi, burned the city's gambling halls and lynched five allegedly crooked professional gamblers. Eastern Puritans and Quakers and frontier evangelists had never liked legalized gambling. Their ranks were swelled during the early nineteenth century by reformers who included gambling with slavery, drinking, harsh prison conditions, and other social problems as fit objects for abolition. By 1860, legal casinos were confined to the frontier. Twenty-one of the twenty-four states that once allowed lotteries had banned them.

In banning the first-wave lotteries, some states chose to rely not on legislation, which could be easily repealed, but on their constitutions. As a delegate argued at New York's 1821 constitutional convention, "Legislatures were always under a strong temptation to resort to lotteries as a mode of raising revenue; and from a temptation to which it was more than probable that they would yield, the constitution should preserve them. Lotteries, although taxes in effect, were not so in appearance and form . . . and could therefore be laid without any hazard to the popularity of those by whom they were imposed."[2]

The second wave of states legalizing gambling occurred during the late nineteenth century. This wave was less tidal than the first—it was a mostly southern phenomenon and was generally confined to lotteries. Bereft of most other revenue sources, some of the defeated Confederate states revived the practice of authorizing private companies to conduct lotteries and taxing the proceeds. The largest of these by far was the Louisiana Lottery Company, which rapidly extended its operations throughout the entire country. The national network of railroads and telegraphs that recently had been developed allowed the Louisiana lottery—"the Serpent" to its critics—to market its games through the mail and in branch offices connected to headquarters by wire. Ninety percent of Louisiana lottery tickets were sold outside Louisiana.

The other states, distressed by the amount of money flowing over their borders into Louisiana, pressured the federal government to crack down. So did antigambling reformers in the burgeoning Progressive movement. In the 1890s Congress passed its first (and only) antilottery statutes. A federal law enacted in 1890 forbade the postal system to deliver mail referring to lotteries, and an 1895 statute barred all lottery activity from interstate commerce. After 1894, not a single state permitted lotteries to operate legally. All but nine states included lottery prohibitions in their constitutions. Opposition to the lottery as a species of gambling spread to incorporate the entire genus: by 1920, nearly all forms of gambling were illegal throughout the country. Indeed, Arizona and New Mexico were forced to outlaw casinos as a condition of achieving statehood.

The third wave of legalized lottery and casino gambling began in the 1960s and, several decades later, has not abated. Although a number of cash-starved states authorized pari-mutuel wagering on horse and dog racing during the Great Depression, only Nevada legalized casinos. The state bans on lotteries lasted until New Hampshire created a lottery in 1964, followed by New York in 1967. In the 1970s, the lottery dam broke: twelve states, mostly in the Northeast, legalized lottery gambling. During the 1980s, seventeen states and the District of Columbia, representing a majority of every region of the country except the South, followed suit. Since 1990 nine more states, six of them southern, have created lotteries. Indeed, as of 2006 only nine states remain without one: Arkansas, Mississippi, Alabama, Utah, Nevada, Wyoming, Oklahoma, Hawaii, and Alaska. The spread of commercial casino gambling occurred later in the third wave—New Jersey legalized casinos in the 1970s, then nine more states followed suit in the late 1980s and 1990s—and has been geographically focused in the nation's heartland, especially in states along the Mississippi River. Moving on a separate legal track that chiefly (and uniquely) involved the federal government and various tribal governments, casinos have opened on Native American lands in twenty-five states.[3]

Several things distinguish the current wave of legalized gambling from the previous two. First, contemporary lotteries are now owned and operated by state governments, not licensed by them to private firms or charitable institutions. Since New Hampshire sold its first lottery ticket in a modestly marketed raffle-style game, these lotteries have evolved into a congeries of aggressively advertised, widely available, often instantly playable games. Two large groups of states have banded some of their games together into consortia (Powerball and Mega Millions, respectively) that sometimes offer prizes of several hundred million dollars. Although modern casinos are taxed and regulated more heavily by the states than the casinos of the eighteenth and nineteenth centuries, they are still commercial enterprises. With the creation of third-wave lotteries, however, the states entered the business of encouraging people to gamble and profiting directly from the results.

Second, the politics of gambling legalization in the third wave has involved the voters more directly than in the past. In the first two waves, legislatures were the sole arena of state lawmaking. Over the course of the nineteenth century, most of them voted to add to their constitutions bans on lotteries and sometimes on all games of chance. The Progressive Era, however, brought the voters directly into most states' constitution-making process by requiring that amendments be approved at the ballot box, usually after the legislature endorsed them but sometimes at the voters' initiative. As a result, thirty of the forty-one current lottery states and four of the eleven commercial casino states had to secure the voters' approval in order to change their constitutions and admit these new forms of gambling.

Finally, and most interestingly, the South, which was a full participant and sometimes a pace setter during the first two waves of gambling legalization, was the slowest region to embrace the current wave. By 1988, after Florida and Virginia became the first southern states to create lotteries, nearly three-fourths of the nonsouthern states already had done so. As for casinos, only the two southern states that have the greatest historical and cultural roots in nineteenth-century casino and riverboat gambling, Mississippi and Louisiana, have legalized commercial casinos. Indian casinos and high-stakes bingo halls operated by tribal governments on tribal lands are even scarcer, largely because of the paucity of such lands in the South. Of the more than 350 Indian gambling facilities in the country, only eighteen (5 percent) are located in southern states.[4]

## WHAT WE KNOW AND DON'T KNOW ABOUT
## THE POLITICS OF GAMBLING

The politics of gambling during the third wave has not gone unstudied. Although important gaps remain in our understanding of the subject, excellent research has been conducted by economists and, especially, political scientists attempting to explain why some states have embraced legalized gambling and others have not. For the most part, these studies have focused on lotteries or casinos but not, as this book does, on both.

### Lotteries

Scholars have found that a state's decision whether to create a lottery is influenced in part by characteristics particular to the state itself. Some of these are demographic: for example, a state with a high percentage of Roman Catholics (whose version of Christianity is generally tolerant of gambling) and a low percentage of fundamentalists (whose version of Christianity is not) is more likely to adopt a lottery than a state whose religious composition is different.[5] Some characteristics are rooted in a state's history. States that already allow racetrack betting or charitable bingo are more likely to embrace a lottery than states with no such history.[6] Other important state characteristics are explicitly political. A divided government—that is, a government in which the governor's party does not control the state legislature—is more prone to enact a lottery than a united one because "divided governments lack the political resources to increase unpopular mandatory taxes and must instead settle for a less controversial lottery adoption."[7] A state's economic characteristics also matter. For example, states with wealthier populations are more likely to adopt a lottery, again because of their citizens' unusually strong aversion to higher taxes.[8]

In addition to these characteristics of the states themselves, scholars have found that state governments are influenced in their decisions about lottery gambling by the actions of other states, especially those with which they share a border. Considering the corruption-riddled history of lotteries during the first two waves of legalized gambling, many states needed to be assured that lotteries could be run honestly. The corruption-free experience of the first few lottery states of the third wave provided this assurance. More important, perhaps, because money flows out of a state when its people cross the state line to gamble (and usually lose) in a neighboring lottery state, states with lotteries on their borders have a strong incentive to adopt lotteries of their own, however reluctant they may be to do so. The greater the number of lottery states that border on a state, the more likely it is to adopt a lottery.[9]

Finally, campaigns to create lotteries in the various states are furthered by the presence of pro-lottery "policy entrepreneurs"—energetic advocates with the ability "to define the issue in ways that energize their allies and put their opponents to sleep," or perhaps even "persuade their opponents to change their position."[10] For example, a state inclined to reject a lottery that has been promoted as just another way to raise money for the government might embrace his idea if the lottery's chief advocate designates the revenue for a popular purpose such as economic development or, more typically, education.

### Casinos

Many fewer states have legalized commercial casino gambling than have created lotteries, providing strong prima facie evidence that the politics of casino legalization is the more arduous. Indeed, the first study of casino politics, conducted by John Dombrink and William Thompson in the late 1980s, argued that if even one important political factor in a state was adverse to legalization, any campaign to authorize casino gambling there would fail.[11]

At the time of their study, Nevada and New Jersey were the only two casino states, and serious campaigns for casino legalization had recently fallen short in twelve states.

No sooner was Dombrink and Thompson's research completed, however, than a cascade of states, most of them (Iowa, Illinois, Mississippi, Louisiana, and Missouri) along the Mississippi River, decided to legalize, regulate, and tax commercial casinos. Using statistical models, Patrick Pierce and Donald Miller found that, as with lotteries, the presence of neighboring casino states attracting gamblers across the border makes it more likely that a state will legalize casinos of its own. So does the presence of a lottery within a state, mostly because state politicians who weather the storm of a lottery adoption campaign are less likely to fear a political backlash from legalizing another form of gambling. Finally, Pierce and Miller concluded, "The existence of a horse racing industry in the state significantly deters casino legalization." Because racetracks and casinos "appeal to largely overlapping markets," track owners and others who depend on horse racing for their livelihood fight hard to keep casinos out of their states.[12]

### Gaps in the Research

The existing research on the politics of gambling, although excellent in the main, is far from complete. What we know is rivaled by what we don't know. Although lottery and casino gambling have been matters of contemporaneous political debate in many states, for the most part they have been studied separately. As a result, scholars have very little to say about how, for example, a state's consideration of lottery legalization might affect its simultaneous consideration of whether to authorize casino gambling. Most southern states that have considered a lottery considered casinos at approximately the same time, but with varying effects. In Tennessee, for example, the adoption of a lottery foreclosed the possibility of casino legalization. In Arkansas, gambling advocates' focus on casinos has long stifled efforts to enact a lottery. As we will see in the subsequent chapters, some important aspects of the politics of gambling, including the influence of state constitutions, have been neglected or slighted by studies that look at lotteries and casinos in isolation from each other.

A second gap in the research is what we call the *after-politics* of gambling legalization. A state's decision to create a lottery or legalize casinos, which has been the focus of the existing studies, is not the end of the story. Such a decision often sets in motion a series of controversies about how and where the new form of gambling will operate, who will share in the proceeds, and how it will be implemented. Georgia's decision to create a lottery, for example, triggered an ongoing debate about how the benefits should be distributed. Louisiana's after-politics even extended to the trial, conviction, and sentencing of a former governor who took an improperly active role in assigning casino licenses.

Finally, the particularities of the politics of gambling in the South have been overlooked. As we have seen, the South has lagged behind the rest of the nation during the third wave of gambling legalization. Yet nearly all of the existing research ends in the 1980s, before the South became the main arena of gambling politics.[13] Even Pierce and Miller's study of casino legalization, which extends to the mid-1990s, treats all states the same, regardless of region. As a result, some of their general findings—for example, that the presence of horse racing in a state is a barrier to casinos, and the presence of a lottery is a spur—do not apply very well to the South. The racing industry has been the main advocate of casino gambling in Alabama and Arkansas, for example, and casino legalization in Mississippi not only occurred in the absence of a lottery but actually turned the political tide against one.

## UNDERSTANDING THE POLITICS OF GAMBLING IN THE SOUTH

The politics of gambling in the South provides the substantive focus of this book: why individual states made the choices they did about whether to legalize gambling and, if so, in what form or forms. Our theoretical focus is on the larger phenomenon of state policy innovation. We draw on the innovation literature in political science, which is extensive and excellent, in explaining what southern states have done, and we contribute to that literature. In doing so, we employ the case-study method.

### Theory: State Policy Innovation

Although the existing studies of lottery and casino legalization discussed above have used different methodologies, the similarities among them are striking from the standpoint of state policy innovation theory. The *internal characteristics* of each state that has considered legalizing gambling emerged in all of these studies as significant influences on lottery and casino politics. So, in most cases, did what scholars call *diffusion*—that is, the influence of what other states were doing in the realm of gambling policy. The role of *policy entrepreneurs*—enterprising advocates of lotteries or casinos—also has been judged important in some studies. As such, scholars have been led to incorporate the leading models of state policy innovation in their research: diffusion, internal characteristics, and policy entrepreneurship.

*Diffusion.* The diffusion theory of state policy innovation, as introduced in 1969 by political scientist Jack Walker, posits that "the likelihood of a state adopting a new program is higher if other states have already adopted the idea," especially if "the innovation has been adopted by a state viewed by key decision makers as a point of legitimate comparison," usually a "regional pace setter."[14] In Walker's view, states facing a common problem look to each other for examples of successful solutions, looking especially hard at states that are close enough to seem comparable. When Wisconsin adopted worker's compensation, for example, Michigan, Minnesota, and other nearby states were inspired to follow suit.

What we have found in studying the politics of gambling, however, is that not all diffusion is as straightforward as in Walker's understanding of the phenomenon. For a variety of reasons, a policy may be reinvented in the course of being adopted. The later adopter has the benefit of the earlier adopters' experiences with the policy, including flaws that it may wish to correct. The balance of political forces within the later adopter may be different, meaning that changes must be made in the policy as the price of securing its enactment.[15] "Local pride of ownership" in a borrowed state's policy innovation also may lead to reinvention "so that it appears to be a local product."[16] Louisiana, for example, followed Mississippi in legalizing casino gambling, but instead of letting the market decide how many water-based casinos would operate, as Mississippi did, Louisiana fixed the number of floating casino licenses at fifteen. We call this process of adapting while adopting *incremental* diffusion.

Diffusion also may be *anticipatory*—that is, a state may decide to adopt a policy innovation for fear that another state will make that innovation less desirable by adopting it first. In the early 1990s, for example, it was clear to Mississippi lawmakers that if their state did not legalize casino gambling before Louisiana did, Mississippi's ability to attract the casino industry to their state would be much diminished.

Finally, a state may experience diffusion *overload* in its consideration of a new public policy. Overload occurs when a surfeit of popular competing alternatives inspired by neighboring states prevents any one of them from being adopted. In the mid 1990s, for example, west Tennesseans' desire for Mississippi-style casinos clashed with east and middle Tennesseans' desire for a Georgia-style lottery. The result was that neither policy was adopted for nearly a decade.

As we see in the chapters that follow, diffusion theory and all of its variations are critical in explaining the politics of gambling in the South. So is *anti-diffusion,* a further refinement of the theory that emerges from our research into the southern states' experience. Sometimes state political actors will fight to keep a nearby state from adopting a new policy so that they can preserve their regional monopoly on its benefits. Mississippi casino interests, for example, hired a Nashville lobbyist to try to talk the Tennessee legislature out of adopting a lottery.

*Internal characteristics.* In considering policy innovations, a state does not simply respond to what other states are doing. Characteristics of the state itself also affect its approach to new ideas. Much of the existing scholarly research places a state's economic characteristics first in order of importance, especially the availability of "slack resources" (that is, unobligated revenues) to fund new policies. Political characteristics of the state, such as a culture favorable to government solutions and elections in which truly competitive political parties must seek votes by promising new programs, foster innovation. Social characteristics such as the education, urbanism, and religious composition of a state's population also have been found to affect its openness to adopting new policies.[17] Finally, the existing policies in a state shape its stance toward innovation, although in complicated ways. For example, the presence of a lottery in a state may make it more likely or less likely to legalize casino gambling, depending on local circumstances.[18]

As we will see, internal characteristics such as these have had a great deal to do with the way southern states have approached the politics of gambling. So has one state characteristic that generally has been overlooked: state constitutions. Gambling legalization during the third wave usually has required that state constitutions be amended, a more arduous form of innovation than simple legislation.

*Policy Entrepreneurs.* Even in combination, the internal characteristics that make a state ripe for policy innovation and the example of one or more nearby states are not enough to bring about the enactment of a new policy. Diffusion and internal characteristics are potential sources of policy energy that can only be made kinetic through the actions of one or more skillful entrepreneurs.[19] In many studies of state policy innovation, these entrepreneurs have been found for the most part in the ranks of bureaucrats, think-tank analysts, interest group representatives, and legislative and gubernatorial staff members. These policy entrepreneurs "network across state lines to learn about how new policies work (and thus gain credibility at home as experts), make contacts who can testify at hearings in their own states, and learn about strategies for selling an innovation that works."[20]

As this book makes clear, policy entrepreneurship has figured heavily in the politics of gambling in the South. To a one, however, the most effective entrepreneurs on behalf of legalized casino or lottery gambling have been politicians: gubernatorial candidates or state legislators, sometimes advised by political consultants. In other words, policy entrepreneurs typically have been political entrepreneurs selling their causes as a way of selling themselves to the voters.

In nearly all cases these politicians-cum-policy entrepreneurs were Democrats looking for an issue with which to roll back the Republican tide rising throughout the South during the 1980s and 1990s. Raising sales and income taxes to fund new programs was an even less-appealing platform in the South than in the rest of the country during the Reagan and post-Reagan eras. In contrast, raising revenue from a voluntary activity such as gambling, especially if the new funds were designated to support the popular cause of improving education, could be a political winner.[21]

### Method: Case Studies

In an effort to consolidate and advance the theoretical literature on state policy innovation and the substantive literature on the politics of gambling, we use the case-study method. Case studies enjoy a prominent place on any shelf of "great books" in political science. A partial list would include Graham Allison's *Essence of Decision*, Robert Dahl's *Who Governs?*, Herbert Kaufman's *The*

*Forest Ranger,* and Jeffrey Pressman and Aaron Wildavsky's *Implementation.*[22] The case-study method offers a particularly useful way to approach a subject whose literature resembles that on the politics of gambling: full of interesting but sometimes conflicting findings, which case studies may help to sort out, and marked by large omissions (the South, the 1990s and 2000s) whose terrain case studies, like voyages of exploration, may help to map.[23] In ways complementary to existing studies of gambling politics that have deployed a set of independent variables to explain the phenomenon statistically, our case studies offer analytic narratives of how, why, and whether the phenomenon occurs. As John Gerring has argued, they "allow one to peer into the box of causality . . . to 'see' X and Y interact."[24]

Case studies also alert the careful observer to developments that research focused on particular data sets or hypotheses might neglect. Statistical studies can measure the relationship between known variables, but what about variables that are important but still unknown? For example, state constitutions—which no study of gambling has taken into serious account—have emerged from our research as critical in shaping the politics of gambling in the South. In addition, our study encompasses both leading forms of legalized gambling, casinos and lotteries, not just one form, as most previous studies do. Although case studies do not render other methodologies unnecessary, they may provide the sort of insights that make the use of other methodologies more effective.[25]

Many of the virtues of the case-study method are present when even one case is presented with the "detail, richness, completeness, wholeness" we strive for in this book.[26] But in order to capture the variety of the states' approaches to legalized gambling in the South, as well as the causal interconnections between one state's approach and another's, we offer case studies of seven of the eleven southern states. One of these, Mississippi (chapter 1), is the only southern state with casinos but no lottery. Georgia (chapter 2), South Carolina (chapter 3), and Tennessee (chapter 5) are states with a lottery but no casinos. Alabama (chapter 4) and Arkansas (chapter 6) thus far have legalized neither form of gambling, although in both states some political leaders continue to press for a lottery and electronic gambling machines, which critics say are indistinguishable from slots, have appeared. Louisiana (chapter 7), is the only state with both casinos and a lottery. Although these seven cases encompass all the possible combinations of casino and lottery gambling—both forms, neither form, casinos only, and a lottery only—we also refer when appropriate to the remaining four southern states: Virginia, Florida, Texas, and North Carolina, each of which resembles Georgia, South Carolina, and Tennessee in having a lottery. Similarly, other forms of gambling, such as pari-mutuel betting, charitable bingo, and tribal gambling, also appear in our book when their place on a state's political agenda has affected its consideration of commercial casino gambling or a lottery. Our conclusions about the politics of gambling and state policy innovation theory appear at the end of the book.

At one time or another in recent years, all of the southern states discussed in this book considered creating a lottery and legalizing casino gambling. Every chapter begins by telling the story of how a state decided what to do about these matters, then proceeds to analyze why it chose to do what it did in terms of our theory of state policy innovation. In addition, each chapter about a state that has approved gambling describes and analyzes the after-politics of gambling legalization—the political controversies that were triggered by the inauguration of a lottery, casinos, or both. These stories are important and suspenseful, and we try to do them justice. Taken together, they help tell the larger story of how the South—sometimes reluctantly, sometimes enthusiastically—decided to join the gambling nation.

# ONE

# MISSISSIPPI

Casinos Come South

In the mid-1990s, one of the easiest ways to stump (or even win a small wager from) your friends was to ask them to name the three states with the most casinos. Nearly everyone knew that two of the three were Nevada and New Jersey. Almost no one knew the third: Mississippi. Yet by 1996, Tunica and Biloxi, Mississippi, each had more casinos than Atlantic City. In terms of revenues, Mississippi had become the third-largest casino gambling state in the nation. In terms of prevalence, its twenty-nine casinos and 1.2 million square feet of gambling space made it second.[1]

By the mid-2000s, careful observers of the politics of gambling noticed that Mississippi stood out in another way. Unlike forty-one other states, including a majority of those in the South, Mississippi has no lottery. This was especially odd because in 1989 Mississippi had elected Democrat Ray Mabus, the first southern governor to champion a lottery in his election campaign.

By 2006, more than four-fifths of the states had enacted lotteries, while only around one-fifth (eleven) had legalized commercial casinos. The South has not embraced either form of gambling as ardently as the rest of the country. One-third of the nation's remaining nonlottery states are in the South, and just one southern state besides Mississippi (Louisiana) allows commercial casinos to operate. But in the South and elsewhere, lotteries have been much more likely to win legislative approval than casinos. Why did Mississippi decide to become the first state in the South to legalize casino gambling? Why has it chosen not to create a state lottery?

Mississippi stands apart from the rest of the South in another way. Its decision to legalize casino gambling was made quietly, with little notice by the news media and, consequently, little public debate. Even the handful of legislators who were paying close attention when they and their colleagues passed the casino legalization bill in 1990 had no idea how large a presence casinos would become in the state. The result of this submerged politics of gambling has been an *after-politics* in which Mississippi has struggled to come to terms with what has become its largest industry. This struggle captured national attention in September and October 2005, when state legislators fought bitterly over what to do about Biloxi and Gulfport's casinos after Hurricane Katrina ravaged the Gulf Coast.

## LOTTERY AND CASINO POLITICS

When the 1990 session of the Mississippi legislature began its work in January, the stage seemed set for the adoption of a state lottery. In the preceding ten years, nineteen states had created lotteries, including two in the South: Florida in 1986 and Virginia in 1987. Two of Mississippi's neighbors, Tennessee on its northern border and Louisiana to the west, were actively considering lotteries. Mired in recession, the state treasury had experienced several consecutive years of budgetary shortfalls. Governor Mabus, eschewing a tax increase, had made a lottery the financial centerpiece of his proposed Better Education for Success (BEST) program to improve Mississippi's notoriously poor public schools. Mabus argued that a lottery would generate more than $50 million per year for the state. Lotteries were an increasingly routine part of state government operations, he added, and the experiences of these other states (including Virginia and Florida) had shown that a well-designed lottery would operate honestly, generating almost no political or financial corruption. A January 7, 1990, poll by the *Jackson Clarion-Ledger* revealed that 62 percent of Mississippians agreed with him.[2] In a state that had voted overwhelmingly Republican in recent presidential elections and had elected two Republicans to the U.S. Senate in the past seven years, Mabus felt confident that by seeking new funding for education without raising taxes, he had found a way for a Democrat to withstand his state's GOP tide.

In order for Mabus and the legislature to create a lottery, however, some high constitutional hurdles would have to be surmounted. Since 1868, Mississippi's constitution had included a provision banning lotteries. To end this prohibition, an amendment removing the ban would need to pass the legislature by a two-thirds vote of both the House of Representatives and the Senate and be approved by a majority of voters in a statewide referendum. The legislature would then have to pass a law creating a lottery by a three-fifths majority of both houses in order to fulfill the state constitution's requirement for enacting a "revenue bill."

Religious organizations in the heavily Protestant state, especially the Mississippi Baptist Convention, fought the lottery when it came before the legislature. Mabus's proposed constitutional amendment barely prevailed in the House, which approved it on June 19, 1990, by eighty-three to thirty-nine, one vote more than the constitutionally required two-thirds majority. Two days later, however, the Senate defeated the amendment. Although senators supported it by twenty-eight to twenty-three, they fell six votes short of two-thirds.

The Senate vote killed the lottery for the 1990 session, disappointing Mabus's hope to create a funding source for educational reform. But legalized gambling as a new public policy in Mississippi was very much alive. Quietly, outside the gaze of the media and interest groups so intent on publicizing the lottery controversy, legislators from the state's three southernmost Gulf Coast counties and from several of its eleven Delta counties, which border the Mississippi River, were working to secure legislative authorization to bring casino gambling to their constituencies.

In 1990 the Gulf Coast counties (Hancock, Harrison, and Jackson) and their largest cities, Biloxi and Gulfport, were down-at-the-heels vacation destinations. The coast's tourism industry had never recovered from the devastation wrought in 1969 by Hurricane Camille, still the strongest hurricane ever to hit the continental United States. The routing of Interstate 10 north of the coast reduced drive-through traffic by east-west travelers. The once-prosperous fishing industry had suffered severely since the 1980s from strong Asian competition.[3] In addition, the coast was still feeling the long-term effects of the crackdown on casino gambling that had begun after Sen. Estes Kefauver's organized crime committee came to Biloxi in 1951. Kefauver's investigators found that during and after World War II more than three hundred nightclubs, hotels, and other facilities offering slot machines and table games had sprung up around the new and massive Keesler Air Force Base in Biloxi. In a typical month, airmen from the base lost $500,000 of their $4 million payroll in the illegal games. State law enforcement officials, prodded by elected politicians who were embarrassed by the extensive national notoriety Mississippi received from the Kefauver hearings, cracked down severely. The perspective of the coastal counties themselves was different. "Once Kefauver came," lamented one local official, "it was never the same."[4]

If the hope of the Gulf Coast counties in 1990 was to revive the local economy, the challenge for the Delta counties along the Mississippi River was to create one where, for all intents and purposes, none existed. Tunica County, for example, had long been known as the poorest county in the poorest state in the country. According to the 1980 census, Tunica had the nation's lowest per capita income and highest proportion of people living in poverty. In 1985 civil rights activist Jesse Jackson called Tunica "America's Ethiopia" and led the CBS News program *60 Minutes* on a tour of "Sugar Ditch," an open sewer that ran through a Tunica neighborhood whose residents lacked indoor plumbing. Government efforts to attract industry to the county had consistently failed. Tunica, according to Benjamin and Christina Schwarz, "was so isolated, and its population so miserably educated, that even state monetary incentives and federal tax breaks could not entice business."[5] An attempt in the mid-1980s to legalize racetrack gambling in Tunica and coastal Pascagoula had passed the Mississippi House of Representatives, but it foundered in scandal when a state senator's demand for a bribe from the horseracing industry was discovered by the Federal Bureau of Investigation.

Gulf Coast representatives were the first to place casinos on the state's legislative agenda. They did so during the late 1980s, in a seemingly insignificant and technical way. In December 1987, much to the delight of Biloxi's depressed tourism industry, a 157-foot-long Panamanian-registered casino ship, the *Europa Star,* docked in the city's harbor and began offering round-trip cruises in the Mississippi Sound. After sailing three miles out to what its owners claimed were international waters, the *Star* would open its onboard casino to passengers, cruise around for a couple hours, then close the casino when it reentered state waters on its return voyage. (In casino industry parlance, these are known as "cruises to nowhere.") Mississippi's attorney general, however, soon ruled that the state's waters actually extend three miles past a series of offshore barrier islands and into the Gulf of Mexico, which meant that the *Star* had to sail much farther, thus spending an unprofitably long portion of each cruise with its casino closed.

After a state court upheld the attorney general's opinion, local businesses and elected officials petitioned Gulf Coast legislators to seek a modification of state law that would authorize cruise ships to open their casinos while still in the sound. The legislature was torn between its reluctance to make Mississippi the first state to allow casino gambling in state waters and its longstanding norm of deference to members on matters of local concern. It resolved the tension by authorizing the gambling cruises but adding a requirement that the casino ships be at least three hundred feet long. When one such ship, the *Pride of Mississippi,* began offering gambling cruises out of Biloxi, its owners found that they could not attract enough customers to operate so large a vessel profitably.[6]

Because the legislature treated the cruise-to-nowhere bill as a routine matter of local concern, it triggered little media interest or public controversy when it was approved in March 1989. But in the course of considering the bill, a few Mississippi legislators took note of a new law legalizing casino cruises on the Mississippi River which the Iowa legislature had approved that same month. Iowa, the first state to legalize riverboat casino gambling, enacted the law for several reasons. One was particular to Iowa's situation: under the terms of the new federal Indian Gaming Regulatory Act (IGRA) of 1988, a number of land-based tribal casinos were about to open in neighboring Minnesota and Wisconsin, which meant that Iowa would feel the effects of casino gambling no matter what it did.[7]

Iowa's other reasons for legalizing casinos, however, seemed more applicable to Mississippi's situation. The farm equipment manufacturing industry in Bettendorf and Davenport, two cities on the Mississippi River, was severely depressed. Riverboat casinos, some legislators thought, might help to revive local economies by attracting gamblers from across the river in Illinois, including not-too-distant Chicago. In terms of public opinion, the romantic mythos of the antebellum riverboat gambler made water-based casinos more palatable to Iowa legislators than the gaudy land-based casinos in Nevada and Atlantic City.

Businesses and legislators representing Mississippi's Gulf Coast, eager for the state legislature to open the door wide enough that national casino companies would find it profitable to come in, were persuaded by Iowa's action to seek a law allowing ships to operate casinos while cruising in the Mississippi

Sound. Legislators from Tunica and some other Delta counties were inspired along similar lines. Officials from both regions of the state feared that Louisiana would soon decide to legalize casino gambling, raising the specter of New Orleans casinos draining money from Mississippians' pockets and diverting even more tourists from the state's declining Gulf Coast counties.[8]

Out of this confluence of interests, examples, and fears, a number of Gulf Coast and Delta legislators quietly formed an alliance to promote the legalization of water-based casino gambling in Mississippi. Their chief strategist was one of the House's most powerful and respected members, Democratic representative H. L. "Sonny" Merideth from the Delta city of Greenville. Merideth realized that most of his fellow legislators, as well as the voters of Mississippi, would recoil at the thought of legalizing as extreme and, at the time, unusual a form of gambling as casinos. Thus, he and other influential casino supporters, such as Sen. Tommy Gollott of Biloxi, did their best to avoid drawing public attention to their efforts.

Merideth and Gollott were aided in this strategy by the prominence of the lottery in Governor Mabus's legislative agenda, which diverted media attention from their efforts to draft a casino bill. Meetings of the Senate Finance Committee, which was considering the lottery, were packed with spectators while a Merideth-chaired subcommittee of the House Ways and Means Committee worked on casino legislation in obscurity. (One reason for the lack of publicity was that the *Clarion-Ledger*, recently acquired by the Gannett newspaper chain, had reduced its legislative bureau to one reporter.) "The 'antis' were focused on lotteries," recalls a strong casino advocate from the Delta, Rep. Charlie Williams of Senatobia. "The cat was out of the bag [on casinos] before they started chasing it."[9] Rev. Paul Jones, the executive director of the Mississippi Baptist Convention's Christian Action Commission, agrees. "We just flat out missed it," he says.[10]

In addition to adopting a low-profile strategy, casino proponents in the legislature developed arguments that they hoped would appeal to the conservative majority of senators and representatives when they brought the bill to the floor. Merideth, Williams, and their allies in the House pointed out that in contrast to a lottery, which would put the state government into the business of running a gambling operation and encouraging people to wager, casinos would be private enterprises that might help revive local economies.

A casino, they noted, is a major private-sector capital investment that employs many people and, if properly designed and situated, attracts tourists from out of state. A lottery, on the other hand, would employ few people, involve little capital investment, and bring in few tourists.

Casino advocates also appealed to state pride, reaching deep into the state's antebellum past to argue that surely Mississippi had a better claim than Iowa to the riverboat gambler tradition, as well as warning that Louisiana might soon supplant that claim.[11] Furthermore, they presented casinos as a measure of local rather than statewide interest, relying on the legislature's unwritten rule that members should defer to each other on constituency matters whenever possible. Under the bill Merideth and his colleagues developed, casinos would be confined to at most fourteen of the state's eighty-two counties: the three Gulf Coast counties and the eleven counties whose western border is the Mississippi River. Even in those counties, the casinos could not be built on land but would float in the gulf or river—a fine distinction whose purpose was to dilute the objections of those opposed to casinos "on our soil." Thus, unlike a lottery, which would operate throughout the state, "the riverboat gambling idea seemed to confine the sin," according to Democratic state committee-man Wilson Golden, "because it was for a few counties and not everybody's county."[12] Finally, the proposed law would not impose casinos on any county that did not want them. The bill included a provision that allowed either 1,500 voters or 20 percent of a county's registered voters (whichever number was smaller) to demand a local referendum barring casinos from the county for a year.[13]

In arguing that casinos could be of great benefit to the small minority of counties that might choose to have them, advocates tried to reassure their colleagues that the effect on the state as a whole would be modest. Williams, for example, spoke in terms of at most "three [casino] boats on the coast, three on the river, with $18 million in tax revenue to the state."[14] This lowball estimate was of strategic as well as rhetorical value. Deemphasizing the fiscal consequences of the casino bill in favor of its effects on tourism and local economic development helped preserve the bill's status as simple legislation and thus kept it from triggering the state constitution's three-fifths requirement for enacting revenue measures. So did the provision that any or all of the fourteen eligible counties could vote to reject casino gambling, which meant that conceivably the state could end up with no casinos and, more to the constitutional point, no casino revenues, at all.

Eager though Merideth and his colleagues were to lower their fellow legislators' estimate of the consequences of passing the casino bill, they also wanted to create a favorable climate for potential investors. Merely to legalize casino gambling, advocates knew, would not attract casinos to Mississippi. "It might end up being sort of a joke," recalled Williams. "Mississippi? The Bible Belt?" Thus, Merideth's subcommittee wrote the law to be industry-friendly. Once again, the Iowa example was instructive, this time as a lesson in what not to do. In enacting its own casino law, Iowa had established loss limits for each gambler of five dollars per bet and two hundred dollars per cruise and had taxed casinos on a steeply rising scale that peaked at 20 percent. In short order, Illinois's legislature legalized casino gambling in Joliet and other river cities close to Iowa. Illinois imposed none of the betting limits that typically drive off high-stakes gamblers, who are the casino industry's most prized customers. As a result, Illinois's casinos cut deeply into Iowa's business.

With the assistance of Scott Scherer, an International Gaming Technologies lobbyist, Merideth's subcommittee adopted what has been called the "Nevada model" of casino legislation rather than the "New Jersey model," which most casino states have employed. The Nevada model treats casinos as corporate citizens that require close regulatory scrutiny to ensure the integrity of their games and keep out organized crime but that also have much to contribute to the state in the way of jobs, capital investment, and tax revenues. The New Jersey model is stricter and more skeptical of casino gambling. It regards casinos as businesses that, although capable of contributing to the state's economy, must be tightly limited in number, location, and practices, lest they endanger the public welfare.[15]

Merideth's bill provided that in Mississippi, as in Nevada, no restriction would be placed on the number of casino licenses that could be issued. Although background checks for casino operators were required, the cost of obtaining a license would be nominal. No limits were imposed on the amounts gamblers could bet, the losses they could suffer, or the days and hours during which they could wager. The tax rate on casino profits would be about half that in most other states: 8 percent to the state and, at local option, no more than 4 percent to the county in which a casino operated. So closely did Merideth and his colleagues follow Nevada law on these matters that "Nevada" instead of "Mississippi" inadvertently appeared in the bill in some places.

The major difference between Nevada's casinos and the casinos Merideth was proposing for Mississippi was that Nevada's were built on land and located throughout the state and Mississippi's would cruise on waters outside the state's landmass. Or so most legislators were led to believe. But just as the House was about to consider the casino bill, Merideth quietly deleted the words "under way" from the description of the vessels in which casino gambling would be allowed to take place.

Politically, the change was inconsequential, which was exactly what Merideth had hoped. "There probably weren't ten people in the House who understood the extent of the bill," says Rep. Danny Guice, a Republican from Ocean Springs. (If they had, he adds, "it probably would have defeated the bill.")[16] But the legal consequence of the change was enormous. In deleting "under way," Merideth was offering a bill that would authorize casinos to operate at dockside, without ever having to leave shore. Instead of confining casinos to riverboats and paddle wheelers, the modified bill opened the door to large-scale gambling facilities constructed on massive barges moored to the waterfront. What's more, the bill provided, the waterfront in the Delta counties would not need to be on the Mississippi River itself. Instead it could be on any body of "navigable waters" in an eligible county that was fed by the river, including (as it later turned out) a mile-long ditch extending inland that was dug for the sole purpose of creating a commercially advantageous location for a casino.

On March 7, 1990, the House passed Merideth's bill, the Gaming Control Act, by a vote of sixty-six to fifty-two. One week later, the bill passed the Senate without modification by twenty-two to twenty. Ten senators who did not want to vote for casinos but also did not want to interfere in what had been presented as a local matter chose to be absent, with most claiming an undisclosed stomach ailment. "If they weren't going to vote for the bill," said Senator Gollott, "I just asked them to abstain." Governor Mabus signed the Gaming Control Act on March 20. "I frankly didn't think I was signing that important a piece of legislation when I signed that bill," Mabus later recalled. "Neither I nor any of my staff had any idea of what doors we were opening."[17] As the governor's offhand attitude toward the new casino law indicated, Merideth's stealth strategy for getting the bill passed and signed had clearly worked. No one in the state—not the news media, the governor, casino executives, Christian conservatives, Merideth's legislative colleagues, or Merideth himself—claims even in hindsight to have foreseen that, by passing the bill, the legislature was opening the door to what soon would become Mississippi's major industry.

One consequence of these universally clouded crystal balls was that the lottery issue remained alive for a few years after its initial legislative defeat in 1990. Mabus centered his campaign for renomination in the September 1991 Democratic gubernatorial primary on his lottery proposal. He won, and, when ten antilottery legislators lost their own bids for renomination, he claimed a mandate. In truth, the defeats of these legislators had as much or more to do with the redistricting that followed the 1990 census as with the lottery. Mabus himself was defeated in the November general election by Republican Kirk Fordice. But the new governor, although personally opposed to a lottery, said that he would not object if the legislature approved a constitutional amendment to remove the constitution's lottery ban and let the voters decide the matter in a referendum. Louisiana had approved a lottery in 1990, as had Texas in 1991, and Tennessee still seemed as if it might be on the verge of doing so. In early 1992, with the first casino yet to open and the state government's revenue picture bleak, the legislature voted to allow the voters to decide in the November general election whether the constitutional ban on lotteries should be repealed.

As has been the case in almost every state that has put the matter on the ballot, the lottery referendum passed in Mississippi. But, in contrast to most other states, the margin of victory was narrow: 53 to 47 percent. Even then, the referendum only made a lottery constitutionally possible. The legislature still would have to pass a bill to create one. As a revenue measure, a lottery bill would require a three-fifths vote of both the House and Senate. Yet, as legislators analyzed the results of the referendum in their home districts, they realized that the majority of pro-lottery votes had come from just three large counties.[18] Most legislators represented constituencies that had voted against the amendment, primarily in the conservative Hill country of eastern Mississippi.[19]

In addition to conservative opposition, lottery legislation faced a fresh obstacle. Casino supporters at the 1993 session of the legislature worried that the new industry might suffer from competition with a lottery. They pointed to the casinos' early success and the dangers of stifling further growth. In August and September 1992, three casinos had opened on the Gulf Coast, and in February 1993 the first casino on the Mississippi River had opened in Natchez. (Two of these were riverboat casinos that sailed south from Iowa, confirming the shrewdness of Merideth's efforts to make the terms of the Gaming Control Act attractive to the casino industry.) Suddenly, Mississippi was leading the South in job creation, with more than a third of the new jobs coming from the new casinos. From the beginning, the early estimate that casinos would contribute $18 million per year to the state treasury was wildly exceeded—tax revenues from the new casinos exceeded $10 million in the first month alone. What to do with a budget surplus, not where to make midyear budget cuts, was the legislature's new challenge. "It's on its last gasp," casino proponent Williams said of the lottery bill in January 1993. During the 1993 legislative session, the bill never came to a vote.[20]

During the following decade, lottery legislation seldom was introduced and, when it was, it was quickly squelched. Tennessee's adoption of a lottery in 2003, joined with growing budget problems in Mississippi, sparked a modest renewal of interest. Soon after the first Tennessee lottery tickets were sold in January 2004 (some of them to Mississippians crossing the state line), Rep. Alyce Clarke, a Democrat from Jackson, introduced a bill to create a Mississippi lottery. Opposition from Republican governor Haley Barbour, a strong supporter of the casino industry, and from the leaders of both houses of the legislature was so forceful and quick that the head of the Mississippi Baptist Convention said he felt no need to mobilize even a small antilottery lobbying campaign.[21]

## WHY MISSISSIPPI LEGALIZED CASINOS BUT NOT A LOTTERY

Why did Mississippi legalize casino gambling? Why did it seriously consider a lottery but not enact one? The state's decision to embrace casinos while rejecting a lottery was anomalous by any standard. As the economist Richard McGowan has observed, "Mississippi is the great exception" to the rule that "casino gambling is usually the last form of gambling that state officials will recognize."[22] In addition, Mississippi is the only state in the country to remove its constitutional ban on lotteries without promptly creating a lottery by statute.

Part of the answer to these questions lies in a slightly modified version of diffusion theory, which argues that states are often inspired to create new public policies by the example of other states, especially states in their region that they regard as similar to themselves. Another part of the answer involves certain internal characteristics of Mississippi, both the economic characteristics usually invoked by students of state policy innovation and an additional, widely overlooked characteristic: the state's constitution. Finally, the remaining part of the answer lies in the influence of policy entrepreneurs in the state—adroit in the case of casinos, less so when it came to the lottery.

### Diffusion

Diffusion theory helps to explain why both the lottery and casinos appeared on Mississippi's policy agenda in the early 1990s. In proposing the lottery, Governor Mabus was taking his cues from two other southern states, Florida and Virginia, which had recently created lotteries of their own. Far from being an immoral activity engaged in solely by northerners, Mabus argued, lottery gambling was a tax-free way to raise money for schools which other southerners were embracing. As a Democrat in a conservative state that was rapidly becoming more Republican, Mabus saw the lottery as a popular way to raise money for a popular purpose.

Diffusion theory's value in determining why Mississippi seriously considered a lottery when it did is not surprising. Other scholars who have studied the politics of lottery gambling have found that they cannot explain why states create lotteries without acknowledging the influence of the example offered by other states that already have done so.[23] In contrast, most studies of casino legalization have focused entirely on political and economic factors internal to each state.[24] Yet, in proposing casinos Representative Merideth clearly was thinking just as regionally as Mabus was when he proposed a lottery. The difference is that Merideth looked upriver for inspiration to Iowa and Illinois, which like his own state, are part of the Mississippi River Valley. Like Iowa, Merideth thought, Mississippi could benefit from water-based casino gambling. Like Illinois, it could prosper by not imposing restrictions on how much gamblers could lose when they visited a casino or how long they could gamble.

Just as diffusion theory helps explain Mississippi's response to legalized gambling, Mississippi's response to legalized gambling suggests a modification of diffusion theory, which we call *anticipatory diffusion.* Anticipatory diffusion involves a state considering and perhaps adopting a policy innovation for fear that another state will make that innovation less desirable by adopting it first. Much of the impetus for Mississippi to legalize casino gambling came from the widespread expectation that neighboring Louisiana was about to do so, thereby preempting the tourist business that Mississippians thought their state could attract by acting first. As for the lottery, Louisiana and another of Mississippi's neighbors, Tennessee, were seriously considering lotteries of their own in the early 1990s.[25] In addition to embracing a lottery as a useful policy innovation in its own right, Mabus argued, Mississippi needed to act first so that Mississippians wanting to play a lottery did not flock northward and westward across the state line, taking their money to other states.

### Internal Characteristics

Diffusion theory helps to explains why proposals to legalize gambling appeared on Mississippi's policy agenda when they did. So does one of the most important internal characteristics of the state, namely, its economy. In a time of recession, Mabus trumpeted the lottery as a painless source of revenue. The state would raise many millions of dollars each year from an entirely voluntary activity, he argued. With an eye on Mississippi's long-term economic vitality, Mabus also promoted lottery gambling as a way to fund improvements in public education, an essential ingredient for sustained economic competitiveness. As for casinos, although Merideth and other casino supporters downplayed them as an important source of revenue for the state treasury, they defended their proposal as a means of fostering economic development on the Gulf Coast and in the Delta. Inviting casinos into the state, they argued, would stimulate investors to build and operate gambling halls, hotels, and resort facilities that would create new jobs and attract tourists from states that did not allow casinos.

What diffusion theory does not help to explain is why, having considered both a lottery and casinos, Mississippi rejected the former and embraced the latter. A second internal characteristic, the state constitution, does help explain this decision. Because the constitution explicitly forbade lotteries, Mabus's proposal first had to work its way through an amendment process that, as in most states, is long, requires supermajorities in the legislature, and attracts great media and interest group attention when controversial matters are involved. (All of the state's Protestant churches, for example, mobilized to oppose the lottery amendment.) Even after the amendment allowing the legislature to consider a lottery passed, the constitution required that any bill to create a lottery must, as a "revenue bill," secure a three-fifths majority in both the House of Representatives and the Senate. This hurdle proved insurmountable.

In contrast, casino gambling required only that simple legislation be enacted by a simple majority. Thus, although both legislative chambers' votes (House, 66 to 52; Senate, 22 to 20) in favor of the Gaming Control Act fell short of the larger majorities the lottery amendment commanded, they were sufficient to pass the act. Equally important, "casinos never had to go to a statewide vote," notes one of their chief advocates, Rep. Charlie Williams. "If that had been the case, it never would have passed."[26]

The lottery amendment's eventual success secured the constitutionality of casino gambling in Mississippi. Most state supreme courts have classified the slot machines on which casinos rely for most of their profits as lotteries because, like a lottery, a slot machine is a form of gambling that depends entirely on chance. In time, the Mississippi court may have embraced that doctrine in applying to slots its own state constitution's lottery ban, thereby smothering the state's burgeoning casino industry in its cradle. (As noted in the next section, the court showed no early inclination to do so.) When the lottery amendment was enacted, however, the constitutional basis of the Gaming Control Act and the resulting casino industry was secured.

### Policy Entrepreneurs

Although both the lottery and casinos had politically influential champions, Representative Merideth proved a much more effective policy entrepreneur for the casino bill than Governor Mabus was for the lottery. To be sure, Mississippi would not have seriously considered a lottery, much less removed the constitutional ban forbidding the legislature to create one, if Mabus had not placed the issue on the state's policy agenda and fought for it so ardently. Yet even Mabus's admirers do not claim for him the virtues of the skillful smoke-filled room politician and legislative backslapper. The lottery then lost its chief advocate when, after failing in 1990 to persuade the handful of senators whose support he lacked to approve the lottery amendment, Mabus was not reelected in 1991.

Merideth, in contrast, worked brilliantly in the legislature on behalf of his casino bill. The list of politically astute maneuvers that he planned and executed is impressive. Because public attention would have aroused the ire of many groups and tied the hands of many legislators, Merideth kept the bill's profile low, staying well outside the range of the political artillery that gambling opponents trained on the lottery amendment. He built a rare coalition between Delta and Gulf legislators by making water-based casinos on the outer borders of their counties the basis of his bill. After doing so, he played to the hilt the strategic benefits of framing his proposal as the sort of local concern on which Mississippi legislators traditionally defer to each other. Merideth also lowballed the fiscal consequences of casino gambling to prevent his bill from being defined as revenue legislation requiring an unattainable three-fifths majority.

Ironically, Merideth turned critic of casino gambling when he saw its effects on his home town. Greenville, in Washington County, is too far from Memphis, Jackson, and other population centers to attract many out-of-state tourists. As a result, the county's two casinos draw most of their business from local residents. "I think we would have been better off without them," Merideth said in 1999. "There's too much money going into the casinos that ought to be going to food, clothing, and shelter."[27]

## THE AFTER-POLITICS OF CASINO GAMBLING

The politics of gambling in most lottery states has followed a standard pattern: a full-scale public debate, a decision by elected officials to "let the people decide," a successful statewide referendum, legislative enactment, and absorption of the lottery into the fabric of state government. The legalization of casino gambling in Mississippi departed from this pattern in two important ways: there was no full-scale public debate, nor was casino legalization ever approved in a statewide referendum. The abbreviated, low-profile politics of casino legalization in the state spawned an after-politics of continuing controversy that has yet to abate fully.

Even with an industry-friendly law on the books, at least two things had to happen before casinos could begin operating in Mississippi: the way had to be cleared for licenses to be issued by the state, and counties had to decide to allow casinos within their borders. Both of these tasks were initially stymied by litigation.

On April 27, 1990, barely a month after the casino bill became law, a chancery court judge in Jackson ruled that charitable bingo violated the state constitution's ban on lotteries, which was still in effect. The judge based his ruling on a 1989 decision by the Tennessee Supreme Court which defined bingo as a form of lottery. The Tennessee court's definition of a lottery, adopted in full by the Mississippi judge, included any game of chance in which people bet money in hope of winning more money. The judge added that, by this definition, most casino games also were barred by the state constitution.[28]

Although the Mississippi Supreme Court overturned the chancery court decision on December 21, 1990, grounding its ruling in a much narrower definition of *lottery* than the Tennessee court had adopted, casino companies were reluctant to move into the state until the legal climate was stable and favorable. Another controversy arose a few months later when a small casino company announced plans to operate a dockside gambling boat in Tunica County. The owners of the Southland Greyhound Park in nearby West Memphis, Arkansas, hired a consulting firm to try to persuade the U.S. Corps of Engineers to deny the casino—and, by implication, all water-based casinos along the Mississippi River—the wetlands-related construction permit that was required under the federal Clean Water Act. As with the chancery court case in Jackson, this effort was ultimately unsuccessful, but for a time it jeopardized the prospects for casino gambling in the river counties.[29]

The involvement of the Arkansas dog track, a competing gambling enterprise, in Mississippi's effort to undertake casino gambling offers an example of what we call *antidiffusion*. Antidiffusion involves actors in one jurisdiction trying to forestall adverse consequences for themselves by preventing another jurisdiction from enacting or implementing a policy. To be sure, those on the receiving end of antidiffusionary efforts may turn up on the giving end as well. For example, starting in the mid-1990s, Mississippi casino interests intervened in Arkansas, Alabama, and Tennessee to oppose efforts to legalize gambling in these adjacent states.[30] As described below, similar antidiffusionary activities occurred not only across state lines but also across county lines within Mississippi.

### Start-Up: County Votes

Mississippi's casino law allowed a county's voters to petition for a referendum to bar casinos from their county for one year. In some counties, including Tunica, no such petition was filed and the county's board of supervisors quickly authorized casino gambling on its own authority. But in most Gulf Coast and Delta counties, Southern Baptist, United Methodist, and other Protestant clergy organized petition drives and a referendum was held. Typically, opponents of casino gambling offered morally grounded concerns about crime, addiction, and subversion of the work ethic as reasons to keep casinos out of the county, while proponents from the business and, in some cases, the political community stressed job creation, tourism, and other economic benefits.[31] Some counties voted to approve casinos in late 1990. Others initially voted *no* but, in a subsequent referendum, voted *yes*. Still others voted *no* year after year.

Anticipatory diffusion is a helpful concept in understanding some of these county-level decisions. For example, when Warren County voted to bar casinos in a December 11, 1990, referendum, casino companies that had been attracted by Vicksburg's proximity to Jackson and to Interstate 20 began looking closely at locations in neighboring Issaquena and Claiborne counties.[32] Warren County voters, fearing that they would inherit all of the costs but none of the benefits of having casino gambling in the vicinity, changed their minds in another referendum less than two years later. Soon four casinos were operating in Vicksburg.

Antidiffusion helps to explain what happened in some other counties. DeSoto County's position on casinos, for example, was shaped by the tension between its demographic characteristics and its geographical location. A prosperous suburban county that lies just north of Tunica and just south of Memphis, DeSoto voted against casinos in 1991, 1992, and 1996, always by a margin of roughly 60 to 40 percent. Yet the politics of each referendum was different. The 1991 vote, which preceded the subsequent proliferation of casinos in Tunica, followed a low-key campaign dominated by antigambling church leaders. In 1992, with casinos thriving in Tunica, the political and economic stakes were higher. Casino proponents were financed by Harrah's, an international casino company, and Belz Enterprises, a large Memphis development firm, which wanted to jointly operate a casino resort adjacent to Memphis. They argued that DeSoto County was missing out on all the economic benefits that Tunica was accruing from Memphis gamblers, who, to make matters worse, were clogging DeSoto highways in order to get to the Tunica casinos. Church leaders remained active in opposition. More important, however, Tunica casino interests, certain that business would dry up if casino gambling was available in a county closer to Memphis, surreptitiously financed hundreds of thousands of dollars worth of anticasino television commercials. In 1996, when Belz sponsored another referendum in DeSoto County, Harrah's switched sides, having already built a casino in Tunica. "We now have a considerable investment in Tunica County that would be harmed by gaming in DeSoto County," said a company spokesman.[33]

In the end, two of the three Gulf Coast counties (Harrison and Hancock) and seven of the eleven river counties (all but DeSoto, Bolivar, Jefferson, and Wilkinson) approved casino gambling. Because of their low populations and inconvenient distance from a major highway, some of the river counties were unable to attract casinos even after voting to put out the welcome mat.

### Start-Up: Regulatory Commission

The Gaming Control Act of 1990 entrusted casino licensing and regulatory responsibility to the Mississippi Tax Commission, pending the creation of a freestanding gaming commission to oversee casino gambling in the state. Both the tax commission and its successor, the Mississippi Gaming Commission (MGC), which began operating in 1993, defined their role as involving promotion of the casino industry, not just regulation to assure that casinos operated honestly and in the public interest. In August 1993, for example, the tax commission interpreted the law's requirement that casinos be built only on the Mississippi River or one of its tributaries to include a lagoon at the end of a newly dug canal that extended several thousand feet inland from the river. The practical result was that casinos in Tunica County could be built on sites thirty minutes closer to Memphis than an interpretation of the law more faithful to the legislature's intent would have allowed.

Three years after the gaming commission began operating in October 1993, the legislature's Joint Committee on Performance Evaluation and Expenditure

Review, widely known as the PEER committee, criticized the commission because it had "assumed an economic development role not contemplated or authorized by the Gaming Control Act" and had done a poor job of meeting its "ongoing challenge . . . to avoid being co-opted by an industry with substantial wealth and lobbying power." Indeed, the PEER committee reported, the mission statement developed by the gaming commission included "to work with the industry to promote economic development" as one of its goals. Commission investigators were found to spend little time reviewing the financial backgrounds of those who applied for casino licenses. Investigators actually received a substantial share of their on-the-job training from the casinos themselves. The commission's former executive director and deputy executive director had already left for high-level jobs with casinos. The current executive director, Paul Harvey, rebutted the PEER report with a thirty-three-page response, twenty pages of which were a barely relevant critique (supplied by Harrah's) of an antigambling book by Robert Goodman.[34]

Commissioner Robert C. Engram, defending the MGC's generally pro-industry approach, responded, "I think they [the PEER committee] are completely wrong." Other commissioners have regularly echoed Commissioner Victor Smith: "Economic development—that is part of our task." Casino gambling "has been a wonderful boost to our state," said commission chair Bill Gresham in 1999. His successor, A. J. Pitts, praised casinos as "good employers [that] bring in a lot of revenue to our state, and we've got to protect that." In 2000, when a *Wall Street Journal* article linked an increase in drunken-driving accidents to the Mississippi casinos' free-drinks policy for gamblers, the commission's executive director, Chuck Patton, said he saw no need for additional regulation. A year later, in a follow-up to its 1996 report, the PEER committee noted that the MGC's executive director, deputy executive director, and chief of staff had violated the commission's own ethics policy by participating in a charity poker tournament sponsored by two Tunica casinos, further contributing to "the appearance of promotion of the industry."[35]

Governors of both parties have continued to appoint progambling commissioners to the gaming commission, and when some legislators tried in 2004 to transfer the authority to calculate individual casinos' tax bills from the gaming commission back to the state tax commission, their effort foundered on the shoals of strong opposition by the casinos.[36] On May 19, 2006, House

Gaming Committee chair Bobby Moaks's argument that "there is no other regulatory agency in the state that determines what is [taxable] revenue for the industry it regulates" fell on policy-deaf but politically attuned ears.[37]

The combination of friendly regulators, low taxes, a supportive judicial climate, and a mostly welcoming stance by the coastal and river counties, along with the Gulf Coast's appeal as a tourist destination and Tunica's proximity to Memphis, have enabled casinos to flourish in Mississippi. In 1992, five casinos opened for business. The number doubled to ten by 1993 and, within three years, tripled to twenty-nine. In 1996 Mississippi casinos were a $1.7 billion industry employing more than 28,000 people. By the early 2000s, twelve casinos were operating on the Gulf Coast (eleven in Hancock County and one in Harrison County) and eighteen casinos were operating along the Mississippi River: ten in Tunica County, four in Warren County, two in Washington County, and one each in Coahoma, Hancock, and Adams Counties.

### Threats to Casino Gambling

Not everyone was happy with casino gambling as it developed in Mississippi during the 1990s. Some complaints arose from inland counties that, under the Gaming Control Act, are not permitted to have casinos. Seeing how lucrative casino gambling had become, they wanted to share in the wealth. In 1993, for example, the city of Jackson asked the legislature to allow casinos in the state capital. One year later, a bill was introduced by a Greenwood senator to give every county the right to have casinos. In 1997, legislators from some noncasino counties supported a bill to raise state casino taxes from 8 to 10 percent and distribute the additional revenues to counties that can not have casinos. None of these measures was enacted. But the 1997 bill prompted the Mississippi Gaming Association, the trade association of the state's casinos, to hire an executive director to raise and improve its public and legislative profile.[38]

Other critics have wanted to eliminate casinos from Mississippi entirely. The state's dominant religious organizations continue to oppose casino gambling, as does the American Family Association, a conservative Christian organization whose national headquarters is in Tupelo. Polls commissioned by Harrah's consistently found that public opposition to gambling in general is higher in Mississippi than in any other southern state. Sen. Billy Hewes, a casino supporter from Gulfport, is one of many political leaders who agree that Mississippi's "extremely fundamental moral core" means that, "statewide, if [casino gambling] were put to a vote, it wouldn't pass."[39]

Perhaps the most serious threat to casinos in Mississippi came from efforts by Christian conservatives in 1998 and 1999 to place an initiative on the ballot to banish all noncharitable forms of gambling from the state within two years of approval. "We're centering on the fact that the majority of counties have not had a chance to vote on gambling, and it's negatively impacting them," said chief strategist Paul Jones of the Mississippi Baptist Convention.[40] Jones worked closely with the American Family Association and other Christian organizations to launch the initiative campaign.

The campaign to ban casinos and close the door to a lottery failed, in part because of constitutional obstacles. Mississippi's initiative process is perhaps the most arduous in the nation.[41] The state constitution requires that petitions be signed by 12 percent of the number of voters in the most recent gubernatorial election, that the signers be evenly distributed among the state's congressional districts, and that all the petition gatherers be residents of Mississippi. Once on the ballot, the initiative must be approved not only by a majority of those voting on the issue but also by at least 40 percent of all those casting ballots that day, a difficult threshold for any down-ballot measure to reach. Yet it was not these difficulties that stymied proponents of the antigambling initiative. Instead, their efforts foundered on yet another constitutional requirement, namely, that the wording of a measure may be challenged in court on fiscal grounds before signatures are gathered.

Judges smothered each of the three initiative efforts of the late 1990s by ruling that the proposals either did not estimate the fiscal consequence of passage or did so inadequately. (Jones argued that expelling gambling from Mississippi would have no net fiscal consequence because the lost tax revenues to the state would be offset by reduced expenditures on gambling-related social problems.) In one case, the legal challenge to a proposed initiative was lodged by People's Bank, which was heavily invested in casino-related construction on the Gulf Coast. All of the challenges were supported by the state's business and political leadership. "Once you invite an industry like this into the state and require it to invest millions of dollars, to suddenly yank the rug out from under it would send a chilling signal to Wall Street," said Blake Wilson, the president of the Mississippi Economic Council. Declaring himself both antigambling and "a vociferous advocate of economic development," Governor Fordice said that he was "totally opposed, vociferously opposed" to the initiative" because it would violate the casino owners' property rights.[42]

### The Entrenchment of the Casino Industry

Despite this opposition, the casino industry is strongly entrenched in Mississippi. Most of the initial promises for economic development, tourism, and tax revenues have been more than fulfilled, with little clear evidence of serious increases in crime or other social problems. When the National Gambling Impact Study Commission, a body created by the U.S. Congress at the behest of gambling opponents, visited Biloxi in 1998, nearly all the testimony it received about the effects of casinos on the local economy was glowing. By 2002, the number of people employed by the state's casinos had risen to nearly 32,000 and the industry's annual revenues had grown to $2.7 billion. In fiscal year 2002, Mississippi casinos paid $327 million in taxes, funding around 10 percent of the state budget and an even larger share of some county budgets. Tunica County, for example, uses casino taxes to fund more than four-fifths of its annual budget.[43]

In election campaigns, the typical approach taken by candidates for statewide office has been to express personal opposition to gambling but to praise the casino industry for its contributions to Mississippi's economy. Fordice, a conservative Republican, adopted this stance (and consistently accepted political donations from casinos) while serving as governor from 1991 to 1999. So did nearly all the candidates to succeed him in 1999, including the winner, Democrat Ronnie Musgrove.[44] Although Musgrove was defeated in his bid for reelection in 2003, it was not because of his broad acceptance of casino gambling. Indeed, his victorious opponent, Republican Haley Barbour, had spent several years lobbying for the casino industry in Washington.

What has changed in the after-politics of casino gambling in Mississippi is that the state government increasingly supports not casinos per se, but casinos as they developed during the 1990s. Mississippi's initial posture of permissive casino licensing has gradually been tightened to restrict entry. In 1993, for example, the legislature responded to pressure from Harrah's, which was building casinos in Tunica, Vicksburg, and Biloxi, by defeating a bill that would have allowed casinos to be built on any body of water west of Highway

61, some of them lakes more than fifty miles from the Mississippi River. In 1994, House Speaker Tim Ford, a close ally of Merideth in passing the Gaming Control Act, defended the legislature's decision not to allow all counties to have casino gambling by arguing that the existing casinos had been built in good faith that the permissible territory for casino operations would not expand. In 1996, after secretly meeting with lobbyists, the gaming commission responded to pressure from the four Vicksburg casinos by turning down another casino company's request to build a gambling facility on a stretch of the Big Black River twelve miles closer than Vicksburg to the casinos' main feeder market, Jackson. In his majority opinion upholding the commission's authority to make this decision, state supreme court justice Mike Mills nonetheless chided commissioners for encouraging "unabashed, unstructured, and unregulated lobbyist-to-agency interactions" that "do not inspire confidence in the Mississippi gaming system and should be curtailed."[45]

In 1997, a bill was enacted to lengthen the minimum amount of time between casino referenda in a particular county from one year to as many as eight years: the legislature was responding to Tunica casinos seeking protection against possible casino legalization in DeSoto County. Two years later, the gaming commission mandated that anyone bidding to build a new casino would have to spend a dollar on land-based facilities—such as hotels, golf courses, restaurants, or concert halls—for every dollar it spent building the casino itself.[46] By raising the cost of entry, the commission's decision strongly discouraged new, smaller-scale casinos from trying to do business in the state.

The entrenchment of casino gambling reflects an acceptance of the industry in Mississippi but not an embrace. Starting in the mid-1990s, for example, the casino industry failed every year to persuade the legislature to allow any of the state's eight universities and fifteen community colleges to offer courses on casino management. "What we do with every other industry we recruit is tell them, 'If you'll come to our state we will assist you in training your employees,'" complained Sen. Grey Ferris of Vicksburg. "Why are we not able to do that with this particular industry?" In addition to the casinos, the state's college board, which oversees the universities, and the Mississippi Association of Community and Junior Colleges requested legislative permission to create casino management programs, citing New Orleans–based Tulane University's decision to open a branch campus in Biloxi for just that purpose. Whenever such bills came before the Senate, however, the Mississippi Baptist Convention and the American Family Association mobilized their members to jam House and Senate switchboards with their objections. "We might as well teach brothel management or tobacco sales 101," said a representative of the Baptist convention.[47]

Legislators who privately supported the casino-management measure often saw publicly opposing it as a way to satisfy their antigambling constituents without placing the casino industry at serious risk. Despairing of success in the legislature, in 2005 the College Board argued successfully in the Hinds County chancery court that its constitutional authority to determine what programs of study would be offered in public colleges and universities precluded any legislative restrictions such as the one that forbade casino management courses.[48] A casino management program soon began operating at the University of Southern Mississippi's Gulf Park campus.

Until Hurricane Katrina struck in September 2005, heavily damaging or washing away all of the casinos in Biloxi and Gulfport, another goal of the casino industry—namely, to secure permission to move the Gulf Coast casinos from floating barges to dry land, where they would be more secure from hurricanes—also went nowhere in the state legislature. It took Katrina's devastation of the coastal economy and strong pressure from Governor Barbour to persuade the legislature to change the law, and even then it was a near thing. "If we want to rebuild the coast bigger and better than ever," said Barbour in an impassioned speech to a special posthurricane session of the legislature, "I believe we will fail if we don't allow the casinos to come on shore, even if only a few hundred feet." As part of his Gulf Opportunity Zone hurricane relief measure, President George W. Bush promised that, in contrast to nearly all other federal economic development measures, Gulf Coast casinos would be eligible for the same tax benefits other businesses would receive. Yet the Mississippi Baptist Convention and the American Family Association pulled out all the stops to defeat Barbour's proposal. Some legislators reported receiving more grassroots pressure to vote against allowing land-based casinos on the coast than on any issue they had ever dealt with. Representative Moak spoke of letting casinos "crawl up on the land"—an image that may suggest the march of evolutionary progress in Cambridge, Massachusetts, but that sounds more like an assault by creatures from the deep in Mississippi. A bill to allow casinos to build on land within eight hundred feet of the gulf was passed in early October, but only narrowly (by 60 to 53 in the House and 29 to 21 in the Senate). Three casinos reopened near the end of December and took in seven times more money than the entire Gulf Coast casino industry typically made in a week. By the end of summer 2006, five more had been rebuilt, each one bigger than it had been before Katrina, and several more were under construction.[49]

The casino industry also fights hard when bills are introduced to raise to as much as 15 percent the state's comparatively low 8 percent tax rate on gambling revenues. Efforts to increase the tax rate on commercial casinos intensified after a brief economic recession substantially reduced the state government's overall revenues in the early 2000s. The Mississippi Gaming Association responded by launching an aggressive statewide advertising campaign to improve the industry's image. The ads pointed out that the more than $300 million per year the state already receives from the casino industry is considerably greater than all the other revenues gained from corporate taxes combined. The association argued that these funds are used to improve the lives of people throughout the state, not just in the counties with casinos. Casino advocates also have frequently cited a 1999 University of Southern Mississippi study suggesting that even a three-percentage-point tax increase would drive seven of the state's casinos out of business, thereby costing the state more revenue than it would generate. In 2006 Barbour said that "raising the casino tax would be the most foolish thing the state could do."[50]

Mississippi's Choctaw-owned casinos, located on the tribe's land near Philadelphia in the southeastern part of the state, seem even less vulnerable to attack from the state legislature. As recently as the late 1970s, the Mississippi Band of Choctaw Indians lived in desperate poverty on their reservation. In 1979, a newly elected chief, Philip Martin, used federal grants to build an industrial park and, after offering a Third World–style combination of cheap labor and no taxes, secured contracts with Ford, General Motors, Xerox, PepsiCo, and other prominent corporations. When Mississippi legalized commercial casino gambling in 1990, Martin invoked the federal Indian Gaming Regulatory Act of 1988, which entitles each tribe whose lands are in a casino state to negotiate a compact with the state government authorizing tribal casinos. Because tribes are sovereign entities as a matter of constitutional law, their casinos are immune from state taxes. In 1993, Chief Martin and Governor Fordice signed a casino compact, and the following year the Choctaws opened the large and highly successful Silver Star casino resort. In 2002, the tribe opened a second casino, the Golden Moon, on its reservation and expanded the resort facilities.[51] Not surprisingly, the same fiscal woes that caused Mississippi legislators to consider raising taxes on commercial casinos in the early 2000s led some of them to look for ways to tax the Choctaws. Other states had negotiated casino compacts in which tribes agreed to contribute a certain amount to the state treasury, subject to renegotiation when the compact expired. In contrast, the compact with the Choctaws that Fordice signed was perpetual and required nothing from the tribe. Frustrating as this may have been to state officials and to the commercial casinos, Martin showed no willingness to change the compact. "We have learned the white man's ways," said the chief.[52]

Unfortunately, Martin didn't learn the "white man's ways" as well as he thought. To buttress their political status in Mississippi, the Choctaws followed Washington lobbyist Jack Abramoff's advice and hired Capital Campaign Strategies, a political consulting firm headed by Abramoff's friend Michael Scanlon. The tribe paid Scanlon $15.9 million in fees between 2001 and 2003. It is not clear how much the Choctaws benefited from the arrangement—their legal position was already strong. What is clear is that Scanlon grossly overcharged the tribe, in part so that, without the Choctaws' knowledge, he could kick back half of his profits to Abramoff.[53]

The reason Abramoff was able to persuade the Choctaws to part with so much of their money in the early 2000s was that he had served their interests well in 1999. Practicing antidiffusion, the Choctaws initially hired Abramoff to help defeat efforts by elected officials in Alabama to create a lottery and legalize video gambling at the state's dog tracks and by the Jena Band of Choctaw Indians to open a casino in Louisiana. Abramoff in turn funneled part of this money to a leading conservative group in Washington, Americans for Tax Reform, which in turn passed most of it on to the political consultant Ralph Reed.[54] Reed, the former executive director of the Christian Coalition and an outspoken opponent of gambling, was the public face of the Mississippi Choctaws' covert campaign to stifle potential competition from new gambling operations in two neighboring states, Alabama to the east and Louisiana to the west.[55] In both cases, Reed and his allies were successful, and at a reasonable price.[56]

## CONCLUSION

In 1990 Mississippi became the first state in the South to legalize casino gambling, and it remains the only southern state that allows commercial casinos but has no lottery. For all that makes Mississippi unusual, however, its experience illuminates several of the themes that animate the politics of gambling in the states whose stories are told in subsequent chapters. Mississippi's decision to allow casino but not lottery gambling was shaped in part by one of the state's most important internal characteristics, its constitution. Enacting a lottery would have meant jumping several constitutional hurdles: a two-thirds majority in the legislature for an amendment to make lottery gambling constitutionally permissible, approval of the amendment by the voters in a referendum, and then passage of a lottery law by a three-fifths legislative majority because the constitution classified it as a revenue bill. Legalizing casinos required only that a simple majority of the legislature pass a law.

The politics of gambling in Mississippi also was influenced by the level of political skill displayed by various progambling policy entrepreneurs—high in the case of lottery champion Ray Mabus but higher in the case of casinos advocate Sonny Merideth, both Democrats. Mississippi's approach to gambling was further shaped by the diffusionary influence of other states. Most studies of state policy diffusion have emphasized the inspirational effect that one state's good experience with a new policy has on other states, and certainly the examples of two fellow Mississippi River Valley states, Iowa and Illinois, helped inspire Mississippi to embrace water-based casinos. But gambling politics in Mississippi also demonstrates that diffusion is more complicated. Some refinements in diffusion theory are required to explain what happened in Mississippi and why—specifically, *anticipatory diffusion* to account for the way states sometimes act to steal a march on other states (as Mississippi did for fear that neighboring Louisiana would beat it to the punch in legalizing casino gambling), and *antidiffusion* to explain why political actors in other jurisdictions sometimes fight to prevent a state or county from enacting a policy (as Arkansas's dog track did in hopes of keeping Tunica from dividing the gambling market in nearby Memphis, and as Tunica, for the same reason, did to keep DeSoto County from allowing casinos).

Mississippi's approach to gambling illustrates that when a controversial policy decision is made without full public debate, its adoption may trigger a new phase of *after-politics*. By many measures, casinos have been an economic boon to Mississippi. Yet because casino gambling received little scrutiny at the time it was made legal, its presence in the state has never been fully accepted, and it remains an object of ongoing controversy. Even the destruction wrought by Hurricane Katrina in 2005 to the casino counties on the Gulf Coast did not spare the casino industry a bruising fight to rebuild in safer circumstances.

# TWO

# GEORGIA

## Politics and HOPE

While Mississippi was deciding to legalize casino gambling but not to create a lottery, Georgia pursued the opposite course: a new state lottery but no casinos. Georgia was not the first lottery state in the South but, as subsequent chapters show, it set the pace for the region by creating the kind of lottery it did. South Carolina and Tennessee adopted lotteries on the Georgia model, and a governor of Alabama tried to do so.

Until the first Georgia lottery ticket was sold in 1993, legalized gambling in the state was confined to charitable bingo. The General Assembly's decision in 1977 to make charitable bingo legal had provoked little controversy, partly because it was portrayed as a fundraising device for worthy causes and partly because local authorities were not enforcing the existing prohibition on bingo anyway. The story of the decision to create the Georgia lottery is considerably more complicated. So is the more recent controversy over video poker in the state.

Part of the complexity attending the politics of the Georgia lottery is that it intersects at various points with unsuccessful attempts to legalize pari-mutuel betting on horse races. The first attempt to authorize racetrack gambling in Georgia occurred in the late 1950s, when a group of seventeen investors organized a company called Atlanta International Racing. The group purchased land in Henry County, just south of Atlanta and very close to the airport, to provide a site for automobile and horse racing. Although most forms of gambling had been forbidden in Georgia since the state adopted its current constitution in 1877, the investors thought that the profits they earned by staging auto races would allow the facility to succeed until the constitution was changed and horse racing could begin.[1] Their hopes were dashed when proposals to amend the constitution to allow pari-mutuel betting were consistently buried in committee by antigambling leaders of the state's House of Representatives.[2] In the 1982 Democratic gubernatorial primary, the antigambling candidate, Joe Frank Harris, trounced Bo Ginn, a mild supporter of pari-mutuel betting.

## GEORGIA ENACTS A LOTTERY

As the pari-mutuel betting controversy waned, Georgians gradually became attracted to a different form of gambling. In the 1970s and 1980s numbers-style lotteries and other illegal games were widespread in the poorer areas of the state. For example, two gambling suspects were arrested in a Tifton funeral home in 1983 when state agents seized $17,000 in cash and a variety of gambling paraphernalia. The arrest represented the fourth major illegal gambling operation uncovered in Georgia that year.[3] A lottery ring attracted betters throughout south Georgia, who wagered as much as $2 million per year. The illegal "bug lottery" was especially popular. This numbers game was based on predictions of butter and egg (hence "bug") prices that were published in newspapers around the state.[4]

If nothing else, the success of illegal lotteries testified to the desire of many Georgians to gamble on such games. Along with the spread of legal lotteries during the 1970s, mostly among the northeastern and Midwestern states, it contributed to the growing interest of some political leaders in the possibility of a state-run lottery in Georgia. As early as 1977, individual members of the House of Representatives had occasionally introduced lottery measures, albeit to little effect. But in preparation for his 1990 campaign for governor, Democratic lieutenant governor Zell Miller became the first gubernatorial candidate in the state's history to lead a movement for a lottery. Miller announced on January 12, 1989, that he wanted Georgia to create a lottery, abandoning his long-standing position that to legalize pari-mutuel betting or a lottery might open the door to casino gambling, which he strenuously opposed.[5] During the 1989 legislative session Miller, who had been lieutenant governor for the past sixteen years, fought to have a lottery amendment placed on the 1990 ballot as a constitutional referendum.

As in most American states, the process of amending the Georgia constitution has grown easier (but not easy) over the years. Until Georgia's 1877 constitutional convention wrote the current governing document, an amendment had to be approved by two-thirds of two consecutive general assemblies, then by the people—a process one convention delegate described as "amount[ing] to a declaration that this constitution shall be as unchangeable as the laws of the Medes and Persians." The revised amendment process requires only a single two-thirds vote of the General Assembly and approval by the voters in a referendum scheduled in conjunction with "the next general election which is held in even-numbered years." On January 27, 1989, the Georgia Senate, in which the lieutenant governor plays a substantial leadership role, began the process of amending the constitution by handily passing a resolution allowing the voters to decide in November 1990 if they wanted to repeal the constitutional ban on lotteries, with the profits from any lottery the legislature might then create earmarked for education. (The vote was 42 to 14, four votes above the constitutionally required two-thirds of the entire membership.) Miller's proposal met substantial opposition in the House of Representatives, however, where the antilottery (and anti-Miller) influence of Speaker Tom Murphy and Governor Harris ran deep. On February 7, 1989, the House Industry Committee voted narrowly to kill the bill. But committee chair Roy H. "Sonny" Watson, who voted against the amendment, switched sides on a subsequent motion to reconsider it at a later time, and the reconsideration motion passed nine to seven. These votes came one day after hundreds of mostly Southern Baptist and United Methodist ministers organized by Rev. Emmett Henderson, a longtime antigambling activist and the director of the Georgia Council on Moral and Civic Concerns, appeared at a committee hearing to oppose the lottery resolution.[6]

The lottery issue was revived in the House in early 1990, partly at Miller's initiative and partly because of lobbying by E. Jack Smith, who had worked the legislature on behalf of horse owners for years and was one of the original investors in Atlanta International Racing. Smith hoped to attach a provision legalizing pari-mutuel betting to Miller's proposal for a state lottery. Even if that effort failed, Smith hoped that adopting a lottery would pave the way to legalizing horse racing in Georgia by softening the state's official opposition to gambling. On January 30, 1990, the House Industry Committee voted eleven to six in favor of a do-not-pass recommendation, which, according to House rules, allowed the lottery amendment to remain alive because any

member of the House could call a floor vote challenging the committee's recommendation not to approve the measure.[7] Although one member did that,
the House voted 143 to 24 to let stand the Industry Committee's do-not-pass
recommendation.

### Zell Miller's Campaign for Governor, 1990

The House committee's action and the subsequent floor vote defeated the proposal for a lottery amendment in the 1989–1990 General Assembly. But Miller
shrewdly spun legislative defeat into rhetorical victory in his 1990 campaign
for governor. He and other lottery advocates now could argue that politicians,
especially the House leadership, were denying Georgians the opportunity to
vote on a lottery even though a statewide public opinion poll conducted by
the *Atlanta Journal and Constitution* showed that 72 percent of voters wanted
one and only 22 percent did not. Miller mounted this charge the day after the
lottery's defeat in the House, declaring that the lottery "is an issue that's not
going to go away. It will be with us this summer on the campaign trail for the
governor's office." Miller went on to claim that his longtime nemesis in the
legislature, Speaker Murphy, had mobilized the leadership of the House to
make sure that representatives upheld the Industry Committee's decision by
invoking the legislative norm of deference to committees. Miller's point was
that the large margin of defeat for the proposed constitutional amendment
did not mean that a lottery was unpopular among representatives, only that
members had adhered to legislative norms.[8]

In addition to the popular illegal lotteries and the failed push for a legal
state lottery in the General Assembly, the wellsprings of Miller's 1990 gubernatorial campaign included the large sums many Georgians were already
spending on the recently created lottery in Florida, a neighboring state. Seven
of the top ten sales points for the Florida lottery were along the Georgia
border. The state of Florida estimated that it was earning $50 million per year
from Georgians playing the Florida lottery. Nor were these players confined
to the southernmost part of Georgia, where the Florida border lies. In August
1990 two men were arrested outside a warehouse in Norcross, an affluent sub-
urb of Atlanta, for selling one-dollar Florida lottery tickets for $1.50 apiece.[9]

Miller's campaign for governor, then, took place in a state where people
were already spending money on lottery gambling illegally or in another state

and wanted to do so legally in Georgia. With the counsel of Democratic political consultant James Carville, whom he hired in 1989, Miller further primed the Georgia electorate and other state politicians by tying the idea of a lottery to increased funding for education. Except for state senator Roy Barnes, a steadfast lottery opponent, all of Miller's rivals for the 1990 Democratic gubernatorial nomination, including former Atlanta mayor Andrew Young, said that even though they personally opposed a lottery, the voters should be allowed to decide the issue. In fact, Miller may have primed the electorate too effectively. House Republican leader Johnny Isakson, Miller's opponent for governor in the 1990 general election, eventually endorsed and even campaigned on the basis of his own proposal for an education lottery.[10]

What remained for Miller was to convert the lottery issue—the most prominent policy proposal of his campaign—into victory at the polls. This was a task that Carville had already helped to accomplish for Kentucky gubernatorial candidate Wallace Wilkinson in 1987. Miller says that Carville's success in electing Wilkinson, a previously unknown businessman, on the strength of the lottery issue was "the thing that really sold me" on hiring the consultant. Carville brought more than just shrewd advice to the campaign. He also introduced Miller to a Kentucky lawyer for GTECH, the Rhode Island–based manufacturer of lottery equipment. The lawyer, Danny Briscoe, held a major fundraising event for Miller in Louisville.[11]

In waging his campaign, Miller emphasized to the voters that any revenues the state of Georgia earned from a lottery would not go into the state's general fund but into a new education trust fund controlled by a commission appointed by the governor and devoted exclusively to funding new education programs for college students and preschool children. Isakson argued that revenues from a lottery instead should go directly to local school boards, a narrower proposal that would not directly benefit two sizable constituencies: the parents of college-bound students and the parents of young children. Nor did Isakson's proposal reassure skeptical education groups like the PTA and the Georgia Association of Educators, which had seen Florida raise funds for education with a lottery while simultaneously reducing education spending from the general fund.[12]

Besides instituting a lottery for education, the major policy proposals of the Miller campaign were boot camps for drug offenders and abolishing the sales tax on groceries. The popularity of these ideas, along with Miller's ability to stay focused on them throughout the campaign, helped him to defeat Young in the Democratic primary runoff and Isakson in the general election.[13] The lottery was an especially helpful issue in the primary. It gave Miller, whose political base had long been among conservative whites in north Georgia, a way of broadening his appeal to include south Georgians used to playing the Florida lottery and African American voters who liked playing the bug lottery. (Even against Young, who was famous for his leadership in the civil rights movement, Miller received around 20 percent of the black vote in Atlanta.) Miller's campaign war chest included contributions from GTECH and a number of other national lottery corporations, including Atlanta-based Scientific Games.[14]

Difficult as it was, Miller's campaign for the governorship proved easier to win than the three subsequent battles awaiting his lottery proposal: securing legislative passage of his resolution for a constitutional amendment to be placed on the ballot, passing the enabling legislation for the lottery, and winning the referendum on the proposed constitutional amendment.

### Proposing a Constitutional Amendment, 1991

The campaign proposal that Miller parlayed into victory in the 1990 election called for any revenues that Georgia raised from a lottery to be spent on new college scholarships, a prekindergarten program, and new funding for public school equipment and construction, with the authority to distribute funds among these programs resting with the governor. Miller's proposal for the new programs emerged after a three-year period of sluggish economic growth in Georgia and in a year when state budget estimates indicated a $332 million revenue shortfall.[15] The state's economic woes favorably influenced the public and legislative response to Miller's lottery, which promised to provide new education programs for young people and financial assistance for their parents at a time when budget cuts were likely to occur in other areas.

Speaker Murphy despised Miller and was reluctant to cooperate with him. During the 1990 general election campaign he had referred to Miller as one of "those two jackasses" running for governor. When the newly inaugurated governor said that his legislative proposals "deserve to be voted on by the full House of Representatives . . . not buried in the Murphy mausoleum," the speaker replied, "I wish I did have a mausoleum. If I did, I guarantee you there would be another person interred in it." Eventually, however, Murphy admitted that it would be politically impossible to deny a vote on the lottery to a new governor who had been elected on the issue. The speaker conceded at the start of the 1991 legislative session that although "everybody knows that I'm not going to vote for a lottery, . . . I think it's time for the people to vote on it."[16]

Despite Murphy's acquiescence, interests collided when the General Assembly began debating the exact language of the proposed constitutional amendment. Horse-racing advocate E. Jack Smith and Shannon Staley, who represented a new group called Georgians for a Lottery Referendum during the 1991 legislative debate about the proposed constitutional amendment, attempted to persuade the House Industry Committee to alter Miller's proposal by removing its accompanying prohibitions on casino gambling and, more important to them, on pari-mutuel betting. The governor deflected their effort by stating that he would not object to a separate constitutional amendment on the pari-mutuel issue. The logic of Miller's concession, which expressed his openness to a constitutional amendment that would undo in part the constitutional amendment he was busy championing, did not extend beyond the political.

The Industry Committee approved Governor Miller's lottery amendment on January 29, 1991, by sixteen to seven and, two days later, the House passed it by 126 to 51, eight votes more than the two-thirds majority that the state constitution requires for a constitutional amendment. Reflecting the support that both Miller and Isakson had given to a lottery in the 1990 election, House Democrats (102–40) and House Republicans (24–11) supported the amendment in nearly equal proportions. Along with Speaker Murphy, several members made clear during the course of the debate that even though they personally opposed a lottery, they would not stand in the way of "letting the people decide." As veteran representative Denmark Groover argued in his speech closing the House debate, "The Constitution of this state says that all government of right emanates from the people. And this man [Miller] had the guts to propose a lottery and he was the only one that did. He ran on it and was elected on it. The people want an opportunity to vote on it themselves."[17]

Among the national lottery corporations lobbying for Miller's amendment were Scientific Games and Dittler Brothers Printing, both of which are based in Atlanta, and Rhode Island's GTECH Corporation. As prospective retailers of lottery tickets, the Georgia Association of Convenience Stores also lent active support to the lottery amendment. The opposition included the Georgia Council on Moral and Civic Concerns, the Georgia Baptist Convention, and the Georgia Coalition for Traditional Family Values. Their champion in the legislature, Rep. Roger Byrd, argued against Miller's amendment but conceded that it was a "noble attempt" at a constructive lottery.[18] Byrd was referring to the section of the proposed amendment specifying that lottery revenues would be used for education and prohibiting "all forms of pari-mutuel betting and casino gambling." As it had done with Miller's 1989 proposal for a lottery amendment, the Georgia Senate approved his 1991 proposal. The measure passed on February 8 by a vote of forty-seven to nine, well above the required two-thirds majority.

The proposed amendment to revise Georgia's constitution to allow a lottery differed from related proposals that were being considered at the time in other southern states, such as Mississippi, Louisiana, Tennessee, and Texas. Miller's proposal stipulated that the revenues Georgia received from the lottery would be used to fund new education programs, not existing ones. The governor would be required by the amendment to include all of these revenues, as well as all of the education programs on which they would be spent, in a separate budget item called "Lottery Proceeds." Placing this language in the state constitution helped ensure that Georgia would not follow the lead of Florida and many other states by substituting lottery revenues for existing state appropriations for education. It also made Georgia the pacesetter for several other southern states that, in subsequent years, adopted or at least considered lotteries of their own.

### Passing the Enabling Legislation, 1991–1992

Because Georgia's constitution requires that constitutional referenda be held in conjunction with a statewide general election, the lottery amendment could not appear on the ballot until November 1992, twenty-one months after it was approved by the General Assembly. The next controversy concerning the lottery occurred during this long interim, when Miller urged the legislature to enact a bill governing the implementation of the lottery in advance of the referendum. This legislation would be contingent—that is, it would take effect only if the referendum passed.

During the weeks leading up to the 1992 legislative session, Speaker Murphy took issue with some of the particulars of Miller's proposed bill. The main question, according to Murphy, was who would control the distribution of the revenues the state earned from a lottery. Murphy insisted that the governor not be in charge of parceling out these funds to his preferred education programs. The speaker was trying, at a minimum, to ensure that the General Assembly would have a voice in deciding how revenues from the lottery would be spent. To underscore his seriousness, Murphy appointed another longtime Miller opponent, Rep. Bill Dover, to chair the Ways and Means Committee, which of necessity would play a leading role in writing the enabling legislation for the lottery. Soon after Dover was appointed, Miller backed off from his proposal to have the governor oversee the distribution of lottery funds.

The compromise that Miller and Murphy reached, which proved to be illusory, was to have the enabling legislation specify that revenues from the lottery would be divided equally among Miller's three educational priorities: a new and voluntary prekindergarten program, funding for new school construction and equipment, and a new HOPE (Helping Outstanding Pupils Educationally) scholarship program that would allow talented low- and middle-income students to attend college within the state tuition-free. In November 1991, estimating that the lottery would earn the state government around $250 million per year, Miller told business and political leaders that he planned to ask the legislature to allocate 30 percent of these new revenues to each of his three new programs. (The remaining 10 percent would be set aside as a reserve fund to carry the state through years when lottery revenues might be insufficient.) Passing the enabling legislation during the 1991–1992 General Assembly would "give the public a chance to know the details of what they are voting for before they vote" in the referendum, the governor argued. Expecting that the voters would approve the lottery amendment by as much as a two-to-one margin, Miller seemed unconcerned that he might alienate some potential supporters by making clear in the law that others would benefit directly from the programs that the lottery funded, but not them. "There is no doubt in my mind it's going to pass," he boasted.[19]

Much to Miller's dismay, when the lottery bill emerged from the House Industry Committee in February 1992, it said merely, "It is the intent of the General Assembly that appropriations from the Lottery for Education

Account shall be for educational purposes only." As Bill Shipp, a longtime chronicler of Georgia politics, noted at the time, this meant that there was "no specific dedication of lottery funds in the bill" beyond the general allocation to education and, more importantly, that the General Assembly would determine specific appropriations for education.[20] The Industry Committee's version of the bill, which broke Miller and Murphy's compromise agreement to divide lottery revenues equally among the prekindergarten, college-scholarship, and school-building programs, passed the House by 127 to 32. The House amended the bill during the floor debate, specifying that a special sales tax of four cents would be levied on each lottery ticket and that the revenue from the tax would go into the state's general fund. With Miller's campaign promise of a lottery that would generate revenue for—and only for—new education programs now in jeopardy, he looked to the Senate for help.

The Senate version of the lottery bill, like the original version introduced in the House, allocated lottery revenues equally among Miller's new prekindergarten, school construction, and HOPE scholarship programs. The Senate also deleted the sales tax provision, which Miller opposed. A House-Senate conference committee took up the two versions of the bill and, in the end, Miller and the House leaders forged a compromise. Lottery revenues would go to Miller's three programs but the General Assembly would determine the distribution ratio and, in subsequent years, could adjust it. The final bill also established a governor-appointed, seven-member lottery board to evaluate bids for major contracts, such as those for scratch-off tickets and on-line games. The board would hire an executive director for the new state lottery corporation, and neither the governor nor the legislature would be able to intervene in contractual or other operational decisions. Miller signed the bill in May 1992.

### Campaigning for the Lottery Referendum, 1992

The final test for Miller's lottery proposal was the November 1992 referendum to remove the state constitution's prohibition on lotteries and thus allow the newly enacted lottery law to take effect. This proved to be a narrow, hard-fought victory for the governor even though, as gambling opponent Roger Byrd noted, lawmakers in early 1992 had regarded the public's support for a lottery as being "so strong, they were afraid not to go along." In the November referendum, 52 percent of Georgia's voters said *yes* to the lottery amendment and 48 percent said *no*. Lottery opponents had been encouraged by an *Atlanta Journal and Constitution* poll indicating that support for the proposed constitutional amendment had fallen from 72 percent in 1990 to 53 percent in late October 1992, as well as by a recent plunge in Miller's popularity caused by his proposal, which he later rescinded, to remove the Confederate battle emblem from the state flag.[21]

The campaign for the lottery amendment was spearheaded by a new group called Georgians for Better Education (GBE), which had been formed by Miller and was chaired by David Garrett III, a widely respected Atlanta businessman and a longtime advocate of educational reform. The week before the referendum, Betsey Weltner, the director of GBE, brought executives from three lotteries to Atlanta to describe their success in raising lottery revenues for their states. GBE also can be credited with keeping the debate centered on education and on the revenue the state was losing because Georgians were playing the Florida lottery. Attacked by critics who questioned why he had abandoned his long-standing opposition to a lottery, Miller said, "Of course I changed my mind on the lottery when I saw the money going from Georgia to Florida, and thirty-five other states with a lottery."[22]

An example of GBE's efforts to frame the debate was an article by Garrett in the *Journal and Constitution*'s Sunday "Perspective" section on the eve of the referendum. According to Garrett, "More than 200 million Georgia dollars have flowed into the Florida lottery since 1988." Garrett also emphasized the overcrowded school buildings, outdated laboratories and computers, and the "scrimping" by Georgia's parents to send their children to college. His article cited the abundance of lottery proceeds in states such as Iowa, Pennsylvania, and New Jersey. Finally, Garrett claimed that "what happened with Florida's lottery funds"—that is, substituting lottery revenues for funds previously appropriated for education—"cannot happen here. We have learned from Florida's mistakes and will avoid them."[23]

To label GBE's funding as superior to that enjoyed by antilottery groups is to understate its advantage. GBE had a budget of $722,671, more than five times greater than the budgets of all the antilottery committees combined ($136,167). Among the large contributors to the pro-lottery organization were Miller's campaign committee, which gave $29,500; the Georgia Association of Convenience Stores, which gave $80,000; and the Marathon Oil Company, which gave $24,373. (Convenience stores and gas stations, of course, would be prime outlets for lottery ticket sales.) Several Georgia banks and law firms, eager to curry favor with the governor for reasons unrelated to the lottery, also were on the list of significant contributors.

Opponents of the lottery amendment included clergy from the United Methodist, Southern Baptist, Episcopal, Presbyterian, and Roman Catholic churches. A combination of antilottery groups pooled their funds to air radio commercials featuring the popular former Atlanta Braves star Dale Murphy, a prominent Mormon. In the end, the opposition ran a surprisingly strong campaign. By astutely focusing its efforts outside lottery-friendly Atlanta, it decreased public support for the proposed amendment. The antilottery groups argued fervently that the lottery was a regressive source of revenue; that for the state to encourage gambling was immoral; that the lottery would erode the work ethic of citizens who became persuaded that purchasing lottery tickets would solve their financial problems; and that no matter what Miller promised, the legislature would use the new lottery as an excuse to reduce existing spending on education. An additional argument—that adopting a lottery would open the floodgates to other forms of legalized gambling—gained credence when, shortly after Miller's election as governor on a lottery platform, a variety of legislators introduced bills to legalize casinos, dog racing, horse racing, and offshore gambling cruises. "For the past ten years we have been saying that when you pass legalized gambling, what you have done is broken the dam to become a gambling culture," said Reverend Henderson. Finally, Miller's decision to pass the enabling legislation in advance of the referendum cut both ways politically. It reassured voters about what they would be getting if they approved the constitutional amendment. But, in defining who would benefit directly from the lottery, it also defined who would not.[24]

The steep decline in public support for the lottery during the 1992 referendum campaign suggests that the fight could have gone either way. As noted earlier, however, proponents of the lottery enjoyed two major advantages over critics: dramatically superior funding and a huge lead at the start of the campaign. A third reason for the passage of the lottery amendment was the voters' perception that the state's economy was still in recession. Many Georgians doubted that new education programs could be enacted during times of economic hardship and budgetary constraint unless they were funded by a new source of revenue such as a lottery. Additionally, the lottery benefited from being on the ballot in a presidential election year, when the turnout among occasional voters, many of them disposed to favor a lottery, would be at its highest. Finally, the white clergy of Georgia failed to coordinate their antilottery efforts with the state's African American clergy. Rev. William T. Neal asserts that he and other white clergy shoulder most of the blame for this lack of coordination because they failed to reach out to the black clergy early enough in the campaign. Many leaders of African American churches preached in general terms on the dangers of gambling but remained silent regarding the lottery amendment. Rev. Timothy McDonald, the African American pastor of the First Iconium Baptist Church, went so far as to say, "If the black clergy had come out against it, it would've been defeated."[25]

## WHY GEORGIA CREATED A LOTTERY

The narrow passage of the lottery amendment suggests that nothing about the politics of gambling in Georgia was inevitable. To understand why Georgia decided to create a lottery requires taking account of the diffusionary influence of other states, certain internal characteristics of Georgia itself, and the efforts of Zell Miller as a policy entrepreneur.

### Diffusion

States are influenced by other states in a variety of ways. In this case, Georgia was influenced by Kentucky in the person of a non-Georgian and non-Kentuckian whose focus was on politics rather than public policy. James Carville, a political consultant from Louisiana, was looking for a way to make Miller his client in the 1990 Georgia gubernatorial election. Carville had helped parlay the lottery issue into success at the polls for Wallace Wilkinson, his client in Kentucky's most recent election for governor, and saw no reason why the issue would not work further south. Carville also thought that focusing on a new and controversial idea like a lottery would refurbish Miller's image, transforming him from a colorless, familiar figure on the Georgia political scene to a change agent and champion of innovative ideas. For a Democrat in particular, championing new education programs without new taxes was a way of pleasing his party's base without playing into the hands of antitax Republicans.

One reason Carville's advice worked so well for Miller in 1990 was that the influence of neighboring Florida had already prepared Georgians for the campaign that Miller would wage on behalf of a state lottery. Many voters had learned to play the lottery by crossing the border into Florida. They wondered why they could not place their bets closer to home so that, even if they lost, they would lose in a way that benefited their own state. Florida also offered an example of how successful a lottery could be in raising revenues without raising taxes.

In other ways, Florida served as a useful counterexample for Georgia. Miller frequently pointed out that after Florida adopted its lottery with the promise that the new revenues would improve education in the state, it had broken that promise by substituting lottery revenues for revenues that would have been spent from the general fund. Appealing to state pride, Miller promised that Georgia's lottery would be even better than Florida's because, by constitutional definition, its proceeds would be placed in a separate account and spent only on new education programs. Thus, although the Georgia lottery in some ways exemplifies the traditional diffusion of a policy from one state to another, it also represents a variation on diffusion theory, which we call *incremental diffusion.* Incremental diffusion describes how a borrowed policy may be made more appealing in a state by being altered and, arguably, improved before being adopted in its new setting.

### Internal Characteristics

A state experiencing fiscal woes in an era of declining subsidies from the federal government and widespread hostility to new or higher taxes is a prime candidate for any new funding source that relies on voluntary contributions. Georgia in the early 1990s was no exception. Because Georgia is the home of Scientific Games, a major national lottery corporation, it did not lack for reminders from within that a lottery was exactly that kind of source.

Tying the lottery to new college scholarships added another element: it spoke to the concern Georgians had about their state's "brain drain," exemplified by the three-fourths of Georgia's brightest high school seniors who left the state to attend college elsewhere, many of them never to return. The provision that lottery revenues would fund new prekindergarten programs also broadened its appeal, especially to the African American community. In Georgia, as in most states, organized opposition to a lottery was centered in the churches. In the South, such opposition is especially potent when it spans racial lines, uniting black and white clergy in a coordinated campaign. Appropriately, white clergy members in Georgia fault themselves for not reaching out to their African American colleagues during the 1992 referendum campaign. To be sure, the success of such efforts would have been limited by the promise that lottery funds would be spent to provide prekindergarten education for the low-income families whom many black clergy serve. But considering how close the vote to pass the lottery amendment was, a cross-racial alliance among the clergy could have made the difference.

The influence of Georgia's constitution on the politics of lottery adoption was important but complex. The amendment process in Georgia is less arduous than in many southern states. The General Assembly must approve an amendment only once before it appears on the ballot, and a simple majority of those voting in the referendum is all that it takes for passage. Because enacting a lottery in Georgia required a change in the state constitution, this aspect of the amendment process helped the cause. The constitutional requirement that referenda on amendments be held in conjunction with a general election, however, cut both ways. By delaying the referendum for twenty-one months after the General Assembly voted to place the amendment on the ballot, it gave the opposition plenty of time to mobilize. But it also assured a higher turnout among precisely those groups of voters who tend to support lotteries than if the referendum had been held on an unfamiliar date. As it happened, 1992 was a presidential year, when turnout among these groups is especially high.

### Policy Entrepreneur

Zell Miller's efforts as the policy entrepreneur for the Georgia lottery succeeded to an extent matched by few other policy entrepreneurs at any level of government. He placed the lottery at the top of the political agenda at a time when no other prominent political leader in his state was willing to do so. His decision to define the lottery as an education initiative was crucial to his campaign to sell it to a traditionally antigambling electorate. He skillfully pursued enactment at every stage of the extended policy process: legislative approval of the amendment repealing the constitutional ban on lotteries, legislative passage of the law creating the lottery, and support by a majority of the voters in the lottery referendum. Not surprisingly, as subsequent chapters show, lottery supporters in Tennessee, South Carolina, Alabama, and other states turned to Miller's example and, often, to Miller himself for guidance. Georgia set the pace for much of the South on the lottery issue, and Miller set the pace for Georgia.

To be sure, Miller paid a political price by deciding to pursue enactment of the enabling legislation for the lottery in advance of the referendum. In identifying who would benefit from lottery revenues, chiefly the parents of preschool and college-age children, Miller also identified who would not benefit, including senior citizens, law enforcement officials, and other groups that might otherwise have seen a direct stake for themselves in passing his version of the lottery. But parents are no small constituency, and, in promising tangible and substantial new benefits for their children, Miller energized them not only for the fight to create a lottery but also against any future effort that might be made to change or repeal it.

## THE AFTER-POLITICS OF THE GEORGIA LOTTERY

Lotteries seldom generate an extended after-politics. No state that has enacted a lottery in the modern era has seriously considered repealing it. Although Georgia did not depart dramatically from this pattern, the lottery referendum's narrow victory set the stage for a brief period of continuing debate about the legitimacy of the lottery. Over the longer term, the lottery's tremendous success in raising funds for education secured not only its permanence but also its immunity to politically effective criticism.

### Securing the Lottery, 1993–1994

Postenactment controversies concerning the Georgia lottery began even before ticket sales started on July 1, 1993. In the spring of 1993, some actually thought that the lottery might be an impediment to Miller's 1994 reelection. Tom Perdue, a leading Republican campaign consultant, began counseling would-be gubernatorial challengers to claim that the lottery violated Miller's pledge of no new taxes or user fees. Ambitious Georgia Republicans such as state representative Matt Towery agreed that the lottery could be used against Miller in the election. Towery alleged that suspicious ties existed between administrators of the Texas lottery and GTECH, one of the companies contracted by the Georgia lottery. Senate minority leader Arthur "Skin" Edge was among several legislators who questioned why GTECH had been awarded the largest contract instead of Automatic Wagering International, which was the low bidder and had operated the Florida lottery efficiently.[26]

In the fall of 1993, however, revenue from the sale of lottery tickets began pouring in to the state treasury in unexpectedly large amounts. As Bill Shipp wrote, "Governor Zell Miller's 'education lottery' has succeeded beyond the Governor's most optimistic predictions. Millions of new dollars from the lottery will go into thousands of [college] scholarships for worthy students." By the end of its first year, Georgia had received $330 million from the lottery, with nearly all of the revenues going to education. Credit for the creation of the Georgia lottery was showered on Miller, while credit for the unexpectedly strong sales of Georgia lottery tickets went to Rebecca Paul, who was chosen to run the Georgia Lottery Corporation by the Miller-appointed lottery board on the strength of her record as the overseer of the state lotteries in Illinois and, more recently, Florida. The early revenue surge, the immediate provision of college scholarships and capital improvements to schools, the planning for the new prekindergarten program, and the lack of any specific evidence concerning unethical state contracts with lottery corporations made the lottery a positive element in Miller's 1994 reelection bid. Johnny Isakson, Miller's defeated Republican rival in 1990, said, "All three of the chosen programs qualify as 'good ideas.'"[27]

Nonetheless, the beginning of the 1994 session of the General Assembly witnessed a new round of controversy. At least twenty-eight bills and resolutions were introduced to change substantially the way the lottery was conducted. Proposals for change ranged from disallowing ticket sales on Sunday to making lottery administrators predict ticket sales five years in advance to help the legislature allocate money for programs. One antilottery politician, after reading a hastily prepared legislative report, claimed that lottery proceeds were being distributed disproportionately to schools in Democratic leaders' districts. (The report proved false.)

As lottery revenues continued to accumulate, however, controversies and proposals for dramatic changes died down. Perhaps the best evidence that the existence of the lottery was no longer a matter of serious dispute was the behavior of Miller's Republican opponent in the 1994 gubernatorial election, Guy Millner. Millner, who had voted against the lottery amendment in the 1992 referendum, initially argued that the lottery should be brought back before the voters every four years and that, in the meantime, lottery revenues should go to the state's general fund. After polls showed that these positions were overwhelmingly unpopular, he ran commercials promising to "leave the lottery alone." Governor Miller consistently and effectively campaigned as the man who had created the lottery and, despite a national Republican tide, was reelected.[28]

### Entrenching the Lottery, 1995–2006

Measured in strictly political terms, the Georgia lottery has continued to rise from strength to strength. Surveys taken in 1998 and 2000 found that 75 to 78 percent of the state's voters would support the lottery if it reappeared on the ballot. Active opposition among religious leaders and groups vanished. Some of the clergy members who had fought against the lottery referendum in 1992, such as Rev. Timothy McDonald, the president of Concerned Black Clergy, acknowledged that the lottery "used to be a real hot topic for us. But once our students started to get a college education that they never would have been able to do otherwise, we do not talk about the lottery as much." The Georgia Council on Moral and Civic Concerns, a conservative Christian organization, refocused its antilottery efforts on the weaknesses of the state's modest program to help the victims of lottery-induced problem gambling.[29]

In the electoral arena, the 1998 gubernatorial contest matched major-party candidates who originally had opposed the lottery but now outdid each other in professing their support. Millner, once again the Republican nominee, was bested in this regard when his Democratic opponent, state representative Roy Barnes, secured unanimous legislative approval for an amendment to enshrine the state's commitment to the lottery-funded HOPE scholarships and prekindergarten program in the state constitution. Persuaded by Barnes's zeal to "get into the constitution the highest covenant the state of Georgia and the General Assembly have with the people," the voters approved the amendment and elected its sponsor as governor. Four years later, Barnes was unseated by Republican Sonny Perdue, another erstwhile opponent of the lottery who now pledged his fealty to it.[30]

Georgians were confirmed in their devotion to the lottery by the accolades it received from political leaders around the country. President Bill Clinton, in his 1997 State of the Union address, praised Georgia's HOPE scholarships as a "pioneering program" and borrowed the name for his own proposed federal tuition-assistance program. (Ironically, the existence of Georgia's program meant that students in Georgia would be ineligible for Clinton's version of HOPE.) HOPE-style merit scholarship programs for college students were adopted by several states during the late 1990s and early 2000s, although only South Carolina and Tennessee followed Georgia in creating a lottery to fund the new scholarships. "If in one hundred years someone tried to do a case study on state lotteries in the second half of the twentieth century," boasted Rebecca Paul, "Georgia would be the case study of how to do it right."[31]

Much of the popularity of the Georgia lottery owes to the rapid expansion of both its benefits and its ranks of beneficiaries. Uncertain about how much revenue the lottery would generate for the state treasury, Governor Miller and the General Assembly initially limited the coverage of the new education programs. The first round of HOPE scholarships financed two years of tuition at any state college or university for students who earned a 3.0 grade-point average in high school and whose family income was $66,000 or less. (College students at private institutions in Georgia received a smaller benefit, $500 per year.) Federal Pell Grant recipients had their HOPE scholarships reduced. Similarly, only children from low-income families were eligible for the new prekindergarten program for four-year-olds.

But when annual lottery revenues reached $500 million in 1995, double the amount Miller had estimated during his 1990 election campaign, he and his successors as governor persuaded a compliant legislature to open the floodgates. The family income ceiling for HOPE recipients was raised to $100,000 per year, then lifted altogether. The requirement for a 3.0 high school GPA was diluted to the point that around one-third of HOPE scholars did not have to meet it. Students who maintained a 3.0 average in college were allowed to keep their scholarship until they graduated, however long that took. Not just tuition, but also the cost of books and fees was added to the medley of lottery-funded benefits. The scholarship for students attending private colleges was raised to $3,000 per year. Other new scholarship programs, including one to help public school teachers seek graduate degrees and another to fully subsidize students in special programs at Mercer University and Georgia Military Institute, two politically well-connected private institutions, were placed under HOPE's full-tuition umbrella.[32] Eventually, Pell recipients were allowed to receive full HOPE scholarships on top of their federal grants.

The revenues the state treasury received from the lottery increased every year, a record of growth unmatched by any other state lottery and attributable, Paul argued, to the support of "citizens who feel so closely connected with how the profits are spent."[33] During the lottery's first seven years, it generated enough surplus funds that the state could spend vast sums on public school construction and technology assistance. Although the rising cost of the HOPE scholarships and the prekindergarten program brought spending on public school assistance to a halt in 2001, full college tuition continued to be offered to every student, regardless of age, income, or scholastic aptitude, at the state's thirty-three technical schools.

The popularity of the HOPE scholarships immunized them from political attack. As eligibility for the scholarships spread to encompass many thousands of families, and as the size of the benefit increased each year, HOPE became a classic distributive program, as politically untouchable in Georgia as Medicare and Social Security are at the federal level. Nonetheless, scholars and journalists published serious criticisms of the program. Among the problems they identified were these:

1. Although lottery gambling has been heaviest among African Americans and the poor, the beneficiaries of HOPE college scholarships have been disproportionately white and middle class. Thus, concluded a study by the Carl Vinson Institute of Government at the University of Georgia, the lottery is "regressive as a source of state revenue" and the "distribution of the benefits of lottery-funded programs tends to exacerbate the inequities." Although Peter Brown of Mercer University exaggerated when he claimed that the lottery "soaked the poor to benefit the children of the rich," he did not overstate the case by much. University of Georgia professors Chris Cornwell and David Mustard found that only 4 percent of HOPE recipients needed the scholarships in order to afford college.[34]

2. Grade inflation and loose definitions of a B average in many of the state's high schools have made HOPE scholarships easy to get but difficult

to keep. State education commissioners reported that in 1997–1998 only 36 percent of HOPE recipients in college earned the 3.0 average required to renew their scholarships past the freshman year, and only one-fourth kept them until graduation. An effort to tie eligibility for the scholarships to end-of-year statewide exams in high school was shot down in the General Assembly, as was Governor Perdue's suggestion in 2003 that a minimum score of 1,000 on the SAT be required. (He later reduced this to 900, but that was rejected as well.) Frustrated by the unwillingness of high schools and legislators to impose realistic standards of achievement on high school students, state school superintendent Linda Schrenko lamented that "nobody ever wants to talk about the problems of HOPE because they are afraid of being labeled anti-HOPE." Referring to the vast number of woefully unprepared students who enrolled in college with HOPE scholarships, she added, "The notion that we are somehow serving those children is crazy."[35]

3. Georgia's leadership in creating new merit-based college scholarships was accompanied by the state's repeal in 1999 of nearly all of its need-based assistance to college students. A study by Thomas Mortenson, the editor and publisher of *Postsecondary Education Opportunity,* ranked Georgia last among the states in likelihood that an economically disadvantaged student would be able to attend college.[36] The merit basis of the HOPE scholarship program has not prevented Georgia from consistently trailing all forty-nine other states in average SAT score.

Defenders of Georgia's new lottery-funded education programs responded to these criticisms by pointing out that Georgians of all kinds were benefiting from scholarships to postsecondary technical schools and that poorer families were the heaviest users of the new prekindergarten facilities. They praised HOPE for enticing many of the state's middle-class students to stay in Georgia for college, pointing out that since HOPE was created, the proportion of the state's students with 1500-plus SAT scores who enrolled in a Georgia institution of higher education had risen from 23 to 76 percent.[37]

Most of the state's elected officials, however, paid little attention to criticisms of the wildly popular program. (Had they paid them greater attention, they likely would have ceased to be elected officials.) In 2003, a HOPE Scholarship Study Commission was appointed after the state's Office of Planning and Budget estimated that within four years, the projected cost of lottery-funded programs would begin to exceed projected lottery revenues by several hundred million dollars per year. The commission, which consisted of legislators, education officials, students, and lottery representatives, refused to consider reimposing income ceilings on eligibility for the scholarships, recognizing that HOPE had become a politically invulnerable middle-class entitlement program. Deferring to strong opposition from the legislative black caucus and other minority groups, the commission also ruled out Governor Perdue's suggestion for a minimum SAT score, even though recent data showed that 81 percent of HOPE recipients who scored below 900 lost their scholarships after their freshman year in college. Instead, in November 2003 the commission recommended that, in the future, HOPE cover only tuition, not books and fees (an estimated savings of $827 million over five years); toughen up the requirement for a 3.0 GPA in high school (saving an estimated $105 million over two years); and take several smaller belt-tightening measures.[38]

Perdue quickly endorsed the commission's recommendations. At the beginning of the 2004 legislative session, commission co-chairs Bill Hamrick, a Republican and the chair of the Senate Higher Education Committee, and Louise McBee, a Democrat and the chair of the House Higher Education Committee, introduced legislation to enact the recommendations into law. Knowing that any attempt to reduce HOPE's benefits would be politically difficult, Hamrick and McBee operated as a bipartisan team to provide political cover for their legislative colleagues in a year when all 236 representatives and senators faced reelection. But Democratic lieutenant governor Mark Taylor, positioning himself to run for governor against Perdue in 2006, toured the state's college campuses attacking the proposal to eliminate book and fees subsidies as a burdensome tax increase for students. He accused Perdue of "beginning the gutting of the HOPE scholarships program."[39]

By the end of February 2004, Hamrick was conceding that his and McBee's bill "was dead" as long as it included the provision to eliminate books and fees, and that substantially modifying the provision was the price for securing legislative authorization to standardize the way B averages were measured in state high schools. With support from the governor, the General Assembly passed a bill in April to standardize the B average and to eliminate the book and fees allowances only if lottery revenues declined for two and three consecutive years, respectively. To discourage colleges and universities from continuing to raise student fees, the bill also froze at their January 1, 2004, levels the amount of fees that HOPE would cover.[40]

Fearing that Taylor had positioned himself to run for governor in 2006 as the defender of the HOPE scholarship program against an incumbent who wanted to trim it, Perdue seized the political initiative in June 2005 by proposing a "HOPE Chest" constitutional amendment requiring that all lottery revenues be spent on HOPE scholarships and prekindergarten programs. Taylor upped the ante with a proposed constitutional amendment to protect HOPE from cuts unless two-thirds of the legislature and a majority of voters approved them. With Republicans in control of both legislative chambers, Taylor's proposal was buried in committee. Nonetheless, the Senate fell three votes short of the two-thirds majority needed to approve Perdue's amendment and the House came up eighteen votes short.[41] Perdue was easily reelected.

### Video Poker

As was the case in Mississippi, the highly visible controversy over whether to enact a lottery in Georgia diverted public and media attention from some quiet legislative actions that were designed to open the door to another, less popular form of gambling. In 1991, while the General Assembly debated and approved Gov. Zell Miller's request for a lottery amendment to the state constitution, legislators also enacted the first in a series of video gambling bills. The 1991 law, like most of those that followed, was written at the behest of Les Schneider, the lobbyist for the powerful Georgia Amusement and Music Operators Association, and was sponsored by Democratic representative Sonny Watson. The law amended the state's broad antigambling statute so that "prohibitions against gambling shall not apply to certain games or devices"—specifically, games that require "some skill" and devices that pay off in noncash prizes valued at five dollars or less. Watson explained to legislative colleagues that his purpose was innocent: to protect family-oriented businesses that allowed children and their parents to play arcade games in hopes of winning stuffed animals and similar prizes. The Six Flags Over Georgia amusement park and the Chuck E. Cheese pizza restaurants were Watson's leading examples. The largest beneficiaries of the new law, however, were the bars, truck stops, convenience stores, and gambling arcades that now could operate video poker and similar gambling machines legally.[42]

Other Schneider-inspired bills followed, usually sponsored in the early 1990s by Watson and in the late 1990s by Democratic representative Alan Powell. Watson and Powell's persuasiveness among their colleagues was reinforced by campaign contributions from the amusement operators association and various gambling-related donors. A 1992 law exempted video gambling revenues from taxation and removed from public inspection the names of those possessing state licenses to operate the machines. In 1998, the law was changed so that gamblers could let their winnings ride for as long as they played instead of having to stop and collect a prize every time they won. The term *noncash* prizes was stretched to the point that it lacked all meaning. Some operators paid off in Wal-Mart or Home Depot gift certificates that could be converted into cash at the stores; others handed out "pet rocks" that they then bought back for cash.[43]

Many operators simply ignored the law and paid off directly in cash. Legislators made violating the law in this overt way easier. For years the state had prohibited local governments from regulating doctors, funeral directors, and seventeen other businesses and professions that were already regulated by a state agency. In 1999, the same year that the final report of the federal government's National Gambling Impact Study Commission described video poker as the "crack cocaine" of gambling, the General Assembly added video gambling operators to the list of professions exempt from local regulation, even though no state agency regulated the operators. Law enforcement officials said that it was almost impossible to prevent operators from running casino-style gambling parlors. The only thing that distinguished video gambling devices from slot machines was that the player pushed a "skill stop" button to make the spinning images come to rest. Operators argued that this skill-free exercise of "some skill" is what made their machines legal.

The flow of video gambling machines into Georgia became a flood when South Carolina's state supreme court declared video poker unconstitutional in October 1999. Expelled from the state by July 1, 2000, tens of thousands of the machines were moved by their owners to Georgia, at first to cross-border cities like Hartwell and Augusta and then throughout the state. Noticing that a street in his neighborhood had become a video gambling strip, a young Hartwell businessman named Arch Adams launched a richly detailed website eponymously named stopvideopoker.org. Adams outed Representative Powell as being the husband of a video gambling company owner, and statewide media organizations publicized the revelation. In fall 2000, Adams also persuaded a local television news station to send an undercover investigative reporter to a video gambling arcade and videotape operators illegally paying off gamblers in cash. The reporter showed the tape to Roy Barnes and asked the governor, a longtime recipient of campaign contributions from video gambling companies, what he intended to do.[44]

Barnes ordered state law enforcement officials to crack down on illegal video gambling, hoping that tough talk and a brief flurry of raids would lay the matter to rest. Responding to a bill introduced by Republican senator Mike Beatty at the start of the 2001 legislative session which would make possessing a video gambling machine illegal, Barnes endorsed a different bill that would increase the penalties imposed on owners who were convicted of paying off gamblers in cash. Schneider and the amusement operators association favored this bill, knowing that police and prosecutors lacked the resources to do the undercover investigations necessary to enforce it. So did two other prominent Democratic leaders who, Adams revealed on his website, had been the beneficiaries of video gambling donations, Lt. Gov. Mark Taylor and House Speaker Tom Murphy. When the Republican-controlled Senate overwhelmingly passed Beatty's ban on gambling machines, Murphy kept the bill off the House floor until 11:30 P.M. on March 22, thirty minutes before the General Assembly was scheduled to adjourn for the year. At 11:30 sharp Murphy recognized a leading video gambling supporter, Democratic representative David Lucas, who filibustered the bill until midnight.[45]

Murphy's late-night maneuver triggered a media firestorm, with Barnes on the receiving end for not doing anything to prevent it. Adams's website, which had become a regular stop for Georgia reporters, pointed out that as governor Barnes had signed three of the bills that eased the way for video gambling to spread throughout the state. Republican House and Senate leaders demanded that Barnes include anti–video gambling legislation in his call for a special summer 2001 General Assembly session that originally was meant to focus exclusively on legislative redistricting. Christian clergy members around the state urged their parishioners to flood the governor with phone calls and faxes demanding that he accede to this request.[46]

Looking for a way to cut his political losses, Barnes not only joined the antigambling parade, he raced to the front of it. "Video gambling is like a cancer that is quickly spreading throughout Georgia," the governor declared in August, and it "will no longer be allowed in this state." In an effort to criminalize video gambling machines while protecting Chuck E. Cheese–style children's games, Barnes followed South Carolina's approach, which barred any machine that uses cards, craps, keno, or slot-style lineup devices. (In a sense, both the problem of rampant video gambling and its solution had diffused from South Carolina to Georgia.) The governor began campaigning against video gambling around the state, often surrounding himself with supportive district attorneys and deputy sheriffs.[47]

When Lieutenant Governor Taylor joined Barnes in cutting his political losses by supporting a ban on video gambling machines, the Senate unanimously passed the bill on August 28, 2001. Before the vote took place, Republican senators lined up at the microphone to pay tribute to Senator Beatty, who had introduced and championed the ban while the governor and lieutenant governor still opposed it. Yielding to the inevitable, Speaker Murphy also abandoned his opposition to the bill and the House passed it by 158 to 12 on September 6. (Murphy continued to grumble that the state would have to reimburse the owners for the cost of their machines, overlooking the obvious fact that they could sell or move them to another state.) In May 2002 the state supreme court unanimously overturned a superior court judge in Fulton County who had ruled in January that the new video gambling statute was unconstitutionally vague.[48] Barnes ordered the machines out of the state by June 30, 2002.

## CONCLUSION

Twenty years ago, it would have been as hard to imagine Georgia adopting a lottery as to imagine Mississippi legalizing casinos. Today the political sanctity of the Georgia lottery could not be greater. As one indicator of what a sacred cow the lottery has become, each of Georgia's last three governors has proposed his own constitutional amendment to buttress it and the education programs its proceeds fund.

One consequence of the lottery's success has been to undermine any other forms of gambling that might divert revenues. In 2002, video gambling was sent packing. In 2003, Fulton County Commissioner Robb Pitts's plea for a constitutional amendment to allow casino gambling in Atlanta failed even to get a hearing in the legislature. "Legislators fear a casino industry would be in direct competition with the lottery," noted one journalist, "potentially endangering the money available for scholarships."[49]

Georgia was not the first southern state to adopt a lottery: Virginia was, followed by Florida. As a candidate for governor in 1990, Zell Miller learned from neighboring Florida's experience that a lottery would raise money for the state treasury in a politically painless way. But he also learned that unless this money was set aside for new programs, it would merely take the place of money from the general fund that was already being spent on existing ones. From political consultant James Carville's recent success on behalf of candidate Wallace Wilkinson in the 1987 Kentucky gubernatorial election, Miller became aware that championing a lottery could be a winning issue at the polls. Applying all of these lessons, Miller invented the lottery-funded HOPE scholarship program and rode it to victory at the polls.

As the next few chapters show, would-be policy entrepreneurs elsewhere in the South, especially Democrats seeking a politically painless way to fund increased state spending on education in an era of rising Republican conservatism, learned and tried to apply the same lessons in their states as Miller had in Georgia. In every case, policy entrepreneurship coincided with political entrepreneurship. Ambitious Democratic politicians strove to further their own careers by translating proposals for lottery-funded college scholarships into electoral success.

# THREE

# SOUTH CAROLINA

## "We Just *Luuuvv* South Carolinians Playing Our Lottery"

As in Mississippi and Georgia, South Carolina's political agenda was, for the most part, devoid of gambling-related issues until the 1980s. Since then, however, gambling has emerged—sometimes quietly, sometimes raucously— as an important subject of political controversy with repercussions for everything from the policies of the state government to its personnel. For a time in the 1990s, South Carolina gained national notoriety as the video poker capital of the world. Yet by the end of the decade, video poker was illegal in the state.

Even as one form of gambling was dying, however, another was being born. In 1998, Jim Hodges ran for governor on an "education lottery" platform modeled on fellow Democrat Zell Miller's 1990 gubernatorial campaign in Georgia. Like Miller, Hodges rode the issue of improving education without raising taxes to victory in an increasingly Republican state. In 2000 Hodges secured the voters' approval for a constitutional amendment that authorized the state's General Assembly to create a lottery. At his urging, legislators did so in 2001, and the first ticket was sold in January 2002.

The provision of South Carolina's constitution which, until the 2000 referendum, stood in the way of a lottery had been part of the document since 1868: "No lottery shall ever be allowed or be advertised by newspapers, or otherwise, or its tickets be sold in this state."[1] Over the years, the General Assembly banned nearly every other form of gambling by statute. An exception for bingo "when conducted by charitable, religious, or fraternal organizations exempt from federal income taxation" was made in 1974 in the form of a constitutional amendment. In 1993 the Catawba Indian Nation, South Carolina's only federally recognized tribe, secured the right to operate bingo halls on two sites as part of the settlement of its lawsuit against the state asserting tribal claims to large swatches of land.[2]

## SOUTH CAROLINA ADOPTS A LOTTERY

The state constitution's prohibition against lotteries was first challenged in 1991, when a newly elected Democratic state representative, John Scott, introduced an amendment to overturn it. Scott envisioned a lottery whose proceeds would be spent primarily to improve the state's public school system.

Because Scott's lottery proposal required a constitutional amendment, it faced two significant hurdles that simple legislation did not. First, it had to be passed by a two-thirds majority in both houses of the General Assembly. Second, it had to be approved by a majority of those voting on the amendment in a general election. Scott's bill failed to gain any momentum in the legislature. Even if it had, the governor at the time, Republican Carroll Campbell, had stated publicly that he would fight against any proposed lottery.

It is no coincidence that 1991 was the year that South Carolina, which shares borders only with Georgia and North Carolina, first examined its longstanding ban on lotteries. Zell Miller had been elected governor of Georgia on a lottery platform the year before. Scott recalls that his lottery bill "was inspired by the one in Georgia."[3] By 1991 Miller was working with the Georgia legislature to determine how a lottery would operate and how its proceeds would be spent. He also was cultivating public support with an eye toward placing a lottery referendum on the ballot in 1992. Miller was successful in both efforts.

In July 1993 lottery tickets went on sale in convenience stores and other locations all over Georgia. Many of these tickets were purchased by South Carolinians driving south across the state line. In 1994 students in Georgia started enrolling in college with lottery-funded HOPE scholarships, which provided free tuition for qualifying students. Lottery-playing South Carolinians were funding a significant portion of these scholarships.

In 1994 Nick Theodore, the Democratic candidate for governor, proposed a South Carolina lottery modeled on Georgia's. Although Theodore did not make the lottery the centerpiece of his campaign—indeed, he only raised the issue a few weeks before the election—he came surprisingly close to beating Republican nominee David Beasley, losing by just two percentage points.[4]

After Beasley became governor in 1995, the lottery assumed a minor place on the state's political agenda. Two trends were at work that helped prevent proposals for lottery gambling from being considered seriously. First, by the mid-1990s South Carolina had become by some measures the most Republican state in the South.[5] In South Carolina and elsewhere, lotteries usually have been less attractive to Republican politicians, whose Christian conservative constituents tend to oppose gambling on moral grounds, than to Democrats. During the 1990s, South Carolina Republicans won a majority of statewide elections and a majority of congressional seats. By 1996, they controlled the state's House of Representatives, and in 2001 they took control of the state Senate. Most important, once he became governor, Beasley made clear that like Governor Campbell, his Republican predecessor, he strongly opposed a lottery.

The second trend at work in South Carolina which helped to keep the lottery off the policy agenda during the mid-1990s was the proliferation of video poker as a large and, for a time, powerful industry in the state. To the extent that gambling issues were discussed in South Carolina in this period, video poker eclipsed the lottery.

### Video Poker

In the 1980s and early 1990s video gambling machines that allowed customers to play for prizes and, in practice, for money began to spread rapidly throughout South Carolina.[6] The General Assembly, without understanding what it was doing, had sanctioned these machines. In 1986 Jack Lindsay, the chair of the Senate Finance Committee, quietly introduced an amendment to a thousand-page budget bill that deleted the words "or property" from a law banning gambling machines that distributed "money or property to a player." Lindsay buried the provision among the hundreds of technical amendments that are customarily made to the annual budget bill, and neither Governor Beasley nor Lindsay's fellow legislators noticed it.[7] As Lindsay intended, however, video poker operators interpreted the change to mean that they could distribute slips of paper ("property") to gamblers entitling them to free plays, and that these free plays could be redeemed by the machine operators for cash. In this favorable legal climate, the number of video poker machines in South Carolina started to increase.[8]

Video poker's legality was tested when a group of Lancaster County citizens filed suit against video gambling operators, claiming that the payouts system was illegal. They lost their suit: the state supreme court ruled in 1991 that the video machine payout slips were a form of property and thus a legal prize under the Lindsay amendment. Having secured the court's endorsement, the video poker industry in South Carolina continued to grow.

In 1993 the General Assembly passed the Video Game Machines Act (VGMA), which was intended to rein in the burgeoning industry. According to the act, no establishment could operate more than five machines, each of which would be taxed by the state at an annual rate of two thousand dollars. Winnings were capped at $125 per day per gambler. The video poker industry thwarted the first of these restrictions by creating gambling malls in which as many as twenty licensed "establishments" with five machines each were housed under one roof. As for the $125 daily cap on winnings, it was unenforceable from the start. If a gambler won $500 playing video poker, for example, the machine would print four $125 paper slips that could be cashed on different days. More commonly, gambling operators simply ignored the law, advertising giant jackpots and cashing winning tickets regardless of amount. They did so knowing that the state lacked the resources to enforce the law and that occasional busts like those that generated $429,000 in fines in one nine-month period were simply a cost of doing business.[9] The most important consequence of VGMA was to open the floodgates to even more video gambling machines.

In response to pressures from constituents upset by the proliferation of gambling malls in their towns and counties, a new round of opposition to the video poker industry developed among legislators in 1994. They passed a bill that scheduled local-option referenda on video poker throughout the state. Voters would decide whether video poker would be legal in their counties.

The referenda backfired on video gambling's opponents. Only twelve of forty-six counties voted to remove the machines. On a statewide basis 58 percent of South Carolinians voted to keep video poker legal in their home counties. Then, in 1996, the state supreme court ruled by four to one that the legislature had violated South Carolina's constitution when it let each county decide the fate of video poker. The majority's rationale was that the state constitution requires a uniform statewide criminal code, with no variation from one county to another. Once again, video poker was legal throughout South Carolina. Its spread continued unabated.

By the late 1990s, video poker had become a significant lobbying force in the legislature and, in terms of machines and dollars, a major industry in South Carolina. Between 1989 and 1999 the number of video poker machines in the state grew from 7,000 to nearly 37,000. The amount bet by gamblers on video poker rose an average 20 percent per year, climbing above $3 billion in 1999, with annual industry profits approaching $835 million.[10] Although video poker generated only about $65 million per year for the state treasury in taxes and licensing fees, it appeared to be popular as well.[11] Confirming the results of the 1994 county referenda, a 1996 poll showed that 60 percent of South Carolinians wanted video poker to remain legal.

As for the lottery bills introduced by Democrats in the General Assembly during this period, the persistence of the ongoing controversy about video poker meant that they were never politically viable. In the House, Scott's bills always fell at least ten to twenty votes short of the two-thirds majority required for a constitutional amendment. The Senate seldom even voted on the lottery. "Without a governor who's supportive of gambling, it's going to be hard to implement any more gambling in this state," said Rep. Billy Boan.[12]

Another problem plaguing lottery bills was the lack of unanimity among Democratic legislators. In a 1996 roll call, for example, five Democratic state representatives abstained on Scott's bill and thirteen voted against it. The Democratic opponents included House minority leader Jim Hodges. Hodges represented Lancaster County, which had brought the 1991 lawsuit against the video poker industry. Lancaster was also one of the twelve counties that voted to ban video poker. Meanwhile, many South Carolinians continued playing the Georgia lottery.

### Gambling and Politics, The 1998 Election

After a decade of sporadic consideration, the campaign to enact a lottery began in earnest with the 1998 gubernatorial election. By fall 1997 most of South Carolina's leading Democratic politicians had decided that four years of economic prosperity in the state had made Governor Beasley unbeatable for reelection. Only Hodges, long an outspoken opponent of gambling, stepped forward to seek the Democratic nomination.

Relatively unknown among South Carolina voters, Hodges was a would-be policy entrepreneur looking for a politically popular policy that a Democrat could ride to victory. Convinced that his best chance for success was to run a campaign focused on remedying the state's serious educational problems without raising taxes, Hodges was persuaded by his chief political consultant, Kevin Geddings, to spend a week in Georgia studying that state's lottery as a possible funding mechanism for new education programs. Conversations with the president of the University of Georgia and with South Carolinians who had moved to Georgia to take advantage of the new lottery-funded HOPE scholarships persuaded Hodges to center his campaign on an "education lottery," which would fund new scholarships for South Carolina's college students as well as new programs for elementary and secondary schools.[13] A December 1997 poll that showed 68 percent of the public supporting such a lottery seemed to confirm the political wisdom of Hodges's sudden conversion.[14]

Hodges was not the only gubernatorial candidate who was unconvinced of Beasley's political invincibility—so was Beasley. The governor had alienated a substantial number of social conservatives within the Republican Party by running as a supporter of the Confederate flag in 1994, only to argue two years later that the flag should no longer fly over the state capitol.[15] Looking for a way to win back these core Republican voters, as well as to head off a potential primary challenge from Charlie Condon, the state attorney general and a prominent flag supporter, Beasley turned his January 1998 State of the State address into a plea to the legislature to excise the "cancer" of video poker by making it illegal in South Carolina.

Beasley's speech accomplished its immediate goal of heading off a primary challenge. But it also stirred the video poker industry to pour money into a campaign to defeat him in the general election. The roughly $3 billion-per-year industry donated around $1 million to the Hodges campaign and spent another $2 million to defeat Beasley in the form of independent expenditures and contributions to the state Democratic Party.[16] Around half of the $6 million spent to elect Hodges—an enormous sum for a challenger in a South Carolina gubernatorial election—came from video poker.

Beasley tried to portray Hodges as a pawn of the video poker industry. "You might have been for sale, but you didn't come cheap," he told Hodges in a televised debate.[17] But Hodges handled the issue adroitly. Noting that most of video poker's growth in South Carolina had occurred while Beasley was governor, Hodges pledged to seek legislation that would tax and regulate the lightly taxed and weakly regulated industry. Hodges further proposed that the public decide in a statewide referendum whether to ban video poker entirely. Meanwhile, Democrats in the state senate tied in legislative knots Beasley's proposal to ban video poker. Video poker operators rallied gamblers by programming their machines to flash "Beat Beasley."[18]

Hodges's promise to crack down on video poker sounded more severe than it was. In truth, the industry already realized that some amount of regulation would establish its legitimacy in the state and that a reasonable but nonetheless substantial tax would make state budget makers dependent on the income derived from a flourishing video poker industry. After winning most of the county referenda in 1994 and persuading the state supreme court to declare the others unconstitutional, the industry had little fear of a statewide referendum or an adverse court decision.

Hodges also framed his lottery-based campaign in a politically skillful way. One set of campaign ads focused on the state's near-bottom rankings on a variety of educational measures, then offered Hodges's "education lottery" as the solution. Another featured Bubba, a good-ole-boy convenience store clerk wearing a red Georgia Bulldogs tee shirt. In the course of thanking the people of South Carolina for sending young Georgians to college by buying $100 million worth of Georgia lottery tickets, Bubba bragged on what the lottery had done for his state's students and teased South Carolinians for not having a lottery themselves. "Just reelect Beasley and keep buyin' our lottery tickets, won'tcha?" Bubba urged. "Here in Georgia, we just luuuvv David Beasley."[19] When Beasley, in unspoken acknowledgement of the popularity of Hodges's lottery campaign, promised to "drop my opposition to the public vote on a lottery," Hodges reminded the voters that Beasley had also flip-flopped on the Confederate flag issue.[20]

Hodges won the election by 53 to 45 percent, the first Democrat to be elected governor of South Carolina in twelve years. Hodges and Alabama Democrat Don Siegelman, who centered his own gubernatorial campaign on a proposal for a Georgia-style lottery, gained national notoriety as the only two candidates in the country to defeat incumbent Republican governors in 1998. Exit polls showed that three-fifths of South Carolina's voters supported

Hodges's lottery proposal. More ominously for the video poker industry, more than 60 percent also told exit pollsters that they now opposed video poker.

### The Lottery Amendment and the End of Video Poker, 1999–2000

The first challenge that Hodges and other lottery advocates faced when he was inaugurated as governor in January 1999 was to persuade the General Assembly to approve a constitutional amendment repealing the state constitution's ban on lotteries. If Hodges could obtain two-thirds approval from the House and the Senate for his proposed amendment, then according to the state constitution it would go before the voters in November 2000, the next regularly scheduled general election. Lt. Gov. Bob Peeler and a number of other Republican leaders in the legislature made clear shortly after Hodges took office that they had gotten the voters' message and would not stand in the way of such a referendum. "Though all of us may not agree on the merits of the lottery itself," Peeler said, "we're unanimous in our agreement that it's high time the people of South Carolina got to vote on this issue."[21]

By early April 1999, the Republican House and Democratic Senate had voted to approve a lottery amendment for the November 2000 ballot. Although Hodges had featured the Georgia model in his 1998 gubernatorial campaign, especially by emphasizing lottery-funded college scholarships, the text of the proposed amendment was sufficiently general that public school teachers and other educational interests in the state could see possibilities for additional funding for themselves. The amendment stated that after paying "all operating expenses and prizes for the lotteries . . . the remaining lottery revenues must be credited to a separate fund in the state treasury styled the 'Education Lottery Account,' and the . . . proceeds may be used only for education purposes as the General Assembly provides by law."

Hodges's request for an additional referendum on a proposed statute to ban video poker was more controversial. Legislators from both parties supported the referendum but disagreed on when it should be held. Fresh from the 1998 election, in which video poker money had helped the Democrats defeat not just Beasley but also several Republican legislators, Republican leaders did not want a repeat performance in 2000. They pressed to schedule the video poker referendum in November 1999. Led by Rep. Terry Haskins and Sen. Wes Hayes, they also urged that the legislation authorizing the referendum be drawn in such a way that video poker would become illegal on July 1, 2000, unless the voters decided to keep it legal. Thus if, as some constitutional scholars predicted, the state supreme court were to strike the referendum from the ballot as an unconstitutional delegation of the statute-writing power from the legislature to the people, video poker would be forced out of the state. South Carolina's constitution confined referenda to the constitutional amendment process, not to simple legislation.

On July 1, 1999, Republicans legislators prevailed on both the November 1999 date for the referendum and the July 1, 2000, demise of the video poker industry, barring approval by a majority of voters in the referendum. They had gained political leverage from the widely publicized release two weeks earlier of the report of the National Gambling Impact Study Commission, which reserved its harshest language for video poker (the "crack cocaine" of gambling) and singled out South Carolina for especially severe criticism.[22] A number of white and black churches across the state urged voters to pass the video poker ban. The sixteen-denomination Christian Action Council even reunited with the state's 725,000-member South Carolina Baptist Convention (the groups had fallen out over the flag controversy) to form an antigambling umbrella group called Changing South Carolina.[23] Tom Grey, a United Methodist minister and the director of the National Coalition Against Legalized Gambling, came to South Carolina to lead a week of training seminars for opponents of video poker.[24] The state's 2,300-member Chamber of Commerce pledged to contribute $1.6 million to the opposition campaign. The chamber regarded video poker as a sordid activity that created a bad climate for attracting industry to the state.[25]

When a late September poll showed that voters favored banning video poker by a margin of 61 to 16 percent, Joytime Distributors and Amusement, a Greenville-based video poker company, filed suit to have the law authorizing the referendum overturned on the grounds that it exceeded the General Assembly's constitutional authority.[26] On October 14, the state supreme court overturned the section of the law that authorized the referendum, holding that "it is clear that our constitution does not give the people the right of direct legislation by referendum."[27] But, much to the company's (and the industry's) dismay, the court left intact the section of the law that declared video poker illegal as of July 1, 2000.

In some ways, the controversy over video poker in 1999 adversely affected Hodges's efforts to obtain a lottery. Although the governor declared that he had voted against video poker by absentee ballot before the court struck down the referendum, some voters associated the lottery with gambling rather than with the governor's preferred theme of education. The same poll that had video poker losing by nearly four to one also showed that support for a lottery had fallen to 49 percent. The grassroots network of church-based opponents of video poker redirected its energies to defeating the lottery in the November 2000 referendum. Many of the political newcomers who had mobilized to fight video poker in the referendum campaign, such as Changing South Carolina chairwoman Kathy Bigham, had become battle-hardened activists.

In other, perhaps more important ways, however, the video poker controversy worked to the advantage of Hodges and his lottery proposal. Although the events of 1999 followed a circuitous path, the combination of legislative and judicial actions that legally eliminated video poker also removed it from the state's political agenda.[28] In addition, for as long as the video poker controversy was raging, Hodges was able to place the lottery on the political back burner and see what he could learn from Governor Siegelman's campaign to enact an Alabama lottery in 1999.

The lessons Hodges learned from Alabama's experience turned out to be important to the eventual success of his campaign for a South Carolina lottery. As shown in chapter 4, soon after taking office in January 1999, Siegelman had secured from the legislature not just a lottery amendment but also enabling legislation defining how the lottery would operate if the state's voters approved the amendment. The Alabama referendum was scheduled as a special election in October 1999. In a surprising result, the voters defeated the lottery amendment by 55 to 45 percent. "We spent a lot of time studying Alabama," says political consultant Kevin Geddings, whom Hodges recruited to run his South Carolina lottery campaign in 2000.[29]

The first lesson Hodges and Geddings learned from the failure of Siegelman's effort in Alabama was that to pass enabling legislation in advance of a referendum was certain to disappoint some groups that otherwise might think they would benefit from the proceeds of a lottery. To the extent that the legislation tied lottery revenues to college scholarships, for example, public school teachers would lose interest. Although Hodges and Geddings did not want enabling legislation in place before the lottery amendment was voted on, however, they felt that the governor must appear to want it, lest he be accused of asking the voters to approve a lottery on faith. Clearly, Hodges had a political tightrope to walk during the 2000 legislative session.

The second lesson that Hodges and, especially, Geddings learned from the Alabama defeat was not to frame the South Carolina lottery as the "Hodges lottery" in the same way that Siegelman had personalized his lottery proposal in Alabama. This strategy was especially important in a presidential election year. South Carolina's recent record of giving overwhelming support to Republican presidential candidates meant that in order for a lottery to pass in the November 2000 election, at least one-fifth of those voting Republican for president would also need to vote for the lottery. "We didn't make it the Hodges lottery because we needed the votes of those [Bill] Clinton-hating white males," says Geddings.[30]

Lottery supporters applied this second lesson in two ways. First, Hodges minimized his public involvement in the referendum campaign until a few weeks before election day. He quietly raised money to fund the campaign early in the year but allowed Geddings to become the lottery's public face as chair of the South Carolina Lottery for Education Coalition. Geddings, not Hodges, campaigned across the state and handled requests for media interviews.[31] Second, lottery advocates concentrated much of their effort on persuading supporters of Republican presidential nominee George W. Bush to vote for the Democratic governor's proposal. "Bubba" commercials were revived in full force (especially on sports programs aimed at white men), this time with Bubba speaking the tag line: "Just remember, here in Georgia, we *luuuvv* South Carolinians playing our lottery."[32] A host of radio and print ads reminded voters that the lottery in Bush's home state of Texas was the third largest in the country. One radio commercial even featured an actor impersonating Bush's father saying, "Now don't forget, go with my boy George Dubya on Nov. 7 and vote 'Yes' at the end of the ballot on Question 1, for a Texas-style, South Carolina education lottery."[33] George W. Bush refused to comment on the lottery issue in South Carolina, saying it was a state matter that did not concern him as a candidate for president.[34]

Implementing the first lesson of the Alabama defeat—namely, that the governor should appear to seek enabling legislation in advance of the referendum but not actually obtain it—was more difficult. Hodges's approach was to embrace with great fanfare a generous $150 million annual estimate of the amount of revenue a lottery would bring to the state treasury and call on the legislature to pass enabling legislation earmarking these funds for college and technical school scholarships, technology upgrades in the public schools, and a scholarship program for teachers. But his proposed legislation was silent concerning how the lottery actually would work, including what kinds of games and advertising would be needed to generate this much revenue. In any event, as one veteran capitol reporter wrote well into the General Assembly's 2000 session, "The enabling legislation has gone nowhere because Hodges's office has not pushed it." The bill died in a House subcommittee.[35]

With midsummer polls showing that support for a lottery had climbed above 60 percent, the referendum campaign settled into a classic "ground war" versus "air war."[36] As even Geddings conceded, Kathy Bigham's antilottery group, No Lottery 2000, was a genuine grassroots organization with "over 2,000 activists who they cultivated each day" and "yard signs distributed by over 1,000 churches across the state."[37] Conservative white churches were joined in active opposition to the lottery by a few prominent African American congregations, some of them pastored by members of the legislature, such as Sen. Darrell Jackson and Rep. Ralph Canty.

Antilottery commercials constituted a much smaller part of No Lottery 2000's campaign, and also were far less effective. Each of them portrayed a man's hand writing on a blackboard with gratingly squeaky chalk. The words on the board conveyed sledgehammer messages such as "The lottery. It's for losers" and "Citizens = Suckers." One commercial showed "Education Prostitution" and "Education Drug Dealing" on the blackboard as a voice intoned, "So, they want us to have an Education Lottery. That certainly makes state-sponsored gambling okay. Maybe we should also have Education Prostitution. We could sure get some scholarship money from that. And how about Education Drug Dealing? Now there's a funding source for our kids."[38]

The pro-lottery campaign, in contrast, consisted almost entirely of television and radio commercials. "Our campaign never purchased a single yard sign, tee-shirt, or coffee mug," Geddings claimed in a postreferendum memo. "TV beats field [campaigning] every time."[39] Not only was Bubba revived by the South Carolina Lottery for Education Coalition, but additional commercials featured the promised benefits of a lottery and a roster of prominent lottery supporters. Freed from the burden of enabling legislation describing the full range of lottery games required to generate $150 million per year for the state, Geddings was able to claim: "It's not gambling. Buying a $1 education lottery ticket is no different than buying a $1 raffle ticket at Rock Hill High School for band uniforms."[40] Hodges picked up this refrain when he began active campaigning for the lottery a few weeks before the election, plugging in the name of the high school in the town where he was speaking.

Except for the churches, which funded the lion's share of the approximately $1 million campaign by No Lottery 2000, most of South Carolina's leading political organization abstained from the referendum. The General Assembly's black caucus endorsed the lottery by a seven-to-six vote and the board of the Urban League voted to oppose it by eight to seven, but neither group became actively engaged in the campaign. Both the chamber of commerce and the NAACP elected to take no position at all. The state's political parties did their best to keep the debate from being perceived as strictly partisan, even though most Republican activists opposed the lottery and most Democratic activists supported it. Nearly half of the $1 million the pro-lottery South Carolina Lottery for Education Coalition raised came from out of state donors. These included the Pantry, a convenience store chain that thought lottery ticket sales would be good for business, and the investment firms Salomon Smith Barney and Lehman Brothers, each of which was hoping to win a contract from Hodges to underwrite the issuance of bonds related to the state's share of the recent national tobacco settlement.[41]

On election day, as Bush carried South Carolina by a three-to-two margin, the voters approved the lottery amendment by 55 to 45 percent. Exit polls indicated that the lottery received strong support from voters under 30 (64 percent), Democrats (70 percent), and voters who defined the issue in terms of education (98 percent). Senior citizens (63 percent), Republicans (59 percent), and voters who defined the issue in moral terms (95 percent) were the lottery's strongest opponents. Whites, who constituted three-fourths of the electorate, opposed the lottery by 53 to 47 percent. African American voters gave the lottery its margin of victory, supporting it by 76 to 24 percent.

## Implementing the Lottery, 2001

Because enabling legislation for the lottery was not passed before the 2000 referendum, Hodges still had the task of persuading the General Assembly to pass one or more bills specifying how the South Carolina lottery would be implemented and how its proceeds would be spent. Although each party wanted to shape the legislation with its own goals in mind, Republican leaders accepted that the voters wanted a lottery. During the 2000 campaign, Republican lieutenant governor Bob Peeler had conceded that if the voters approved a lottery, "then it'd be up to us to make sure it's the best-run, best-operated lottery in the nation." After the lottery referendum passed, even antigambling activist Kathy Bigham said, "We don't want the lottery to fail. The people of South Carolina have spoken."[42] But Hodges could not count on Republican legislators to accept his understanding of what the lottery should be, especially since they again controlled both houses of the General Assembly.

For tactical reasons, Republican legislators insisted on dealing with implementation first and in a bill separate from the spending measure. South Carolina's constitution authorizes the governor to veto "any one or more of the items or sections contained in any bill appropriating money" but denies the governor a similar line-item veto over other kinds of legislation. Keeping the spending aspects of the lottery out of the implementation bill, the Republicans would prevent Hodges from vetoing items defining how the lottery would operate.

Led by House speaker David Wilkins, Republicans channeled most of their efforts concerning the implementation bill along two lines. First, they wanted to ensure that the regulatory provisions governing the lottery sealed any potential loopholes like Lindsay's 1986 "or property" amendment, which had opened the floodgates to video poker. "We wanted to write the law in such a way that it would cover the issues that would come up rather than try to play catch-up the way we did with video poker," recalled Sen. Jim Ritchie.[43] Related to this cautionary effort was the Republicans' attempt to prevent any governor (but especially the Democrat Hodges) from having unchecked control of the lottery. This concern was made manifest in a House-sponsored provision that empowered the governor, the speaker of the House, and the president pro tempore of the Senate to appoint three members each to the nine-member lottery commission rather than, as Hodges preferred, allowing the governor to appoint a majority of the commissioners.

Second, Republicans, mostly in the House, wanted to place restrictions on the lottery that they thought would be popular among South Carolinians who had voted *yes* in the referendum as a way to improve education but were uncomfortable with the idea of the state encouraging people to gamble. For example, Republicans wanted to prohibit the South Carolina lottery from participating in multistate lottery games such as Powerball. In addition, they wanted provisions banning the sale of lottery tickets on Sunday or by vendors who also sold alcohol.

Democratic legislators, in contrast, aimed their efforts at creating the most profitable lottery possible so that the state could raise the $150 million per year that Hodges had pledged during the campaign. Only with this amount could the lottery fully fund the governor's pledges for new college scholarships, free tuition to state technical schools, and technology upgrades in the public schools. The Democrats' version of the implementation bill authorized the governor to appoint five of the nine lottery commissioners, placed no restrictions on how the lottery would be advertised, and allowed the lottery to participate in multistate games. The Democratic bill also offered lottery retailers a generous 7 percent commission on ticket sales, in part to offset the losses some convenience store and gas station owners had suffered when video poker was banned.

In April 2001 the Senate passed the Democratic version of the implementation bill by a vote of thirty-six to nine. A month later the House approved the Republican version by sixty-three to fifty-five. A conference committee was created to iron out the differences. On most issues, support in conference from Senate president pro tempore Glenn McConnell, a pro-lottery Republican, enabled the Democrats to prevail. Except for including language that disallowed advertising targeted at minority groups, the law authorized the lottery commission to advertise freely. Lottery ticket sales would be untaxed, could occur on premises that sold alcohol, and would take place seven days a week. Lottery retailers would receive a 7 percent commission on ticket sales. Finally, a toothless provision was included stating that proceeds from the lottery would have to supplement, not supplant, existing spending on education from the general fund.

Republican legislators were able to influence some provisions of the implementation law. The House's ban on participation in multistate lottery games without explicit approval from the General Assembly remained. Despite Hodges's request that the lottery commission enjoy administrative autonomy, the law subjected the commission to the state's Administrative Procedures Act and its procurement code.[44] As Sen. Scott Richardson, who along with Senator Ritchie pushed hard for this safeguard, recalled, "I wasn't for the lottery but if it was going to happen I wanted it to run right."[45]

The issue of control—who would appoint the lottery commissioners—was the final sticking point in conference. The Republican plan for three appointments each by the governor, the House speaker, and the Senate president pro tempore prevailed, mostly because, in a gentlemen's agreement, McConnell assured the governor that the appointments he made as president pro tempore would go to lottery supporters. The conference report on the implementation bill passed the General Assembly on June 7, 2001, by 105 to 16 in the House and forty-one to five in the Senate. Hodges signed the law six days later but made clear that repealing the ban on South Carolina's participation in multistate games would be "one of my administration's top legislative priorities." Two months later, the newly appointed commissioners hired Sen. Ernie Passailaigue, a Charleston Democrat and a friend of Hodges and McConnell, to serve as the lottery's executive director. The commission had essentially preordained Passailaigue's appointment when it defined the job as requiring "extensive knowledge of South Carolina and South Carolina State Government" and "the ability to interpret accounting reports and records and to analyze accounting data." Passailaigue was a veteran legislator and a certified public accountant before resigning from the Senate to accept the post.[46]

### Spending Lottery Revenues, 2001–2006

The second piece of enabling legislation concerning the lottery, the one governing how the proceeds would be spent, took considerably longer to enact than the implementation bill. One reason was that political leaders and groups in the state began staking claims to large chunks of the expected revenues. Although Hodges had focused on college scholarships and capital improvements in public schools during the 1998 and 2000 campaigns, the language of the constitutional amendment was sufficiently broad as to accommodate any "education purposes as the General Assembly provides by law." Thus, in October 2001 alone, Lieutenant Governor Peeler urged that nearly half the revenues be spent to buy new buses for the state's public schools; the state Commission on Higher Education offered a plan to expand existing merit-based college scholarship programs and create a new one; and Hodges himself proposed that nearly one-third of the money be used to attract major research professors to Clemson University, the University of South Carolina, and the Medical University of South Carolina. When ticket sales exceeded expectations after the lottery was launched on January 7, 2002, the line of claimants grew even longer. African American legislators, for example, demanded that part of the lottery revenues be used to fund construction and renovation projects at the state's historically black colleges.[47]

Not surprisingly, how to spend the money the state received from the lottery was the major item on the General Assembly's agenda when it convened for its 2002 session. Hodges proposed a spending plan that, with the support of Republican Senate leader McConnell and nearly all Democratic senators, passed the Senate largely intact on February 27. The Senate bill offered free tuition to every South Carolina student who wanted to attend a state technical or community college, created a new HOPE scholarship program for aspiring college students who had a B average in high school but whose low scores on standardized tests disqualified them from the state's existing LIFE and Palmetto merit scholarship programs, and increased the amount of the LIFE and Palmetto awards. Estimating that lottery revenues would be one-third higher than the amount projected by the state's Board of Economic Advisers, the Senate also included substantial funds for new school buses, aid to low-performing public schools, and research professorships at the state's major universities.[48]

Two weeks later, on March 14, 2002, the House approved a substantially different spending bill, with considerably more money going to public schools and considerably less to new college scholarships. The House bill, for example, did not include the HOPE scholarship program and tied technical and community college tuition waivers to academic performance. Democratic legislators complained that by continuing to keep the eligibility bar high for scholarships, the Republican-dominated House was freezing out many African American students. In a state that was 30 percent black, they noted, more than 80 percent of the state's college scholarships already went to white students. The House bill, unlike the Senate version, would do nothing to alter that situation.[49]

Meanwhile, pressure to join the twenty-two-state Powerball consortium grew increasingly difficult to resist. South Carolina's own lottery games were drawing many betters from North Carolina, which at the time had no lottery, but few from the other state with which South Carolina shares a border, Georgia. South Carolinians continued to buy Georgia lottery tickets whenever the jackpot for Mega Millions, the multistate lottery in which Georgia participates, rose above $100 million, the usual threshold for frenzied betting. (A state lottery could affiliate with Powerball or Mega Millions but not both.) By offering Powerball, Hodges argued, South Carolina would be able to sell tickets to Georgians as well as North Carolinians when the Powerball jackpot grew large.

As monthly lottery revenues continued to exceed projections throughout 2002 and the General Assembly moved toward approving participation in Powerball, the basis for a compromise on how lottery revenues would be spent emerged from a House-Senate conference committee. Essentially, both houses got what they wanted: a new HOPE scholarship program, expanded funding for the LIFE and Palmetto scholarships, nearly free tuition for state technical and community college students, research professorships at the major state universities, financial assistance to the state's historically black colleges, and substantial new funding for public schools. African American legislators, however, were less satisfied with the final bill than their white colleagues. "What about the financially needy parents whose kid struggled through high school and got a C+ grade point average?" complained Senator Jackson. "They're the ones that got shafted." Sen. Robert Ford added, "The people that would benefit from needs-based scholarships are the people who play the lottery."[50] An additional source of unhappiness was that federal Pell grants received by minority students would count against the amount of any lottery-funded scholarship for which they qualified.

Revenues from the lottery grew during each of its first three years of operation, rising to an estimated $289 million in 2005. Because the overall state budget faced substantial deficits every year, however, the temptation was great for legislators to substitute lottery revenues for tax revenues in funding ongoing education projects, such as testing, data collection, and elementary school reading, math, and science programs. Complicating the lottery's problems, North Carolina began selling its own lottery tickets in March 2006. Because

North Carolinians had previously accounted for around 15 percent of South Carolina's revenues from the lottery, state economists predicted that South Carolina's treasury stood to suffer as a result. From March to June 2006, however, lottery sales increased by 5.5 percent over the same period in 2005.[51]

## TRIBAL GAMBLING, 1993–2006

Taken together, the success of South Carolina's new lottery in attracting gambling dollars and its abolition of video poker had an adverse effect on the Catawba Indian Nation. In 1993, as part of a legal settlement with the state over disputed lands, the Catawbas were authorized to open two bingo halls, one on its reservation in York County and one elsewhere in the state. These halls could be open twelve hours a day for six days per week and offer prizes as high as $100,000. The agreement also provided that "the Tribe may permit on its Reservation video poker or similar electronic devices to the same extent that the devices are authorized by state law."[52]

In 1997 the Catawbas opened one of the largest bingo halls in the country on their York County reservation, just across the border from North Carolina. They added video poker two years later, but when South Carolina banned video poker in 2000, the tribe was ordered to remove its machines. After the state began selling lottery tickets in 2002, the tribe's profits from bingo fell from more than $2 million in 2001 to less than $1 million in 2002.[53]

Launching a campaign to recoup their losses, the Catawbas found land to open a second bingo hall in Santee, South Carolina, near the busy junction of Interstate 95 and Interstate 26. To help make both bingo halls profitable, they persuaded U.S. senator Ernest Hollings, a Democrat, to introduce a bill in Congress that would bring the halls under the coverage of the federal Indian Gaming Regulatory Act of 1988 (IGRA) and thus allow the tribe to offer larger jackpots and unlimited hours of operation. (The Catawbas are one of a small handful of federally recognized tribes not covered by IGRA.) Hollings's Republican colleague, Sen. Lindsey Graham, was initially inclined to support this effort. "The day we got in the lottery business, we became a competitor" of the Catawbas," he said. "We've got nobody to blame in South Carolina but ourselves." But Graham was soon persuaded by the newly elected Republican governor, Mark Sanford, to block Hollings's bill for fear that federal involvement might someday open the door to casino gambling. Sanford, who had defeated Governor Hodges by 53 to 47 percent in a Republican sweep of the state's major elective offices in 2002, insisted that under the terms of the 1993 agreement only the General Assembly could authorize the Catawbas to conduct a form of gambling that was otherwise illegal in South Carolina.[54]

In 2004, as a way of pressuring the General Assembly to allow his tribe to open the high-stakes bingo hall it wanted in Santee, Catawba chief Gilbert Blue sued the state for denying it the right to offer video poker at its York County facility. The Catawbas' legal claim was that they were forever entitled under the 1993 agreement to sponsor whatever forms of gambling were legal in South Carolina that year. Under this claim, the state's abolition of video poker in 2000 did not affect the tribe's right to continue offering it. "The goal is not to open a casino in Rock Hill," said a member of the Catawbas' legal team. "The goal is to open a bingo facility in Santee." The General Assembly, strongly supported by Governor Sanford, refused to yield on the Santee issue. But on December 13, 2005, a state judge ruled in the Catawbas' favor, prompting further efforts in the legislature to authorize the tribe to open a Santee site in return for its agreeing not to offer video poker. These efforts did not succeed during the 2006 session of the General Assembly.[55]

## WHY SOUTH CAROLINA BANNED VIDEO POKER
## AND CREATED A LOTTERY

Events peculiar to South Carolina led to the creation and rapid expansion of its video poker industry during the late 1980s and 1990s: a seemingly innocuous amendment snuck into a budget bill by a powerful pro–video poker legislator, some helpful court decisions, and the Democratic support gained by the industry as it prospered financially. Adverse national publicity, shrewd legislative maneuvering by Republican opponents of video poker, and a state supreme court decision that went against the industry later brought about video poker's demise.

The state constitution figured heavily in the rise and fall of video poker. Because the constitution requires a uniform statewide criminal code, county referenda that banned video poker in some jurisdictions but not others were declared invalid in 1996. Consequently, for a time video poker was legal everywhere in the state. But because the constitution confers exclusive statute-writing authority on the General Assembly, a statewide referendum on whether to prevent video poker from becoming illegal on July 1, 2000, was also declared unconstitutional.

Explaining how and why South Carolina created a lottery is a less idiosyncratic enterprise. The explanation lies in the state's internal characteristics, in policy diffusion, and in an element that stands at the intersection of the two: policy entrepreneurship.

### Internal Characteristics

South Carolina's constitution and partisan makeup clearly affected lottery politics in the state. In order to remove the constitutional ban on lotteries, Hodges and other supporters had to attain a two-thirds majority for an amendment in both houses of the General Assembly, then persuade a majority of voters to approve it in a referendum held as part of a regularly scheduled general election. Compared with the amendment process in Tennessee, for example (see chapter 5), which requires at the referendum phase that the change be approved by a majority of citizens who cast votes in the gubernatorial election rather than just on the amendment, modifying the constitution in South Carolina is easier. The bare majority required for approval of the lottery was a boon for supporters, including the governor.

In other ways, however, and in contrast to states such as Arkansas (see chapter 6) which require only a simple majority of the legislature (or a sufficient number of signatures on a petition) to place a constitutional amendment on the ballot, the amendment process in South Carolina is marked by significant impediments. These impediments required lottery supporters to adopt shrewd strategies in order to succeed. Part of the reason that Hodges delayed pressing for enabling legislation until after the referendum, for example, was so the lottery would appear to the public to be a panacea for all of the state's education problems. Earlier passage of the enabling legislation would have deflated that perception before the voters went to the polls by making clear which programs would be funded by the lottery and, by implication, which would not.

Another notable part of the amendment process in South Carolina is the requirement that citizens can only vote on changes to the state constitution in a regularly scheduled general—as opposed to a special—election. This stipulation is in marked contrast to the amendment process in Alabama (see chapter 4), where voters rejected a lottery in a 1999 special election. As a rule, the groups of voters who turn out at a disproportionately higher rate in general rather than in special elections include African Americans, young people, and Democrats—all of whom strongly supported the lottery in South Carolina.

South Carolina's character as a solidly Republican state also affected the politics of the lottery.[56] Lottery supporters knew that in 2000, when George W. Bush was almost certain to carry South Carolina in a landslide, winning a substantial number of Republican votes for the lottery was an essential challenge. This goal influenced everything from the content of pro-lottery advertising to the decision to keep Hodges in the background during the referendum campaign.

After the lottery referendum passed, the Republican-controlled legislature used its influence to write enabling legislation that restricted to three the number of lottery commissioners appointed by Hodges and future governors, shored up any ambiguities or oversights in the lottery legislation which might open the door to another video poker–style fiasco, and targeted many of the benefits of the lottery's proceeds at the high-achieving children of middle- and upper-income South Carolinians, who tend to be Republicans.

### Diffusion

As important as South Carolina's internal characteristics were in influencing the shape that the politics of gambling took in the state, diffusion theory helps even more in explaining the outcome of the lottery controversy. South Carolina is one of the few states in the country to share a border with only two states. As a consequence, it receives fewer policy signals from its neighbors than do most other states. During the 1970s and 1980s, neither Georgia nor North Carolina had a lottery or allowed casinos or any other form of state-sponsored or commercial gambling. In the early 1990s, however, Zell Miller's lottery-centered campaign for governor of Georgia and Georgia's decision to enact a lottery attracted great interest in South Carolina. As Rep. John Scott recalls, his decision to sponsor the first major lottery bill in South Carolina and dedicate its proceeds to education was "inspired" by the Georgia example.

By 1998, when Hodges ran for governor, the Georgia lottery had been up and running long enough that he was able to invoke it as an issue by citing the number of Georgia students whose college tuition was funded by HOPE scholarships, the amount of money that South Carolinians had lost betting in the Georgia lottery, and even stories about people moving from South Carolina to Georgia so their children could benefit from lottery-funded scholarships. To be sure, the lottery has not been of unalloyed benefit to Georgia. A number of studies have suggested that the lion's share of lottery scholarships go to middle-class students but are funded by the disproportionately high lottery play of poor and working-class people. But neither Hodges's opponent in the 1998 election nor the leading opponents of the lottery referendum in 2000 stressed these disadvantages of the Georgia lottery in their campaigns, focusing instead on traditional moral objections to gambling.

### Policy Entrepreneurship

Interwoven with the influence of South Carolina's internal characteristics and, especially, of policy diffusion was the policy entrepreneurship provided by Jim Hodges. In 1998 Hodges was an ambitious Democratic politician seeking an appealing issue that would enable him to win an uphill race for governor in a Republican state.

Advised at every turn by political consultant Kevin Geddings, Hodges engaged in a series of adroit political maneuvers, both in the 1998 gubernatorial election and the 2000 lottery referendum, to raise the lottery to the top of the state's political agenda, and he was instrumental in securing its enactment. In preparing to help launch Hodges's campaign for governor, Geddings learned what he could from the example of Wallace Wilkinson, the relatively unknown Democrat who had seized on the lottery issue as his ticket to victory in Kentucky's 1987 gubernatorial election. (Wilkinson got the idea from his own Democratic consultant, James Carville, as did Zell Miller in Georgia.) The Hodges campaign also finessed the video poker issue in 1998. Hodges took the industry's money but, in his speeches and commercials, offered himself to the voters as a critic of video poker.

In 2000 Hodges managed to walk another political tightrope. Having learned from the failure of the 1999 lottery referendum in Alabama that to pass enabling legislation in advance of amending the constitution would give lottery critics targets to shoot at, Hodges allowed such legislation to die of neglect, then blamed his opponents for defeating it. During the referendum campaign itself, Geddings's pro-lottery television commercials focused on what Georgia was gaining because it had a lottery and what South Carolina was losing because it did not. Radio and print ads invoked the Texas lottery in an effort to persuade those who voted for Bush in the presidential election to vote for the lottery as well. In all, Hodges borrowed politics from other states as much as policy.

Hodges was less astute in crafting a constitutional amendment that did not, as Georgia's lottery amendment did, explicitly set aside lottery revenues for new education programs rather than "for education purposes as the General Assembly provides by law." The door Hodges opened to "substitution" was a familiar one—many states have created a lottery in the name of education or some other popular purpose only to see their legislatures substitute lottery revenues for spending that otherwise would have come from the general fund.[57] Some of the uses that Hodges and the General Assembly instantly made of lottery funds, such as school bus purchases and increases in the amounts of existing scholarships, were clearly of this kind.

# FOUR

# ALABAMA

## The Governor, the Churches, and the "Sin Legislator"

An old saw in Alabama holds that "nothing about Alabama politics is predictable"; a more recent one is that "politics in Alabama can be peculiar."[1] These axioms have been borne out by the state's approach to gambling. During the late 1990s, Alabama seemed to be on a course nearly identical with South Carolina's. In 1998, South Carolina Democratic gubernatorial nominee Jim Hodges ran on a pro-lottery platform inspired by the perceived success of the lottery in Georgia, which borders South Carolina on the south. In that same year, Alabama Democratic gubernatorial nominee Don Siegelman ran on a pro-lottery platform inspired by the perceived success of the lottery in Georgia, which borders Alabama on the east. Siegelman, like Hodges, was elected, unseating an incumbent Republican governor. They were the only two gubernatorial challengers in the country to win in 1998.

Both Siegelman and Hodges claimed that the voters had given them a mandate to enact a state lottery based on the Georgia model created by Democratic governor Zell Miller, with most of the proceeds designated for a new college scholarship program. Their legislatures agreed, swiftly taking the necessary steps to place a lottery on the ballot. Although controversies regarding other forms of gambling arose simultaneously with the lottery in both Alabama and South Carolina, political pundits in Montgomery and Columbia forecast easy passage for the lottery referenda.

Unlike the voters of South Carolina, however, Alabama's voters rejected the lottery. Explaining why is one of the challenges of this chapter, but not the only one. For example, how did the lottery rise to such a prominent place on Alabama's political agenda? How has the state dealt with other gambling issues? As with the other case studies in this book, we find that all of the elements of our theory of state policy innovation—interstate diffusion, internal state characteristics, and policy entrepreneurship—help to illuminate the politics of gambling in Alabama.

## ALABAMA REJECTS A LOTTERY

As it entered the 1990s, Alabama's public policies toward gambling resembled those of most other southern states. The Alabama constitution, which was enacted in 1901, provided in Section 65 that, "The legislature shall have no power to authorize lotteries or gift enterprises for any purpose, and shall pass laws to prohibit the sale in this state of lottery or gift enterprise tickets, or tickets in any scheme in the nature of a lottery." The state's courts had interpreted this ban to extend to all games of chance played for money or prizes but not to games that require skill. Over the years the state had legalized charitable bingo and pari-mutuel wagering at dog tracks in Mobile, Birmingham, Macon County, and Greene County.[2]

### Gambling Politics before 1998

In 1986, Florida became the first southern state to enact a lottery.[3] Southeastern Alabama brackets the Florida panhandle, and thousands of Alabamians began crossing the state line to play the Florida lottery. When Siegelman, who was Alabama's attorney general at the time, ran for the 1990 Democratic gubernatorial nomination in a five-candidate field, he reluctantly accepted the advice of political consultant Rick Dent that the best way to break out of the pack was to center his campaign on support for a lottery. Siegelman finished second in the primary but lost the runoff by seven percentage points to Paul Hubbert, the longtime executive secretary of the Alabama Education Association, a powerful force in state politics. Dent argues that the lottery issue explains why Siegelman ran as well as he did—it "got us into the runoff." But he concedes that the statewide political community, including the candidate himself, reached a different conclusion, namely, that Siegelman lost the primary because he advocated a lottery.[4]

The inauguration of commercial casino gambling in Mississippi in 1992 triggered the next wave of gambling legalization efforts in Alabama. Southwestern Alabama, including the city of Mobile, adjoins the Mississippi Gulf

Coast where, as we saw in chapter 1, Biloxi and Gulfport rapidly became leading casino centers. Not only did many nearby Alabamians make the short drive to gamble in Mississippi casinos, but Mobile lost considerable tourism and convention business to the new casino hotels and convention facilities in Mississippi's two Gulf Coast cities. Although the drive was longer, north Alabamians headed west in great numbers to the burgeoning casino center that began operating in Tunica, Mississippi. All four of Alabama's dog tracks suffered severe declines in revenue. By 1998, for example, the handle at the Mobile Greyhound Track was half what it had been before Mississippi legalized casino gambling, even though the tracks had recently begun offering simulcast betting on dog and horse races held at other tracks around the country.[5] Live racing ceased entirely at the Greene County track, which became a simulcast-only facility.

In early 1993 an active political alliance was forged in support of legalizing commercial casino gambling in Alabama. The main parties to the alliance were those who were feeling most severely the pinch of competition from the Mississippi casinos: dog track owner Milton McGregor, a Democratic party powerhouse, and the city of Mobile. They united behind a plan to authorize one full-scale casino in downtown Mobile and an additional casino at each of Alabama's four dog tracks. According to Milo Dakin, a McGregor lobbyist, the coalition attached a state lottery to its casino plan in hopes of increasing public support.[6]

It was clear to all that legalizing casino gambling would require a constitutional amendment. The state courts' interpretation of the Alabama constitution's ban on lotteries applied to slot machines, which casinos rely on for profitability. Because amendments to the state constitution require a three-fifths majority of both the House of Representatives and Senate to get on the ballot, the McGregor-Mobile coalition postponed drafting its casino-lottery measure. The less specific their initial proposal, they believed, the broader the base of support they could assemble.[7]

The casino coalition caught a break in April 1993 when antigambling Republican governor Guy Hunt was removed from office for misusing funds designated for his inauguration. Lt. Gov. Jim Folsom Jr. succeeded to the governorship. Folsom was widely thought to be sympathetic to casinos. In addition, he was openly in favor of a lottery, which had received support ranging from 63 to 66 percent in recent statewide polls.[8] Folsom proposed in August 1993 that a special session of the legislature take up the issue of a state lottery, but legislators demurred because their agenda for the session was already filled with more pressing issues involving ethics and campaign finance.

Folsom entered the 1994 gubernatorial election with a lot going for him, including abundant campaign funding, substantial business support, and credit for the new Mercedes Benz assembly plant that he had helped persuade the German car manufacturer to build in Tuscaloosa. He decided not to deal with the casino or lottery issue until after the November election. To do so sooner would have handed his opponent, conservative Republican Fob James, the opening he was seeking to brand Folsom progambling as part of his morality-based campaign for governor.

A few weeks before the November election, state newspapers revealed that Folsom had used Milton McGregor's private plane to take a vacation in the Bahamas. The revelation reminded the voters of their revulsion against the previous governor's ethical failings. It also fed James's character-based appeal and, along with the year's strong national Republican tide, propelled him to victory. Folsom's defeat took down the McGregor-Mobile casino effort with it. As in 1990, the lesson the political community drew was that for a statewide candidate to advocate legalized gambling was disastrous. Don Siegelman's experience again seemed to bear this out, at least indirectly. Defeated in the 1990 Democratic gubernatorial primary when he ran on a lottery platform, Siegelman was elected lieutenant governor in 1994 after staying silent on the lottery and other gambling issues.

During James's term as governor, McGregor and Mobile continued to press for casino legalization in the Democratic legislature. In view of the continuing financial drain on McGregor's tracks and Mobile's tourism and convention business caused by the flourishing of Mississippi's casinos, they had little choice. But their efforts made no progress with an antigambling governor and a legislature in which even some supporters of gambling had been rendered gun shy by the recent elections.

One significant new gambling measure was enacted into law during the mid-1990s, however, although in a shrewdly disguised form. In 1996 the legislature passed the so-called Chuck E. Cheese bill, which took its name from a popular restaurant chain for children. Purportedly, the restaurants needed legal permission to operate "amusement" games in which kids could win coupons redeemable for prizes with a maximum value of five dollars. In truth, the main lobbyists for the bill represented out-of-state video gambling operators who hoped to move their machines into Alabama if, as seemed possible at the time, video poker was forced out of South Carolina. "I called it the Chuck E. Cheese bill," recalls Rep. John Rogers, an African American Democrat from Birmingham who promoted the bill in the House, "but Chuck E. Cheese had nothing to do with it. I was trying to open the door to gambling machines by making it sound like it was for the kids."[9] In April 1997 the state supreme court issued an advisory opinion affirming that video poker–style gambling machines are games of skill and thus do not violate the constitutional ban on lotteries.

The main effect of the Chuck E. Cheese bill, which sailed through the legislature under the banner of innocent fun for children, was to authorize businesses to operate video gambling machines that seemed to require skill, as long as noncash prizes were all that a player could win. As South Carolinians were coming to realize from their own experience with video gambling (see chapter 3), noncash prizes could take the form of slips of paper redeemable for cash, a distinction without a difference that enabled video gambling operators to argue that they were technically within the law. But neither Alabama's news organizations nor the state's public officials seemed aware of what was going on in South Carolina at the time.

### Siegelman's Campaign for Governor, 1998

The supreme court's 1997 advisory opinion on games of skill and games of chance had repercussions in the state legislature. Although Alabama politics in 1998 eventually would be dominated by a lottery-centered gubernatorial election, the first gambling proposal of the year concerned the state's dog tracks. In March, the Senate Tourism and Marketing Committee unanimously endorsed a bill to allow the Greene County track, the one nearest the Mississippi border, to offer video blackjack and poker, along with high stakes bingo.

"This is about jobs," said Sen. Charles Steele, the sponsor of the bill and a Democrat from Tuscaloosa, the Alabama city closest to the Greene County track.[10] The track had ended live racing in August 1996 in response to the downturn in business fostered by the proliferation of casinos in Mississippi, including a recently opened Choctaw Indian casino in Philadelphia, near Alabama's western border. Steele and the owners of the Greene County track believed that the only way to return the track to profitability was to allow it to offer casino-style games. But, lacking broader support in the legislature, especially in an election year, the bill went no further, and the Greene County track, like the others in the state, continued to feel the pinch from the Mississippi casinos.

Meanwhile, Alabamians living near the state's eastern border were crossing it in growing numbers to play the Georgia lottery, which began selling tickets in 1993. Many of them wondered why they couldn't play a lottery that would help fund college scholarships in their own state. In 1998, Siegelman decided to base his campaign for the Democratic gubernatorial nomination on a proposal for a Georgia-style "education lottery."

As had been the case when Siegelman ran for governor in 1990, his decision to emphasize the lottery was inspired in large part by his political advisor Rick Dent. It was a hard sell. Siegelman believed that supporting a lottery had cost him the 1990 nomination, and statewide polls showed public support for a lottery decreasing slightly from its 66 percent peak in 1992. But in the eight years since Siegelman's first gubernatorial campaign, Dent had worked with Zell Miller in Georgia and knew the decisive role that a lottery tied to college scholarships had played in Miller's successful 1990 and 1994 campaigns for governor. Dent got Siegelman an audience with Miller, and, in Dent's words, "Miller really persuaded him that it was a political winner for a Democrat." Siegelman also saw that when poll questions identified college scholarships as the purpose of the lottery, support for it rose by around ten percentage points. Siegelman's conversion to a lottery-based campaign strategy was so complete, says Dent, that "we made the lottery the center piece of the 1998 gubernatorial election."[11]

Siegelman stayed on message during the primary campaign, consistently pledging that he would enact an education lottery identical to Georgia's and estimating that it would raise $150 million per year for college scholarships and other educational programs. His only opponent for the Democratic nomination was Lenora Pate, a Birmingham lawyer who was new to statewide politics. Pate ran on an antilottery platform and won 17 percent of the vote, not enough to threaten Siegelman's nomination but enough to suggest that not every Democratic primary voter was a lottery supporter.

While Siegelman was cruising to victory in the Democratic primary, incumbent governor Fob James desperately battled to win renomination as the Republican candidate. James's opponent was Winton Blount Jr., the son of Winton "Red" Blount, a prominent political figure and philanthropist. Blount damaged James with accusations that Siegelman later revived during the general election campaign, charging that James had neglected economic development in Alabama while embarrassing the state with his public behavior. During an appearance before the state Board of Education, James had mocked the theory of evolution by walking across the stage like a monkey. On another occasion, in what seemed like an echo of former governor George Wallace standing in the door to block integration at the University of Alabama, James had threatened to call out the National Guard to protect county judge Roy Moore from a federal court order to remove the copy of the Ten Commandments that he had hung in his courtroom. James was renominated, but only after Blount forced him into a runoff and won 44 percent of the vote.

As a result of the gubernatorial primaries, the 1998 general election campaign was a contest between a challenger empowered by a strong victory and a resonant campaign theme and an incumbent who had barely secured his party's nomination. The first poll taken by Siegelman's campaign showed James ahead by 43 to 42 percent. But when the survey respondents were asked if they would be more likely to vote for Siegelman if he supported a lottery for education and James opposed one, the campaign found that Siegelman's support "moved up to 56–42."[12]

Based on the findings of this poll, the Siegelman campaign launched an early round of television advertisements on July 24, 1998, well before the traditional Labor Day opening of the state campaign season. Advertising on television this early was unprecedented in Alabama gubernatorial politics. Siegelman's ads focused exclusively on the lottery, making the simple point that he was for it and James was against it. According to Dent, "We essentially won the election with the spot, right then."[13]

The James campaign did not respond in an organized way to Siegelman's media barrage for nearly a month. In mid-August, the governor proposed a college scholarship program paid for by Alabama's share of the recent national legal settlement with the tobacco companies as well as from its general fund.[14] But James did not launch television ads championing his "Alabama Scholars" proposal until the first week of October.

James gained ground late in the campaign, in part by running commercials that integrated his familiar emphasis on moral character with Siegelman's advocacy of a lottery. One ad depicted Siegelman as a lying Pinocchio because he claimed that he did not support casino legalization. James managed to cut Siegelman's lead from 25 points in an October 24 poll to 8 points in an election-eve poll. The Alabama Baptist Convention, which represents over one-fourth of the state's population, swung many voters to James by attacking Siegelman's lottery proposal.[15] But the competence-based charges that had first emerged in the Republican primary campaign continued to plague James. The governor also suffered from his inability to match Siegelman in campaign spending. According to campaign finance reports filed after the election, Siegelman outspent James by approximately $8 million to $6 million.

On November 3, the voters elected Siegelman as their governor, the first victory for a Democratic gubernatorial candidate in Alabama since George Wallace won a fourth term in 1978. Siegelman won handily, 58 to 42 percent. An election-day exit poll indicated that 54 percent of Alabama voters supported the lottery. Of those, 87 percent voted for Siegelman.[16]

Siegelman acknowledged that James's weaknesses were among his own strengths. "Fob has done for me what I could never do for myself," he said: "Divide the Republican party and at the same time unite the Democratic party." But that analysis did not stop the new governor from declaring his victory a mandate for the lottery. "I defy anyone," Siegelman said the day after winning the election, "to stand between the people of Alabama and scholarships for the children of this state."[17]

### The Campaign to Enact a Lottery, 1999

Siegelman spent much of the postelection transition period laying the groundwork for his campaign to enact a lottery in 1999. He did so by wrapping his proposal in the cloak of the Georgia lottery and himself in the cloak of Gov. Zell Miller. Siegelman went to Georgia after the election to learn from Miller how he got the lottery through an initially unsympathetic legislature. He was briefed by Rebecca Paul, the head of the Georgia lottery, and other state officials on how the lottery operated. Siegelman invited Miller not only to attend his inauguration in Montgomery but also to administer the oath of office. Miller "is a role model for me in many ways," Siegelman told reporters. "He created the most successful scholarship program and pre-school program in the country." Not surprisingly, the lottery was the centerpiece of Siegelman's inaugural address on January 18. "The people demand it. Our children deserve it. Alabama needs it," the new governor declared.[18]

Constitutionally, three things had to happen for Alabama to create a lottery. First, the legislature had to pass, by a three-fifths vote in both houses, an amendment that repealed the constitution's ban on lotteries. Second, the voters had to approve the amendment by a simple majority vote in a referendum. Third, the legislature had to enact enabling legislation to specify how the lottery would operate. This legislation could be passed either before or after the referendum.

Siegelman's proposed constitutional amendment specifically provided for the creation of an "Alabama Education Lottery" and stipulated that the purpose of the lottery was "to fund the Alabama HOPE Scholarship Program for colleges and universities, and junior, technical, or community colleges; to fund pre-kindergarten programs; [and] to fund technology in the public schools." The amendment anticipated objections that lottery revenues would be substituted for general funds that already were being spent on education, which had happened in Florida and numerous other states.[19] It did so with a provision, similar to Georgia's, to "require the proceeds to be used to increase funding for education and not to take the place of existing education revenues." Persuaded by polls that the voters would be less likely to support a lottery if they thought it might open the door to casino gambling, the amendment also included a provision "to prohibit the operation of casinos." The inclusion of a casino ban was crucial to winning the support of several legislators.

Siegelman's lottery campaign proceeded smoothly and rapidly in the House, where the Democrats enjoyed a two-to-one majority. Organized opposition was confined mostly to conservative Christian groups such as the Alabama Baptist Convention and the state chapter of the Christian Coalition, each of them a mass membership organization with a modest lobbying presence in Montgomery. In contrast, the roster of groups that endorsed the lottery amendment was extensive, including the Alabama Education Association, the Council of College and University Presidents, the Alabama Retail Association, and the Business Council of Alabama. As the state's interest groups took sides on the lottery, the only surprise was that the Alabama Association of Convenience Stores, which represented four thousand stores in the state, decided to stay neutral. In most states, convenience store owners are strong lottery supporters because their facilities sell a large number of tickets. But the group representing the Alabama stores doubted that its members would earn enough in commissions to justify hiring the extra employees needed to handle long lines of players.[20]

A February 1999 public opinion survey found 58 percent support for the lottery. More important at this stage of the amendment process, it found 83 percent support for allowing the voters to decide the issue in a referendum. Siegelman focused his March 2 State of the State address on the lottery. "Eighteen of Alabama's twenty-four daily newspapers carry the Georgia and Florida lottery numbers," he declared, holding up a copy of the *Birmingham News*. "Why? Because they know what you and I know, that their readers are buying lottery tickets." On March 9 the House approved the lottery amendment by seventy to thirty-one, nine votes more than the required three-fifths majority. Although Republican House members opposed the amendment eleven to twenty-three, Democrats supported it by fifty-nine to eight.[21]

The Senate was, if anything, even more disposed to approve the lottery than the House.[22] But senators began their session by getting bogged down in an unrelated rules dispute involving the powers of the lieutenant governor. The dispute lasted until the end of March, consuming eleven of the legislative session's thirty authorized meeting days.[23] During this period, the politics of gambling in Alabama became more complicated because the House took up a bill to allow the state's four dog tracks to operate video poker and other video gambling devices at their facilities. Supporters argued that no constitutional amendment was needed to pass the bill because in 1997 the state supreme court had declared video poker and video blackjack to be games of skill and thus not covered by the constitutional ban on lotteries and other games of chance. On March 23, 1999, the House passed the video gambling bill forty-nine to forty-eight, with strong Democratic support.[24] Proponents of video gambling benefited from news reports that Corporate Relations Management, the Jackson lobbying firm that represents the Mississippi casino industry, had hired a prominent Montgomery lobbyist to oppose the video gambling bill.

Lottery opponents argued that the House's approval of video gambling proved their contention that the lottery would open wide the door to other forms of gambling in Alabama. Their case was strengthened when Rep. John Rogers, a strong video gambling supporter, declared that "around 30 or 35" House members had voted for the lottery only because they expected to get video gambling legalized too. "If we are being double crossed," Rogers said, the Senate would reject the lottery. In addition, state attorney general Bill Pryor issued an advisory opinion declaring that the video gambling bill would allow video poker machines to operate throughout the four counties that had dog tracks, not just at the tracks themselves.[25] Faced with this controversy, Siegelman refused to take a position on video gambling.

On April 14, the Senate debated the governor's lottery amendment. Republicans fought hard to defeat it. As Sen. J. T. "Jabo" Waggoner said, "This isn't some little old bill that doesn't mean much. This is an issue that will affect our lives and our state for generations to come." Invoking the Georgia and Florida lotteries, Siegelman told a press conference, "We all know that hundreds of millions of dollars have left this state to buy lottery tickets in other states. We want to capture those dollars and keep them in Alabama." After the debate ended, the Senate voted to approve the lottery amendment by twenty-four to eleven, three more votes than the required three-fifths.[26]

Procedurally, the next step was to set the date for the referendum on the lottery amendment. The state constitution provided that the referendum could take place on any date agreed to by the governor and legislature, as long as it was more than ninety days after the end of the regular legislative session. If they could not agree on a date, the referendum would coincide with the next statewide general election, which would be in November 2000.

Siegelman persuaded the legislature to approve an October 12, 1999, special election. One reason he chose the date was that it coincided with municipal elections in Birmingham and Montgomery. Siegelman expected the lottery to benefit from a high turnout among the two cities' large African American communities, whom polls showed were the lottery's strongest supporters. In addition, according to Rick Dent, "Our feeling was that the momentum was there, so why not choose an early date? Even Zell Miller said, 'Go for it.'"[27]

Antilottery religious groups had been frustrated during the legislative debate by the absence of widespread indignation about the lottery among their members. But the legislature's nearly simultaneous consideration of the lottery amendment and the video gambling bill enabled the Christian Coalition and other organizations to rouse considerable grassroots opposition among conservative Christians. "What is particularly disturbing," said Lt. Gov. Steve Windom, a Republican with strong support in the evangelical community, "is that less than twenty minutes after the lottery vote took place, we have casino gambling on the floor of the Senate."[28]

Although its role was concealed at the time, Mississippi's Choctaw tribe fought hard to defeat the video gambling bill. At the recommendation of Washington lobbyist Jack Abramoff, the Choctaws hired Century Strategies, a new political consulting firm started by former Christian Coalition director Ralph Reed, to keep Alabama from allowing its dog tracks to install gambling machines that would draw business from the tribe's Silver Start casino in Philadelphia, Mississippi. (Reed had recently emailed his friend Abramoff that he "need[ed] to start humping in corporate accounts! I'm counting on you to help me with some contacts.") Reed boasted that "Century Strategies has on file over 3,000 pastors and 90,000 religious conservatives in Alabama that can be accessed in this effort." Within two months the Choctaws channeled $1.3 million to Reed through Abramoff's firm and Americans for Tax Reform (ATR), a Washington-based conservative group headed by a mutual friend of Abramoff and Reed, Grover Norquist.[29]

Conservative Christians flooded the switchboards at the state capitol with around ten thousand phone calls urging senators to vote *no* on video gambling. Then, after the Senate voted down the bill by twenty to fourteen on April 15, Alabama Christian Coalition director John Giles seized the opportunity to redirect his members' energy into a campaign to defeat the lottery in the October referendum. "The people of Alabama burned up the phone lines and let the Senate know the people do not want gambling," said Giles, who also directed the newly formed Coalition Against Gambling Expansion. Additional opposition developed among some traditional supporters of gambling. Echoing Representative Rogers's earlier prediction that disappointed video gambling advocates would take out their frustration with the governor on the lottery, Democratic House speaker pro tempore Demetrius Newton reported that "quite a few felt like they got out and helped the governor with the lottery and he didn't help them."[30]

On the matter of legislative authorization for the lottery—the remaining stage in the lottery creation process—Siegelman had a choice: seek enabling legislation before the referendum or wait until afterward. Such legislation would take effect only if the referendum was approved and the amendment entered the constitution. But fearing, as Dent put it, that "if we didn't show the voters what they were getting in advance, we'd lose because the people of Alabama are never going to buy a 'Trust Us' argument," Siegelman decided to seek the legislation immediately.[31]

Siegelman drew almost entirely on the Georgia model in drafting the enabling legislation. As in Georgia, the Alabama lottery would be administered by a governor-appointed board, with a maximum of 20 percent of lottery revenues spent on administrative expenses. The enabling legislation also would create offices to administer the new programs funded by the lottery: college scholarships, prekindergarten classes, and educational technology. Both houses passed the legislation, much of it drawn word for word from Georgia's lottery statute. Passage came in May with little controversy after the legislation's sponsors beat back a campaign by the state's convenience store owners to raise the minimum sales commission on lottery ticket sales from 5 to 7 percent. "The education lottery is not about making a profit for convenience stores; it's about scholarships for Alabama children," said Siegelman's chief of staff, Paul Hamrick, who charged the convenience store owners with being "greedy."[32]

As soon as the enabling legislation was enacted, Siegelman launched a full-throttle campaign on behalf of the lottery. On May 27, for example, he traveled by plane to visit elementary schools in Mussel Shoals and Huntsville in north Alabama, Homewood in central Alabama, and Mobile in south Alabama to champion the lottery as a funding source for prekindergarten programs, computers for schools, and the HOPE scholarship program. Siegelman repeated his estimate that the lottery would raise $150 million per year to pay for these new programs. Alabamians, he said repeatedly, were already playing the lottery. Siegelman estimated that they had spent $446 million on Georgia lottery tickets since 1993. Pro-Alabama lottery television commercials showed raucous groups of Georgia college students tauntingly shouting, "Thank you, Alabama!" for funding their scholarships by playing the Georgia lottery.[33]

The governor launched his highly publicized statewide campaign in response to polls that showed support for the lottery at slightly below 60 percent and, he feared, trending downward. These poll results gave pause to Siegelman and his staff because antigambling groups in the state had barely begun to target the lottery. As Rick Dent recalled, "By late spring [1999], right after the session, Siegelman's numbers were dropping and so were the lottery's. If you don't start at 65 percent for a lottery, then it is hard to end above 50 [percent] because of the daily barrage of scrutiny. We knew we didn't start the campaign where we needed to be."[34]

A poll taken in late August indicated that support for the lottery had risen to 61 percent, a sign that the campaign waged by Siegelman and the pro-lottery organization he created, the Alabama Education Lottery Foundation (AELF), was making some progress. AELF was extremely well-funded. More than 80 percent of the $5 million it ultimately raised came in donations of five thousand dollars or more, most of them solicited by the governor himself from companies that did business with the state, despite the privately expressed objections of James Sumner, the State Ethics Commission director. For example, computer companies with no-bid state contracts donated $100,000 to AELF and financial firms that handled the state's investments gave $117,500. Other donors were in the process of seeking help from the state, including HealthSouth Corporation, which contributed $250,000. A court later found that HealthSouth founder Richard Scrushy illegally channeled an additional $500,000 to the lottery campaign in return for Siegelman's appointing him to a state board.[35]

At about that time, however, opposition groups began their counterattack. The Alabama Family Alliance (AFA) made 5,200 copies of an antigambling video called "Gambling in Alabama" and distributed them for showings in churches and homes. John Hill, a senior policy analyst for the AFA, published research that hammered the lottery on two grounds: first, that it would harm existing businesses in Alabama because consumer spending on the lottery would cause spending on nonlottery items to go down; and, second, that the lottery would harm members of minority groups, who would play the lottery more than whites but would receive fewer scholarships.[36]

The Alabama Baptist Convention was active in the antilottery campaign throughout the state. Joe Bob Mizzell, director of Christian ethics for the convention, and Dan Ireland, executive director of the convention's political arm (the Alabama Citizen Action Program), decided to give special emphasis to a longstanding annual event in the national Southern Baptist Convention, "Anti-Gambling Sunday." "Every third Sunday of September," said Mizzell, "is Anti-Gambling Sunday in our denomination. Probably 70 percent of our churches had an antigambling sermon that Sunday."[37] In 1999 Anti-Gambling Sunday fell on September 19, less than a month before the lottery referendum. In a state with more than one million Southern Baptists, the antilottery message reached many voters.

All of Siegelman's rivals for governor in 1998 campaigned against the lottery. Lenora Pate, who had challenged Siegelman for the Democratic nomination, Winton Blount, who had challenged Governor James for the Republican nomination, and James himself spoke against the lottery on numerous occasions during the referendum campaign. Lieutenant Governor Windom did the same, charging that the lottery was not for education but "for the good ol' boys in Montgomery."[38]

Although lotteries typically enjoy strong support from African American voters in state referenda, some prominent black Alabamians, such as Representative Rogers, a longstanding legislative supporter of gambling, helped lead the opposition in 1999. Rogers, along with other black legislators such as Laura Hall, James Buskey, and Yvonne Kennedy, took issue with the lottery's Siegelman-sponsored enabling legislation because it barred federal Pell grant recipients from receiving HOPE scholarships. "I was all over the state saying that his lottery would hurt poor people," said Rogers. "They call me the 'sin legislator' and the 'gambling legislator,' so when I came out against the lottery, people thought there must really be something wrong with it." Conservative lottery opponents welcomed Rogers's opposition. "If John wants to preach that doctrine," remarked Dan Ireland of the Alabama Citizen Action Program, "I'll say, 'Amen!'"[39]

In addition to criticism from African American political leaders, Siegelman's lottery was attacked by a substantial number of black clergy. As Mizzell points out, "The black preachers of the state turned against the lottery and this reduced the black vote from 90 percent for Siegelman in 1998 to only 60 or 70 percent for the lottery in 1999."[40]

Not all the opposition to the lottery was public. Not wanting to face competition from an Alabama lottery any more than they did from video gambling at Alabama dog tracks, the Mississippi Choctaws now funneled $300,000 through ATR to Citizens Against a Legalized Lottery (CALL), a new organization led by Birmingham businessman Jim Cooper.[41] CALL produced the video that was distributed by the AFA and tried to coordinate the antilottery efforts of whites with those of black Alabamians. "My group [CALL] did give some money to black groups to help fight the lottery," Cooper recalled, "for example, around $40,000 for radio [advertising] in Mobile County. And we did win Mobile County."[42]

A poll taken at the end of September indicated that the counterattack had succeeded in moving public opinion. Only 51 percent of the state's likely voters said that they would support the lottery. Forty-two percent said they would vote against it, and 7 percent said they were still undecided.[43] During the final two weeks of the referendum campaign, new political developments helped convert undecided voters and a handful of lottery supporters into lottery opponents. On the eve of the October 12 vote, a scandal tainted the Siegelman administration and, indirectly, its proposal for a lottery. Newspapers reported that members of the administration and high-ranking officials in the state Department of Public Safety had been fixing traffic and speeding tickets for their friends and colleagues. Siegelman's executive secretary, Nick Bailey, and his public safety director, Mike Sullivan, eventually lost their jobs because of the scandal.

The ticket fixing scandal gave lottery opponents ample ammunition to claim that state officials in general and governors in particular could not be trusted to run honest operations, including a lottery. (Two of Siegelman's three most recent predecessors, Hunt and Folsom, had left office amid ethics scandals.) Shortly before the lottery referendum, Jim Cooper asked, "What would have happened if there were hundreds of millions of dollars involved instead of traffic tickets?" Dovetailing with Windom's message that the lottery was for the "good ol' boys of Montgomery," Cooper argued that the lottery is "ripe for all types of corruption" among state officials. Antilottery television commercials had already been playing to voters' suspicions by portraying two overweight, cigar-chewing politicians gloating about the cream they expected to skim off the lottery. Now the news seemed to confirm these concerns. As Rick Dent recalled, the ticket fixing scandal was "the giant straw that broke the camel's back. If the other side's message is, 'You can't trust these guys,' and a scandal breaks a few days before the vote that involves the governor's staff fixing tickets—that's going to kill you."[44]

On October 12, 1999, Alabama voters rejected Siegelman's lottery proposal by 54 to 46 percent. Although pro-lottery groups outspent opposition groups $5 million to $1.2 million, the antilottery position prevailed. Turnout was high across the state but especially in the counties that voted against the lottery. Governor Siegelman admitted defeat. "The people have spoken," he said, "I accept their decision."[45]

### The Post-Lottery Politics of Gambling

With the lottery off the state's political agenda, at least for a time, the politics of gambling in Alabama for the most part morphed into what it had been before the lottery issue arose. Starting with the 2000 legislative session, progambling legislators introduced bills and constitutional amendments to allow the state's still struggling dog tracks to offer video gambling with cash payouts.

The defeat of the lottery colored the legislature's consideration of these proposals. No gambling bill was passed in either chamber in 2000, in part because a sizable number of the representatives and senators who had voted for the lottery were eager to go on record against some form of gambling. As Windom said at the time, "Any senator who votes for gambling after the people rejected gambling last October is going to do so at his or her risk." A poll found that 56 percent of Alabamians opposed allowing video gambling for cash at the dog tracks. Citizens for a Better Alabama, the antigambling organization formerly known as Citizens Against a Legalized Lottery, lobbied against video gambling. So did the state's Baptist churches. Most notably, the Alabama Christian Coalition funded an anti–video gambling campaign with an $850,000 donation from Americans for Tax Reform. The original (and until 2005 unknown) source of the money was the Mississippi Choctaws, who funneled it to the Christian Coalition through ATR for fear that legalizing trackside video gambling in Alabama would cut into the tribal casino's customer base.[46]

Proposals to expand gambling at the dog tracks continued to be pressed in subsequent legislative sessions, however. The defeated lottery remained an important backdrop to these proposals. Legislators were still wary of arousing the substantial and well-organized constituencies that had rejected lottery gambling. Even more important was the indirect effect of two events seemingly separated by time and distance: the Alabama legislature's 1996 passage of the Chuck E. Cheese law and an October 14, 1999, South Carolina state supreme court decision that declared video gambling unconstitutional and forced video gambling operators out of business in that state by July 1, 2000.

Taken together, these events sparked a migration from South Carolina to Alabama of video gambling machines that pay winners in paper slips redeemable for prizes. By 2001, Alabama was estimated to have as many as ninety thousand video gambling machines in operation, most of them either in so-called adult arcades or at the state's dog tracks, which had begun offering video "games of skill" played for prizes. Because the machines do not pay out in cash, adult arcade and track operators argued, their gambling operations were protected by the same law that allowed Chuck E. Cheese and other businesses to let children play games for small prizes. Like the machines in the children's arcades, the video gambling machines were untaxed and unregulated. As periodic raids by law enforcement agencies indicated, a significant number of the machines paid out illegally in cash.

These developments provoked a host of responses. On behalf of the dog tracks, Sen. Gerald Dial, a Democrat from Lineville, introduced a bill to shut down the adult arcades while simultaneously allowing the tracks to offer video gambling with unlimited cash payoffs. To win the support of the Alabama Amusement and Music Operators Association, whose members place small numbers of gambling machines in convenience stores, restaurants, and bars, Dial's bill also would have allowed businesses to have as many as four of the machines. Finally, in hopes of winning broad-based support at a time when the legislature was looking for ways to close a $160 million funding shortfall for the state's education system, Dial endorsed a companion bill in the House to raise $20 to $30 million per year by taxing the machines.

Dial underplayed the benefits the tracks would derive from his bill, presenting it instead as an antigambling, revenue-raising measure that would close down the proliferating adult arcades while helping the state to meet its fiscal needs. Dog-track owner Milton McGregor argued that he needed no-limits video gambling to compete not just with Mississippi's casinos but also with three high-stakes video bingo halls operated by Alabama's Poarch

Creek Indians on sovereign reservation land near Atmore, Montgomery, and Wetumpka.[47] Although the federal Indian Gaming Regulatory Act of 1988 forbade the Poarch Creeks from offering casino games in the absence of a compact with the state government, the act did authorize the tribe to offer high-stakes bingo gambling on tribal land. As one previously antigambling legislator said, the presence of the Poarch Creek facilities meant that "it's no longer a question of should there be gambling in the state of Alabama."[48]

Governor Siegelman endorsed Dial's bill, and, on May 2, 2001, the Senate narrowly passed it by eighteen to seventeen. Opponents of gambling such as Windom, Giles, and Ireland responded by rallying against the bill because it would expand gambling at the tracks. "They may parade it as a bill to close down gambling arcades," Ireland charged, "but it's a guise for the dog tracks to have full-fledged gambling." As for closing down the adult arcades, gambling opponents expected that to happen anyway because of an advisory opinion issued by four justices of the state supreme court when overturning the court's 1997 opinion that some video gambling devices were constitutionally permissible games of skill. The court had been asked if bills such as Dial's were revenue measures that, under the state constitution, must originate in the House rather than the Senate. Three of the nine justices responded directly to this question and two chose not to respond at all. The other four, including the court's new chief justice, Roy Moore, offered a sweeping opinion that declared video gambling machines to be unconstitutional games of chance. Although the proposed legislation described the machines as "skill-dependent wagering games," Moore and his colleagues wrote, "the player's skill cannot determine the outcome." The House decided not to vote on the gambling bill, and it died at the end of the 2001 session.[49]

Not everyone agreed that an advisory opinion issued by less than a majority of the court was binding. Although the opinion placed some of McGregor's existing gambling machines in legal jeopardy and foreclosed his immediate hopes for cash-paying machines, he responded defiantly, installing several hundred more of the prize-giving machines at his tracks. But a number of courts and prosecutors around the state heeded state attorney general Bill Pryor's recommendation to accept the supreme court's advisory opinion as binding and shut down the arcades. To buttress this recommendation, Pryor sought and in December 2002 won a unanimous judgment from the Alabama

Court of Civil Appeals declaring that gambling machines violate the state constitution's ban on lotteries.[50] As Pryor had hoped, the ruling was appealed to the supreme court by the losing party, a machine distributor named Ted's Game Enterprises. Pryor was certain that the court's decision in this case would be consistent with the four-justice advisory opinion, thus removing all doubt that video gambling is illegal in Alabama. His strategy was vindicated in June 2004 when the supreme court upheld the civil appeals court's decision by a seven-to-one vote.

Undeterred by the court's decisions or by his previous failures to win legislative approval for cash-paying machines at his dog tracks, McGregor changed his strategy. In 2003, taking advantage of an obscure but important provision of the Alabama constitution governing the adoption of constitutional amendments that affect only one county, he engineered the passage of amendments to allow bingo-style high stakes electronic gambling machines at the tracks in Greene County and Macon County. The constitutional provision stipulates that a one-county amendment, after clearing the legislature, need only be approved by the voters of the affected county in order to become part of the state constitution.[51] The only African American Republican in the legislature, Rep. Johnny Ford of Tuskegee, allowed his colleagues to vote down one version of the bingo amendments while inserting a slightly different version into another bill that passed. Legislators thought they had defeated the electronic cash bingo measure, and the *Birmingham News* congratulated them in an editorial for doing so.[52] In truth, they had forwarded the measures to the voters of Macon and Greene counties, who approved them as constitutional amendments in referenda that November. By January 2004, hundreds of high-stakes video bingo machines were operating at each track.

With sponsorship by Senator Dial and Rep. Yvonne Kennedy, a Mobile Democrat, McGregor then pushed a constitutional amendment during the 2004 legislative session that would allow him to add video gambling halls to all of his tracks. The amendment was packaged as "Bingo for Books" because the profits from the new cash-paying gambling machines would be taxed at a rate of 14 percent and the revenues used to buy textbooks for the state's public schools. The new strategy was politically astute, winning the endorsement of the Alabama Education Association and the Alabama Association of School Boards. The measure even passed the Senate by the three-fifths majority required for constitutional amendments, with Democratic senators supporting it twenty to three and Republicans opposing it one to six. But it succumbed to a threatened filibuster in the House, where antigambling Republicans were more numerous.[53]

McGregor is nothing if not resourceful, however. In December 2005 he opened a round-the-clock facility at his Birmingham track that, to all appearances, was a slot-machine hall with 1,320 casino-like machines. "I've tried to make it as much like a casino as I could," he declared on the eve of the facility's 2005 opening. What made the machines legal, McGregor argued, was that they constituted "promotional sweepstakes," not gambling. The machines read plastic cards, which customers bought for the ostensible purpose of using the Internet in the track's new cybercafé, to determine which of the cards were winners. (In truth, the computers are scarcely used.) On January 31, 2006, a Jefferson County judge, with gritted teeth, ruled the games legal even though "the sweepstakes operation is a sham. Through careful planning [McGregor] found a loophole in the patchwork of Alabama's anti-gambling laws and has taken advantage of that loophole." At the start of the 2006 legislative session, Governor Riley submitted a bill designed to close the sweepstakes loophole, but it was buried in the legislature's tourism committees. According to Sen. Hank Erwin, the bill's sponsor, and Rep. Johnny Mack Morrow, legislators on neither side wanted to vote on the issue. A *yes* vote would generate a McGregor-funded opponent in the next election and a *no* vote would brand one as progambling.[54]

As for a state lottery, doubt was removed in November 2002 about the prospect of reviving the idea any time soon when Siegelman was narrowly defeated in his bid for reelection by Rep. Bob Riley, an antigambling Republican. Siegelman had revived his proposal for a lottery in modified form in May 2002. Pointing to recent shortages in state funding for public education, Siegelman proposed to designate the $200 million per year that he now estimated a lottery would generate for public school systems rather than for college scholarships. He also argued that Alabama needed a lottery because Tennessee was about to enact one, draining even more dollars from the state as north Alabamians crossed the border to buy Tennessee lottery tickets. (He was right about Tennessee, which approved a lottery referendum in November 2002.) Riley and Windom, his rival for the Republican nomination, outdid each other in professing opposition to a lottery. A pollster found that Siegelman's lottery plan was energizing opponents more than supporters, and Riley won the election.[55] Siegelman and the lottery suffered an additional setback when he ran another "education lottery"–centered campaign for the Democratic gubernatorial nomination in 2006, only to be handily defeated by Lt. Gov. Lucy Baxley.[56]

Riley made clear when he took office that a lottery "is not an option" and that he would veto any bill that explicitly authorized video gambling for cash prizes at the racetracks. "One, I don't think it would generate any money," the new governor said of the track proposal. "Two, I think it's an excess burden on the poor. Three, it sends a message that you can get something for nothing." When the Poarch Creek Indians offered to share their profits with the state in return for a compact authorizing the tribe to turn its gambling halls into casinos, Riley refused to negotiate with them as part of his across-the-board opposition to gambling.[57]

## WHY ALABAMA REJECTED CASINOS AND A LOTTERY

Alabama remains one of only two states in the South with neither a lottery nor commercial casinos. (Arkansas is the other.) This status persists despite the strong push for casino legalization in 1993 and 1994, the raucous debate over a state lottery in 1998 and 1999, the federally authorized opening of several tribal video bingo halls, and ongoing, partially successful efforts to allow video gambling for cash prizes at the state's dog tracks. As with the other states we have examined, any explanation of the politics of gambling in Alabama must draw on a combination of policy diffusion (that is, the examples of Alabama's neighbors), the internal characteristics of the state, and policy entrepreneurship.

The campaign for casino legalization had little going for it. No governor or other prominent statewide official has ever stepped forward as a would-be policy entrepreneur on this issue. Casino gambling is anathema to the state's many and powerful Protestant denominations. Equally important, the workings of policy diffusion on this issue have been of ambiguous political consequence. Mississippi's enactment of casino gambling in 1992 certainly gave Alabama dog-track owners and Mobile tourism officials an argument they could use in demanding the right to offer casino games of their own. But as was shown in chapter 1, Mississippi legislators had legalized casinos quietly, leaving the public unaware of how pervasive casino gambling would become in the state. Even the casino's strongest supporters in Mississippi agree that casino legalization could not have survived close public scrutiny at the time of enactment. Casino advocates in Alabama have never had the luxury of flying below the political radar. The presence of Mississippi casinos made it obvious to all that casino legalization in Alabama would be a major and a highly controversial step.

The politics of video gambling at the dog tracks has been more complex. The four tracks are established legal enterprises and significant employers. No one disputes that they have suffered from the rise of casino gambling in Mississippi and high-stakes video bingo on Indian lands within Alabama. Track owner Milton McGregor is a shrewd and influential figure in state politics who has shown considerable adroitness in his campaigns to install video gambling machines at some of his facilities. That said, Alabama's voters have shown little inclination to support efforts to expand gambling, and Mississippi's Choctaw casino operators have demonstrated their willingness to spend heavily (albeit covertly) to defeat any campaign to do so. In a shifting coalition, the Choctaws, who also have worked to prevent the Poarch Creek Indians from expanding their bingo halls into casinos, allied with the Poarch Creeks in a successful campaign to prevent Alabama's Mowa tribe from securing federal recognition, which would have allowed the tribe to sponsor bingo gambling on its lands north of Mobile.[58]

The campaign for an Alabama lottery also failed but only after coming very close to succeeding. In this case, the workings of diffusion, internal characteristics, and policy entrepreneurship were the most complex of all.

### Diffusion

Diffusion theory helps explain both why the lottery rose to the top of Alabama's political agenda in the 1990s and why it failed to be enacted. By 1998 Alabama was bordered by two lottery states, Florida and Georgia. The creation of the Florida lottery in 1986 had placed lottery gambling on Alabama's political agenda in the 1990 election in a small way, when Siegelman based his first campaign for the Democratic gubernatorial nomination on the issue. But the influence of Florida's example remained limited. For one thing, the

Florida lottery placed only the southeastern part of Alabama on a border with a lottery state, attracting a relatively small share of Alabamians as players. For another, the Florida lottery was widely regarded as a disappointment. Its promise to increase funding for the state's public schools had been compromised by the legislature's pattern of substituting lottery revenues for existing educational spending from the general fund.

The launching of the Georgia lottery in 1993 not only increased dramatically the number of Alabamians playing out-of-state lottery games but also, with its celebrated lottery-funded HOPE scholarship program, offered a popular example of what a lottery could help to accomplish in a state. In 1998, when Siegelman ran again for governor, he had a more politically appealing version of the lottery to present to the voters. Not only did he run an "Education Lottery"–focused campaign, but he and others attributed his victory to his embrace of the issue.

Tennessee's approval of a lottery referendum in November 2002 came too late to help secure Siegelman's lottery-based reelection in that year. But the sale of the first Tennessee lottery ticket in 2004 meant that Alabama was now surrounded on all but its western border by lottery states, each attracting swarms of players from Alabama. (Indeed, all ten of the top sales locations for the Tennessee lottery are just north of the Alabama line.) "I think the people of Alabama are going to demand a lottery when they see Tennessee taking money out of the state, as well as Mississippi, Georgia, and Florida," Siegelman said soon after leaving office in 2003.[59] In 2006, declaring his candidacy for governor once again, Siegelman promised to renew his campaign for a lottery and pledged to negotiate a compact with the Poarch Creek Indians which would allow them to operate full-scale casinos on their lands in return for making substantial contributions to the state treasury.

As governor, Siegelman had immediately pressed for the enactment of a Georgia-style lottery in Alabama. But he neglected the advantages of incremental diffusion—that is, the political benefit that leaders in one state may derive from altering, if only cosmetically, a policy innovation in the course of borrowing it from another state. The dynamics of political campaigning make such alterations advantageous: state pride requires political candidates to avow that, far from simply copying another state's policy, they will improve it and adapt it to their own state's circumstances. That is what Zell Miller did in Georgia when he modified Florida's lottery by explicitly providing that lottery-generated revenues would not be substituted for existing spending on education. It's also what Miller suggested that Siegelman do: as Miller put it, "Every state is different."[60] But Siegelman was so personally—and publicly— devoted to the Georgia example that he failed to modify the lottery in any way that would give Alabamians a sense of pride and ownership in the new policy he was asking them to endorse in the statewide referendum.

The working of antidiffusion in Alabama's politics of gambling should not be overlooked either. The Mississippi Choctaws did not want Alabama to legalize any new form of gambling that might distract their Alabama customers. The tribe was politically astute enough to realize that open opposition to gambling legalization in Alabama would backfire. But in 1999 and 2000, the Choctaws covertly channeled nearly $2 million to antigambling organizations in Alabama that shared their opposition to gambling in that state.

### Internal Characteristics

Diffusion theory accounts substantially for the prominent place of the lottery on Alabama's policy agenda during the late 1990s. The state's internal characteristics help explain the voters' eventual decision not to create one.

Initial public support for the lottery was never as high in Alabama as it typically is in states that enact lotteries. Although Siegelman's sixteen-point margin of victory in 1998 was impressive, especially considering that he was the first Democrat to be elected governor of Alabama in twenty years, the election-day exit poll showed that only 54 percent of the voters favored a lottery. Because Siegelman's party controlled both houses of the state legislature, his lottery proposal enjoyed smoother legislative sailing during his first months in office than this level of public support would have predicted. In South Carolina, by contrast, Governor Hodges required a higher level of public support to win legislative endorsement of the lottery because both houses were controlled by the opposition Republican party.

An additional internal characteristic that contributed to the defeat of the lottery in Alabama, albeit only mildly, is the state constitution. The constitution includes a prohibition on lotteries, which meant that Siegelman needed an amendment in order to secure his proposed new policy. The Democratic legislature did its part, providing the three-fifths majorities needed for passage.

But the amendment process also requires voter approval in a statewide referendum. That requirement is no bar to popular or uncontroversial minor amendments—the Alabama constitution has been amended more than seven hundred times. But, as we have seen, the voters of Alabama were never strongly pro-lottery.

Another characteristic of the state constitution is that it empowers the governor to choose, subject to legislative approval, the date of the referendum. In the case of the lottery, Siegelman decided to hold the statewide vote on October 12, 1999, thinking that the already-scheduled municipal elections in two large cities with substantial African American communities would spur a disproportionately high turnout among lottery supporters.

Giving the governor discretion to choose the date of a referendum creates the possibility that he will choose badly. Siegelman did: his decision backfired. The date he set for the special election on the lottery followed close on the heels of the Southern Baptists' long-scheduled Anti-Gambling Sunday. Alabama Baptists, who constitute one-fourth of the state's population, were already riled by the dog tracks' efforts to win legislative approval of video poker. Roused to action by this more controversial form of gambling, as well as by sermons that portrayed the lottery as the first step toward slot machines on every street corner, they were better organized and more motivated to oppose the lottery than they otherwise might have been.

Less foreseeable but no less significant, the October 12 date turned out to mean that the voters were asked to consider giving the governor more administrative power just as they were hearing news stories about a ticket-fixing scandal directly connected with Siegelman's office. As Rick Dent recalls, "After the ticket scandal, the referendum was about whether we can trust the legislature and the governor with $150 million a year. The voters' answer was, 'Hell no, we can't trust these people.'"[61]

### Policy Entrepreneurship

In several southern states, the politics of gambling has been marked by policy entrepreneurs—usually governors or prominent state legislators—taking the lead in the effort to create a lottery or open the legal doors to casino gambling. Miller of Georgia and Hodges of South Carolina served as policy entrepreneurs for their states' lotteries, and state representative Sonny Merideth was the entrepreneur for casino legalization in Mississippi. Don Siegelman aspired to be the policy entrepreneur who instituted a lottery in Alabama. Although he was, in the words of one observer, "the most adroit political campaigner this state has seen since [former governor and presidential candidate] George Wallace," he failed to do so, for three main reasons.[62]

First, after his election in 1998, Siegelman overinterpreted his electoral victory as a clear mandate for a lottery. In truth, his election in an increasingly Republican state was as much a function of incumbent Fob James's shortcomings as it was of Siegelman's lottery proposal. The narrow majority for the lottery among exit poll respondents suggests that the voters were more interested in changing governors than in inviting a new form of gambling into their state.

As governor, Siegelman and his political advisers proceeded as though the voters had spoken more clearly on the lottery than they had. During the first several months of his administration, Siegelman operated on the assumption that his lottery amendment would pass with only moderate campaigning on his part in the weeks before the referendum. This proved to be a severe miscalculation because, as Dent says, he and Siegelman were not "where we needed to be" in the campaign to win public approval of the lottery.

Second, Siegelman secured passage of the enabling legislation for the lottery before the electorate voted on the constitutional amendment that would activate such a law. This was a considered political judgment, rooted in the governor's belief that a significant number of voters would refuse to buy a pig in a poke—that is, approve a lottery amendment to the constitution without knowing how the lottery would work. But the price of proceeding in this way was high. Because the legislation spelled out how the lottery would operate and how lottery revenues would be spent, groups of voters who might otherwise have thought that they would benefit from a lottery now knew that they would not. Anti-lottery television commercials played on their disappointment with the slogan, "Not *this* lottery, Alabama."[63]

Specifically, convenience store owners were disappointed by the 5 percent commission they would earn from ticket sales, which did not seem to justify the cost of hiring new employees. Some African American voters, led by black legislators such as John Rogers, were upset that Pell Grant recipients would be excluded from receiving lottery-funded HOPE scholarships. Siegelman miscalculated that these groups would come around in the end and provide as much support for the lottery as if their specific concerns had been addressed. The falloff in support among black voters for the lottery is hard to measure in the absence of referendum-day exit polls, but evidence that it made a difference can be found in the fact that majorities in certain areas with sizeable African American populations, including Mobile and Tuscaloosa, voted for Siegelman in 1998 but voted against the lottery in 1999.

Finally, Siegelman was not the only player in the lottery game. In most southern states, conservative Christian white voters have been the chief opponents of lotteries and African American voters, many of whom are theologically if not politically conservative, have been the chief supporters. In Alabama, some Southern Baptist and other white conservative Christian leaders reached across racial lines to forge alliances with black Christian leaders on the lottery issue. African American clergy did not have to campaign against the lottery to hurt its chances. All they needed to do was lie low. As political scientist Paul Johnson found, "With many of the [black] preachers sitting on their hands or campaigning quietly against the lottery rather than exhorting their followers to go to the polls, it is not surprising that voter turnout in the black belt counties was lower than usual."[64] The result was that the pro-lottery vote in the African American community, which was large enough to carry similar constitutional amendments to victory in Georgia and South Carolina, was too small to do so in Alabama.

# FIVE

# TENNESSEE

## "Let the People Decide"

Tennessee shares borders with eight states, as many as any other state in the union. By the mid-1990s, all eight of Tennessee's neighbors had legalized at least one form of gambling. Tennesseans had easy access to Mississippi's casinos, Arkansas's racetracks, Missouri's lottery and casinos, Kentucky's lottery and horseracing, and Virginia's lottery. They could visit North Carolina's Eastern Band of Cherokee Indians casino, buy lottery tickets in Georgia, and experience Alabama's dog tracks and charitable bingo. Fifty-five percent of all Tennesseans lived in counties that shared a border with at least one of these gambling states.

"Tennessee is an island in a sea of gambling." said Ned McWherter, a former speaker of the Tennessee House of Representatives and governor, in a 2000 interview.[1] Diffusion theory—that is, the scholarly model of state policy innovation in which public policies spread from state to state as states learn from each others' experiences—would lead one to expect that the island would have been quickly engulfed. Yet until the early 2000s, Tennessee remained the only state in the South and, along with Hawaii and Utah, one of just three states in the country that allowed no form of legal gambling within its borders. Not only had it consistently rejected the casinos and lotteries prevalent among its neighbors, but it also had abandoned other kinds of gambling—specifically, pinball gambling, charitable bingo, and pari-mutuel wagering—that recently had been legal in the state.

By all accounts, Hawaii and Utah remain disinclined to legalize any form of gambling. But in 2001, Tennessee's General Assembly voted to place on the state's general election ballot a lottery amendment closely modeled on Georgia's. (The amendment explicitly banned casino gambling.) In 2002, the measure was approved by the voters. In 2003, the legislature passed the enabling legislation to create the Tennessee lottery. In 2004, the first ticket was sold.

Several aspects of the politics of gambling help to explain why Tennessee was so slow to create a lottery and why it finally did so. The influence of other states—that is, the working of diffusion—was complex and multidirectional. To be sure, the specter of Tennessee dollars flowing into the coffers of bordering state treasuries and gambling establishments generated strong support for legalized gambling throughout the 1990s. So did the casino-based economic boom in Mississippi, the apparent success of Georgia's lottery-funded college scholarship program, and the general satisfaction nearby states seemed to feel about their own forms of legal gambling. Yet the many and varied examples offered by Tennessee's neighbors divided the efforts of gambling's advocates, some urging casinos and some a lottery, with the result that neither was able to muster a winning coalition for quite some time.

As for Tennessee's own internal characteristics—the second major influence on state policy making that political scientists emphasize—those that are relevant to the politics of gambling often were unfavorable to legalization. Some of these characteristics have to do with Tennessee's constitution, especially its uniquely arduous amendment process. Others are rooted in the state's earlier experience with gambling.

In Tennessee as in Georgia, South Carolina, Louisiana, and Alabama, the banner for the lottery was carried by a prominent Democratic political leader. In this case, however, the policy entrepreneur was a state senator, Steve Cohen, rather than a governor. (Until recently, Tennessee's governors have been unenthusiastic about or hostile to gambling.) Cohen's energies and abilities kept the lottery and, on one occasion, casinos high on the state's political agenda for nearly twenty years. No progambling policy entrepreneur in any state worked so hard for so long as Cohen. Yet Cohen's controversial qualities—both political (he was arguably the most liberal member of the legislature) and personal (he is famously abrasive and impatient)—slowed the progress of the cause he pursued so vigorously.

In this chapter the long and complex politics of gambling in Tennessee is organized chronologically, into four main parts. The story begins with a discussion of Tennessee's experience during the 1970s and 1980s, when pinball gambling, charitable bingo, and pari-mutuel wagering were prominent on the state's policy agenda. It then considers the period from 1990 to 1994 when for the first time lottery and casino legalization received serious consideration. The third part of the chapter treats the politics of gambling from 1995 to 2000, when the prospects for a lottery declined. The final section concentrates on the early 2000s, when the lottery passed from proposal to policy and charitable gambling was revived in a more modest form than in the past.

## PINBALL, BINGO, AND HORSERACING, 1971–1989

Tennessee's consideration of a lottery and casinos in the 1990s and early 2000s followed two decades of unhappy experience with other forms of gambling. This experience cast a long shadow over subsequent proposals to legalize gambling.

Charitable bingo was the first form of gambling to be made legal in Tennessee in the twentieth century. Government-sanctioned private and municipal lotteries had been integral to Tennessee's history from the late eighteenth century until 1834, when lotteries were constitutionally banned in a provision that was incorporated into the 1870 state constitution and remained in force until it was amended in 2002.[2] In 1971, however, responding to requests from the Roman Catholic dioceses of Memphis and Nashville and from veterans groups around the state, the General Assembly voted to allow nonprofit groups to sponsor bingo as a fundraising device. Some of the groups that took advantage of the new law turned out to be charities in name only, donating just a tiny fraction of their revenues to philanthropic causes and pocketing the rest.

At about the same time, the pinball gambling industry, which previously had operated legally only in Nevada, moved into Tennessee. In 1975, the court of criminal appeals ruled that pinball gambling machines were not covered by any of the state's antigambling statutes. Within a short time Tennessee became known as the "Pinball Capital of the Nation," with fifteen thousand gambling machines. Although the machines paid off betters at an extraordinarily low rate—sometimes no more than 20 percent of the amount wagered—they attracted enough players in Tennessee to bring the industry an estimated yearly gross of around $100 million.[3]

Attempts by legislators to close the loophole in Tennessee's antigambling statutes were thwarted by the pinball industry, which flooded state elections with campaign contributions. The success of their efforts left pinball gambling not just legal but also untaxed and unregulated. The election of Gov. Lamar Alexander in 1978 tipped the political balance against pinball, however. Alexander opposed gambling in all forms. "My objection," he says, "was that it was state-sponsored something-for-nothing and that this wasn't the kind of values I wanted to encourage or that the state should encourage."[4] Citing the judgment of law enforcement officials that it was impossible to prevent minors from gambling on pinball machines, the popular Republican governor urged the General Assembly to ban pinball gambling by July 1, 1982. The legislature not only voted to pass the ban but also declared bingo illegal in the same act.

Advocates of charitable bingo quickly attempted to have the ban reversed. "The Catholic bishops came to see me only two times in eight years, once about the death penalty and once about bingo," says Alexander. "The bishops told me that bingo was important to the operation of their churches and their schools, that they were pressed for money. I didn't see bingo in the basement of a parish church as a great threat to the values of our society."[5] Under pressure from veterans groups and religious organizations that raise money from the game, the legislature again legalized charitable bingo in 1980.

Bingo returned to the state's political agenda in 1984, when Attorney Gen. Bill Leech declared in an advisory opinion that the law making charitable bingo legal was unconstitutional.[6] Leech argued that bingo, as a game of chance played for money, violated Article XI, section 5 of the Tennessee constitution, which says: "The legislature shall have no power to authorize lotteries for any purpose: but shall pass laws to prohibit the sale of lottery tickets in the state."

Leech's opinion carried great legal weight. Uniquely among the states, the Tennessee constitution provides that the state attorney general is appointed by the justices of the supreme court and, in addition to representing the state in civil litigation and criminal appeals, "provides formal opinions interpreting state statutes and provisions of the state constitution." The legislature responded to Leech's opinion by considering for the first time an amendment to remove the constitutional ban on lotteries. Some advocates, especially Senator Cohen of Memphis, hoped that repealing the ban would open the door to a state lottery. But most legislators who supported the amendment were mainly concerned about restoring bingo. In 1984, they won majorities for their proposal in both houses.[7]

Unfortunately for the amendment's advocates, this vote was only the beginning. Under the constitutional amendment method that they pursued—the resolution method—two consecutive general assemblies must approve a proposed amendment, the first by a simple majority of the entire membership of both houses, and the second by a two-thirds majority. The amendment then goes before the voters in the next gubernatorial election. For the amendment to become a part of the constitution, a majority of all those voting for governor, not just a majority of those voting in the referendum, must approve it. Because it was widely assumed that many people who vote for governor would leave the voting booth before reaching the part of the ballot where referenda are located, this method of amending Tennessee's constitution had seldom been used.

Having passed the amendment in the 1983–84 General Assembly, the next task for bingo and lottery supporters was to win two-thirds majorities for the measure in both the House of Representatives and Senate in 1985 or 1986. They were successful in the Senate, where they got the necessary twenty-two of thirty-three votes. As in 1984, most Democrats voted for the lottery and most Republicans voted against it. But Memphis Democrat Mike Kernell, the amendment's sponsor in the House, refused to let the measure come to the floor because he lacked the votes to pass it. Alexander's continuing opposition made Republican support difficult to attract.

The bingo industry abandoned its effort to change the constitution, partly because in practice bingo in Tennessee was as widespread as ever. In 1984, as a way around Attorney General Leech's opinion, the legislature passed a statute that classified bingo wagers as charitable contributions rather than as bets. The idea was to allow only legitimate charities and churches to sponsor bingo, and Alexander reluctantly signed the law on that basis. Administration of the statute was assigned to the secretary of state's office.[8]

In February 1989, the five-member Tennessee supreme court ruled unanimously that the constitutional ban on lotteries applied to all games that have three characteristics: payment of money, for a chance, to win a prize. In doing so, the court pointed out that the constitution does "not prohibit all forms of gambling." "Games of skill" such as poker, blackjack, and pari-mutuel betting on horse or dog racing were illegal under state law, but they were not barred by the constitution. But "games of chance"—not just a state lottery but also raffles, and, in the case at hand, charitable bingo—were a form of lottery and therefore unconstitutional.[9] State regulators promptly ordered Tennessee's 160 licensed bingo parlors to close immediately.

In January 1989, a month before the supreme court's ruling, the public learned of a massive federal investigation involving the bingo industry's efforts to corrupt the secretary of state's office and certain legislators. Operation Rocky Top focused on bribes paid to state officials by W. D. "Donnie" Walker, who had been Tennessee's bingo regulator before resigning in 1987 to become a bingo lobbyist. Rocky Top jarred the state, resulting in the indictment of several lobbyists, regulators, and bingo operators, and provoking the suicides of Secretary of State Gentry Crowell and the chair of the House state and local government committee, Rep. Ted Ray Miller. As Democratic state senator Roy Herron of Dresden recalls, "You had this swirl of horribly tragic consequences."[10] To most voters, Rocky Top was about corrupt politicians in general. To legislators it was a more specific warning about the potentially devastating side effects of legalized gambling.

Taken together, the supreme court decision and the Rocky Top scandal sounded the death knell for charitable bingo. More to the point, the history of charitable bingo, coupled with the state's unhappy experience with pinball, complicated the broader politics of gambling in Tennessee. By 1989, lotteries existed in the District of Columbia and thirty-two states, including three of Tennessee's neighbors, Virginia, Kentucky, and Missouri. But when Tennessee finally began to give serious consideration to a lottery later that year, advocates had to deal with negative attitudes about gambling that were still fresh in the minds of the state's political leaders. McWherter says that the scandal "gave the opposition the issues to talk about."[11]

The one new form of gambling that the legislature did authorize during the 1980s also undermined, in a different way, subsequent efforts to create a lottery. Because pari-mutuel betting, as a game of skill, did not violate the constitutional ban on lotteries, the General Assembly was able to legalize horseracing by statute. Most of the impetus to do so came from Memphis legislators, who were distressed by the amount of money that their constituents were betting across the Mississippi River at Southland Greyhound Park, a nearby Arkansas dog track.[12] As the decade unfolded, lobbyists for the Tennessee Farm Bureau also got involved, predicting that if horseracing was legalized, Tennessee would rival Kentucky as a center of horse breeding. Predictions were widespread that pari-mutuel betting on horse racing would generate enormous revenues for the state.

Alexander thwarted legislative efforts to legalize horserace gambling for as long as he was governor. When the state constitution's two-term limit prevented him from running again in 1936, House Speaker McWherter, a Democrat, was elected. McWherter actively supported horseracing as a way to boost the farm economy, especially in his home region of rural west Tennessee. The legislature quickly enacted the Racing Control Act of 1987, which allowed any city of 100,000 or more or any county regardless of population to legalize horseracing by local referendum. Racing advocates came close to passing a referendum in Nashville, but only Memphis embraced horseracing, voting 61 to 39 percent in favor.[13]

None of the predicted benefits of legalizing horseracing ever came to pass. The racing industry regarded Tennessee's tax rate as too high and disliked the Racing Control Act's prohibition against year-round simulcast betting on races at other tracks. In 1993, the legislature began a five-year process of reducing the tax rate and removing the simulcast ban. But by then, casinos had begun to operate in Mississippi, draining gambling dollars from Memphis and reducing the appeal of the Memphis market to potential track operators. In 1998, when the law creating the racing commission came up for renewal, the legislature allowed it to expire.

In sum, Tennessee's experience with legalized gambling during the 1970s and 1980s was marked entirely by failure. Pinball and bingo gambling, which had been legal, were barred from the state because of the corruption they sowed. The apparent lesson from the state's effort to inaugurate pari-mutuel betting was that legalizing a new form of gambling might well bring nothing but unmet expectations and regulatory headaches. As for a lottery, although efforts to repeal the constitutional ban came close to succeeding in the mid-1980s, the demise of charitable bingo stripped the repeal coalition of one of its primary reasons for being. Thus the lottery amendment was not even brought to the floor of the General Assembly during the late 1980s.[14]

Despite the decline in support among Tennessee's political leaders for repealing the constitution's ban on lotteries, the early 1990s should have been a propitious time for the state to adopt one. The combination of a recession-induced decline in state revenues and an expected court decision mandating an estimated $400 million in state funding for rural schools colored Tennessee's gubernatorial election in 1990. So did the debate in Mississippi on Gov. Ray Mabus's lottery proposal and the 1990 gubernatorial campaign in Georgia, in which both major party candidates supported a lottery. The Republican challenger to Governor McWherter's bid for reelection, state representative Dwight Henry, made opposition to a state income tax the centerpiece of his campaign, proposing a lottery as an alternative. McWherter said that he regarded a lottery as a minor and uncertain source of revenue that would neither solve the state's fiscal problems nor reliably fund ongoing state responsibilities. But he also declared for the first time that he would not oppose a lottery if its proceeds were used only to fund one-time expenditures such as school construction. McWherter was handily reelected.[15]

In 1991 the General Assembly took the first steps that, under the resolution method of amending the constitution, were necessary to begin the process of repealing the ban on lotteries. In April the House voted the constitutionally required three times for a Republican-sponsored lottery amendment, by margins that never fell below seventy-four to twenty-two. A month later the Senate followed suit on Cohen's companion proposal in votes of nineteen to fourteen, eighteen to fifteen, and eighteen to thirteen. With the Tennessee Poll showing that support for a lottery among voters had increased from 62 percent in 1990 to 70 percent in 1991, advocates were optimistic that they would be able to get the amendment on the ballot in 1994.[16] All they needed was a two-thirds vote from both houses during the next General Assembly—that is, in 1993 or 1994.

In November 1991 McWherter, seeking additional funding for rural schools, adopted a strategy to persuade the legislature to create an income tax that was designed to take advantage of the lottery's strong support among voters. He proposed a constitutional convention to consider amendments for both tax reform and the removal of the lottery ban. Historically, conventions have been the device that Tennessee usually has employed to change its constitution, with major alterations in state government resulting from conventions held in 1834, 1870, 1953, 1959, 1965, and 1972.[17]

Like the resolution method of amending the constitution, the convention method involves several steps. The first is a majority vote of the House and Senate to call a convention. The governor can veto the convention call, but the veto may be overridden by a simple majority of both houses. The remaining stages in the process are voter approval of the legislature's convention call in a referendum, the election of delegates, the convention itself, and another referendum to approve any amendments the convention proposes. (Both referenda must be scheduled to accompany a statewide general election.) The calling of a constitutional convention forestalls the calling of another one for at least six years.

The legislature rejected McWherter's convention proposal at its spring 1992 session, voting instead to raise the state sales tax by one-half cent and earmark the proceeds for education. But efforts to enact a lottery amendment to the state constitution continued. Republican Lynn Lawson persuaded the Senate to vote nineteen to ten that a thirty-three-member convention meet in July 1993 to consider a lottery, along with tax reform and county government reorganization. But Cohen, who was pursuing his own lottery amendment through the resolution method, attacked Lawson's proposal in words that inflamed the House: "What kind of thirty-three delegates would they be? What if they were like the House of Representatives? . . . Wouldn't that be scary?"[18]

Cohen's harsh remark sank not only Lawson's convention proposal in the House but also his own proposal for a lottery amendment. Cohen had shifted gears since the previous year, now combining into one proposed amendment the lottery, a state income tax capped at 4 percent, and repeal of the sales tax on groceries. But McWherter, satisfied that the half-cent sales tax increase would fund the state's education needs, did not actively support Cohen's measure, and it never came to a vote in the House.

The defeat of Lawson's and Cohen's proposals, although disappointing to lottery advocates, did not undo the 1991–92 General Assembly's earlier vote for an amendment that would simply remove the state constitution's ban on lotteries. But compared with its predecessor, the 1993–94 General Assembly was more supportive of the lottery in one house and less supportive in the other. Legislative reapportionment after the 1990 census had altered the

House and the Senate in drastically different ways . Reapportionment of the House strengthened its Democratic majority by, for example, jamming twelve Republican incumbents into six districts. The Senate, on the other hand, had been controlled since 1987 by the so-called "Wilderbeast," a coalition of Republicans and some Democrats who supported conservative Democrat John Wilder as Senate speaker. The Senate was reapportioned to protect incumbents by making Democratic districts more Democratic and Republican districts more Republican.[19]

Reapportionment played a role in increasing the Democratic majority in the House from fifty-six to forty-three before the 1992 elections to sixty-three to thirty six afterward, thus making the House more inclined to support proposals to legalize gambling. As a result, throughout the 1990s and early 2000s, lottery resolutions would routinely pass the House by large majorities. Another effect of reapportionment was to sharpen the partisan divide on gambling in the Senate. Senators from both parties now had to worry more about primary challenges than about closely contested general elections. For Republican senators, in particular, this meant shoring up their right flank, especially on social and cultural issues such as the lottery.

Meanwhile, supporters of a different form of gambling launched a campaign that further jeopardized the chances for a lottery. In early 1992, with casinos about to open in Tunica, Mississippi, several of Memphis's political and business leaders undertook a procasino lobbying effort in the state capital. In February, the city's newly elected mayor, Willie Herenton, urged the twenty-three member delegation that represented Memphis and Shelby County in the state legislature to unite in support of his effort to bring riverboat gambling to downtown Memphis.

Herenton's effort failed. Rep. Larry Turner, a Republican opponent of gambling from Memphis, not only refused to follow the mayor's lead but sought and received an attorney general's opinion stating that slot machines, the casino industry's most profitable games, are games of chance and thus barred by the state supreme court's 1989 decision. Most important, Senator Cohen, the Memphis legislator who usually took the lead on gambling issues, denounced the proposal as "not legally feasible and not politically feasible."[20]

Cohen's main concern was that the campaign for casinos would cloud his efforts for a lottery. "You had a negative, because they brought casino gaming to the fore," he says, "but they didn't bring any positive to the table because they couldn't move a vote" in the legislature.[21] The political complications introduced by the casino effort were especially frustrating to Cohen because, before the General Assembly convened in 1993, he had developed what he thought was a winning strategy for his lottery amendment.

Cohen's new strategy was to urge doubtful legislators not to declare their personal support for a lottery but rather to "let the people decide" the issue at the ballot box. The shrewdness of this approach, according to statewide political columnist M. Lee Smith, was that "legislators who buy into Cohen's argument can tell lottery opponents that they personally are strongly opposed to a lottery but that they are only voting in favor of giving the people the right to vote on this issue."[22] Faced with the task of winning two-thirds support for his lottery resolution, however, Cohen found that the Memphis casino campaign had awakened fears around the state that repealing the ban on lotteries would open the floodgate to gambling of all sorts.

Representatives of Christian conservative groups such as the Tennessee Baptist Convention and Eagle Forum testified against Cohen's resolution at a Senate judiciary committee hearing. As noted earlier, Republican sponsorship of lottery bills as an alternative to income tax proposals had once been common. The arousal of Christian conservative opposition closed that door for most Republican legislators. In fact, two Republican senators who had voted for Cohen's proposal in 1992 announced that they would vote against it now. "Lottery . . . is a generic term meaning slot machines, roulette, and craps," said Sen. Jim Holcomb from Bristol. Sen. Ray Albright of Chattanooga warned that removing the constitution's ban on lotteries "opens it up for everything . . . Look at the kinds of elements that it would bring in here: casinos, gambling joints, roulette. It's the Las Vegas atmosphere."[23] Lacking the votes to pass his amendment, Cohen did not let it come to the floor in 1993.

For lottery advocates, 1994 loomed as a critical year. The resolution to place a lottery amendment on the ballot, which legislators had approved by a simple majority in 1991, would expire unless it received two-thirds support in the 1994 session. Much to their delight, however, the political tide seemed to be running in the lottery's favor. The Tennessee Poll showed that support for the lottery, already high, had increased from 71 percent in 1993 to 75 percent in 1994. Fifty-five percent of Tennesseans said that they had bought lottery tickets in other states.[24] East Tennesseans watched as the first class of Georgia high school seniors applied for lottery-funded HOPE scholarships. Spurred by envy and admiration of Georgia's popular new lottery, and concerned by a report showing that Tennesseans had bet $72 million in the past year in the Kentucky lottery alone, the Tennessee Municipal League for the first time urged the legislature to approve Cohen's amendment. Because it represents nearly all of Tennessee's 342 cities, the League is traditionally one of the most influential lobbies in the state.

But once again Memphis's preoccupation with casinos arose to undermine the push for a lottery. By the start of the 1994 session, the full implications of casino gambling in Mississippi had become apparent. With several casinos up and running, Tunica was booming, seemingly at Memphis's expense. "The Memphis tourism and hospitality industry is about to become the stepchild of Tunica," warned the president of the Memphis Restaurant Association.[25] Executives of Promus, the Memphis-based parent company of Harrah's Casinos, joined Mayor Herenton and several prominent Memphis business leaders in stepping up their lobbying in Nashville. In an effort to broaden their base of support, Promus issued a report arguing that not only Memphis but also Nashville, Knoxville, Chattanooga, and East Tennessee's Tri-Cities (Bristol, Johnson City, and Kingsport) "would be good markets" for casinos.

Cohen's reluctant response to these intensified pressures from his city's business and political leaders was to modify his lottery proposal by authorizing the General Assembly to give Memphis voters the right to approve casino gambling in their city while banning it everywhere else in the state.[26] In an April 14, 1994, floor speech, Cohen invoked Tunica's success at drawing millions of dollars from Tennessee betters and reminded Middle Tennessee senators that he had supported Nashville's efforts to attract a professional basketball team.[27] Several other West Tennessee senators added their voices to Cohen's plea.[28]

As Cohen had feared, the casino issue only strengthened East and Middle Tennessee legislators' opposition to a lottery. The Promus study had aroused concern that, no matter what Cohen's amendment might say, legalizing casinos anywhere in the state soon would spark efforts to legalize them everywhere. "Once it starts in Shelby [County]," warned Sen. Carl Koella, who represented an East Tennessee district, "it will creep across the state to East Tennessee."

When the roll was called on Cohen's motion to include Memphis casinos in his proposed lottery amendment, West Tennessee senators voted *aye* by a margin of five to two, with two abstaining. The rest of the Senate was overwhelmingly opposed, however. The vote from Middle and East Tennessee senators was four to nineteen. Thus the Memphis casino amendment failed by nine to twenty-one to two.[29]

When the Senate turned to Cohen's original lottery-only amendment after rejecting the Memphis casinos version, it defeated the measure by fourteen to eighteen, well shy of the two-thirds majority required for passage. As a token to senators who had voted *nay* but whose constituents favored a lottery, the Senate voted to call for a constitutional convention on the lottery. But it did so knowing that the vote was an empty political gesture. The legislature was about to adjourn and Speaker of the House Jimmy Naifeh, had vowed not to let the House version of the convention bill out of subcommittee.

### Why Gambling Proposals Failed in the Early 1990s

The 1990s began with a strong tide running in favor of a lottery. By the end of 1994, the lottery was back to square one in Tennessee's arduous constitutional amendment process. What accounts for the lottery's political decline from 1990 to 1994? As one would expect from our theory of state policy innovation, the explanation draws from three elements: interstate diffusion, the state's internal characteristics, and policy entrepreneurship.

*Diffusion.* The defining feature of diffusion theory is its prediction that as states initiate new policies and are satisfied with them, the likelihood increases that nearby states will follow their example. Certainly the spread of lotteries to nearly three-fourths of the states by 1994 suggests that this process had been at work for some time in the politics of gambling.[30] No state that had enacted a lottery had shown any serious inclination to repeal it.

By this reckoning, Tennessee seemed very much in line to join the ranks of lottery states in the early 1990s. Cohen and other lottery advocates offered the experience of other states as one of their leading arguments; they also lamented the dollars that were flowing from Tennessee into neighboring states' treasuries. In doing so, these advocates persuaded even some previous opponents to reconsider their positions. McWherter, for example, says that over the years, "my position softened a great deal as other states made progress with them . . . You've got the lotteries in Virginia, . . . Kentucky, and Missouri, south of us now in Georgia, and our people are spilling across the state line" to play.[31]

The lessons Tennessee learned about gambling from other states became more complicated when Mississippi legalized casinos in the early 1990s. To West Tennesseans, it was the success of casino gambling that was alluring and the flood of Tennessee dollars into Tunica's slot machines that was worrisome.

In sum, the example of most of the state's neighbors led many Tennesseans to support legalized gambling in the early 1990s. But the state was experiencing a kind of diffusion overload. The Mississippi-inspired interest of West Tennesseans in casinos clashed with the influence on Middle and East Tennesseans of the lotteries in Georgia, Kentucky, and Virginia. Because different parts of Tennessee wanted different forms of gambling, the state as a whole legalized no one form of gambling.

*Internal characteristics.* Public opinion polls in the early 1990s showed strong and consistent support for a lottery in Tennessee.[32] Other, less supportive characteristics of the state proved more important, however. One of these was the bad experience that Tennessee had with pinball and charitable bingo in the 1970s and 1980s. "The hangover from Rocky Top created a seedy image of gambling in the body politic, which was reflected in the legislative view of such things," says veteran legislative correspondent Tom Humphrey. The scandal touched many legislators personally when friends and associates were indicted or, in two cases, took their own lives. In the same vein, McWherter says that the pinball and bingo controversies "created a problem about any kind of gambling, including a lottery."[33]

The lines of partisan division also were generally unfavorable to a lottery, much less to casino gambling. In particular, two changes occurred in the state Republican party that made support from Senate Republicans politically untenable. First, the redistricting that took place in advance of the 1992 elections reinforced each party's control of its existing Senate districts. Second, conservative Christian organizations that are influential within the GOP intensified their antigambling activity. The combination of these two changes threatened primary challenges to Republicans who might otherwise have been inclined to support some form of gambling. After 1992, no gambling effort ever attracted substantial Republican support in the Senate.

Finally, lottery advocates were attempting what in Tennessee is an unusually ambitious task: to amend the state's constitution. Fulfilling the intentions of the constitution's framers, Tennessee's amendment processes are the most difficult of any state in the country.[34] The rationale underlying most states' early requirement that a constitutional amendment be approved twice by the legislature, the second time after an intervening election, was that the voice of the people should be heard during the process. Typically, the required second legislative endorsement was dropped when states added the referendum to the amendment process, but not in Tennessee.[35] In addition, lottery advocates in the early 1990s were primarily focused on the resolution method, which historically has been even harder to employ than the convention method. It is no surprise, therefore, that for a time after 1994 the efforts to create a lottery in Tennessee would shift from legislative resolutions toward calls for constitutional conventions.

*Policy entrepreneurs.* The change in the governorship from the Republican Alexander to the Democrat McWherter in 1987 was of some value to lottery advocates. But McWherter never said that he would vote for a lottery if one got on the ballot, and he was adamant that revenues from a lottery not be used to fund "core functions" of state government but rather "one-time projects like state parks and library buildings."[36] This stance closed the door to the politically appealing prospect of a new college scholarship program such as the one funded by the Georgia lottery.

Even with a governor who was not opposed and a House that after the 1990 redistricting was consistently supportive, the lottery suffered in the Senate from the controversial reputation of its chief sponsor and the increasing resolve of its mostly Republican opponents. Steve Cohen is a "fighter," according to former House finance committee chair Matt Kisber, and "I think Steve would admit that at times when he really gets emotionally involved, he can say or do things that upset those he might be trying to persuade."[37]

### THE LOTTERY, 1995-2000

The resounding defeat of the Memphis casino proposal in 1994 effectively removed casino gambling from Tennessee's political agenda. Arguably, this should have quickly cleared the decks for a lottery. Instead, the chances for a lottery receded for several years, due in no small measure to the blunders of its advocates.

### Seeking a Lottery Amendment: The Resolution Method

During the 1995–1996 General Assembly and afterward, Senator Cohen continued to pursue the resolution method of amending the constitution. The election in 1994 of a Republican governor, Don Sundquist, who unlike most Republican legislators was open to the idea of a lottery, had given Cohen hope. With McWherter gone, Cohen was able to add to his proposal the Georgia-inspired idea of earmarking lottery proceeds for college scholarships. This made it more appealing not just to Sundquist but to many others.

Not everything that happened in the late 1990s advanced the prospects for the resolution strategy, however. Although the Georgia lottery had been successful, no other state except South Carolina enacted a lottery in this period. Support for a lottery in the Tennessee Poll fell from its earlier peak of 75 to 66 percent in 1998.[38] In an October 1999 referendum, voters in Alabama decisively defeated a Georgia-style lottery proposal. Even so, enough of Tennessee's neighbors already had enacted lotteries that the likelihood seemed small of a Tennessee lottery drawing many players from other states. A widely circulated study published in 1999 concluded that "Tennessee may have missed the revenue boat by waiting so long to join the lottery game."[39]

Finally, Cohen's lottery resolution suffered from the heightened activity of Christian conservatives, especially Bobbie Patray, the full-time volunteer lobbyist for the Eagle Forum. Patray's reputation on Capitol Hill in Nashville was high: in the assessment of a veteran reporter, "if you did a cost-of-lobbying vs. success-of-lobbying analysis, it's hard to imagine anyone other than Patray topping the list." In the late 1990s, Patray says, "I put aside other issues I was working on" to focus on the lottery. Meanwhile, national lottery supply companies such as Scientific Games and GTECH that wanted to see a lottery in Tennessee treaded water, confining their efforts to monitoring what the legislature was doing.[40]

As usual, both houses of the legislature passed Cohen's proposed constitutional amendment by a simple majority in the two-year General Assembly that ended in 1996. But—again, as usual—the resolution failed to get the necessary two-thirds majority in the Senate during the 1997–98 General Assembly. In April 1998 Cohen's amendment received only sixteen votes, six fewer than the required two-thirds. Yet in the next General Assembly, Cohen again introduced his resolution, winning a seventeen-to-fourteen vote in March 2000 to begin the process all over again. One of Cohen's colleagues invoked the myth of Sisyphus to convey his stubborn persistence in pursuing the resolution strategy: "Steve has been trying to roll that stone up that hill for the two-thirds [majority], and it always rolls back down."[41]

### Seeking a Lottery Amendment: The Convention Method

In 1997, persuaded that Cohen's resolution strategy for amending the constitution would never succeed, Democratic Senate majority leader Ward Crutchfield of Chattanooga announced that he would pursue the convention approach to obtaining a lottery.[42] Crutchfield's district borders on Georgia, and he had recently become concerned about Chattanoogans moving to Georgia to make their children eligible for HOPE scholarships. His proposal, which required only a simple majority in both houses, specified that: the voters would decide in August 1998 whether they wanted a convention; elections for the convention's thirty-three delegates would be on the November 3, 1998, ballot; the convention would begin its work on November 23, 1998; and the voters would approve or disapprove any lottery amendment the convention proposed in 2000. Although each of the delegates would represent a Senate district, all members of the legislature were constitutionally ineligible to serve as delegates.

Momentum for the convention grew when House Speaker Naifeh endorsed a slightly modified version of the Crutchfield plan. On April 15, the House approved it by a vote of sixty-four to thirty. But a host of problems developed in the Senate. One senator, whose support turned out to be crucial in committee, held his vote hostage to an unrelated bill that he was promoting.[43] When his colleagues refused to yield on the bill, he voted against the convention. Other senators insisted that the convention have ninety-nine delegates, one from every House district, rather than thirty-three delegates, one from every Senate district. They were concerned that delegates would use their newfound political prominence as a platform from which to challenge incumbent senators. Governor Sundquist, who had said he might support letting the people vote on a lottery resolution, declared his opposition to a lottery-only constitutional convention because it would foreclose the possibility of another convention during his tenure as governor.[44] Other Republicans were concerned that any lottery-related election or referendum that took place on the same day as a regularly scheduled election would swell the ranks of Democratic voters.

The most surprising problem the convention plan encountered was strong, vocal, and persistent opposition from Senator Cohen. On January 4, 1998, the day Crutchfield introduced his plan, Cohen attacked it as too expensive and, given that conventions can be held only once every six years, a waste of a convention. In late February, when it became apparent that his own lottery resolution was dead, Cohen chose to step up his opposition to a lottery convention rather than get behind it. Although the state attorney general had said that the legislature could confine the convention's agenda to the lottery, Cohen raised the specter of a "runaway" convention that might decide to propose an income tax or impose term limits on legislators.[45] At session's end, the convention bill remained bottled up in committee.

In the 1999–2000 General Assembly, the House once again voted for a convention, this time by a margin of fifty-six to forty-one. Lottery opponents worried that there might be seventeen pro-lottery votes in the Senate, the simple majority needed to set the convention process in motion. Sundquist's renewed threat to veto a convention bill carried some weight in the Senate, as did continuing concerns among Republican members about how a lottery-related ballot measure would affect their bids for reelection. When Crutchfield's convention bill came to a vote in 2000, it failed, thirteen to seventeen. All fourteen Senate Republicans voted *no.*

What was remarkable about the 1999–2000 General Assembly was that all of its proceedings took place in the shadow of a looming fiscal crisis, with annual deficits in the state budget exceeding $350 million. So massive was the estimated shortfall in revenues that Governor Sundquist was willing to alienate many in his party by proposing a state income tax.[46] Most estimates of the annual revenue that a lottery would raise for the state ranged from $150 to $250 million, a substantial amount. Yet a lottery was not enacted, and it never figured seriously in discussions of how to raise new revenues. For one thing, Sundquist and the legislature were consumed with closing the budget shortfalls in 2000 and 2001. Because of Tennessee's elaborate constitutional amendment process, revenues from any lottery were at least three years away. Furthermore, with lottery proposals now linked to a new college scholarship program, those revenues would do nothing to close the state's budget deficit.

## Why the Lottery Failed in the Late 1990s

As the 1990s came to a close, Tennessee's status as a nongambling state became increasingly anomalous. In 1999 and 2000, Tennessee faced the sort of fiscal crisis that has advanced the fortunes of lotteries in other states. Casinos receded from the state's policy agenda, uncomplicating the effort to secure a lottery. A new and influential sponsor emerged in the Senate, Majority Leader Crutchfield, shifting the lottery spotlight from the controversial Cohen.

Yet by the time the 2000 legislative session ended, the lottery seemed further from enactment than ever—defeated, not just insufficiently supported, in the Senate. Once again, the various elements of our theory of state policy innovation help to explain this outcome.

*Diffusion.* As in the early 1990s, the influence of other states' experiences on how Tennesseans thought about gambling was complex. On the positive side, at least for lottery advocates, the Kentucky, Missouri, Georgia, and Virginia lotteries continued to attract Tennessee betters in large numbers. Even more significant was the well-publicized popularity among Georgians of the state's new lottery-funded HOPE scholarships. Diffusion theorist Jack Walker's concept of "regional pace setters" aptly describes Georgia's influence on Tennessee.[47]

In other ways, however, the example of nearby states made Tennessee less inclined to adopt a lottery in the late 1990s than the state had been earlier in the decade. By waiting so long to act, Tennessee seemed to have forfeited the possibility of attracting significant lottery dollars across state lines. "In 1991, we had few states competing with us," said Matt Kisber in 2000. "Today we would pick up a smaller amount of that out-of-state business."[48]

The October 1999 defeat of the lottery referendum in Alabama was even more instructive. Tennessee legislators began to question their longstanding assumption that a lottery would pass if it ever got on the ballot. Polls in Alabama had shown just as much support for a lottery there as in Tennessee until a specific proposal came before the voters. District polls commissioned by at least two legislators found that after the Alabama lottery failed, support for a lottery in Tennessee declined among their constituents.[49]

Even the Georgia experience cut both ways politically. After Cohen tied his lottery resolution to the creation of a college scholarship program in Tennessee, some of the groups that had hoped to benefit from the proceeds of a lottery lost interest. Also, as the sole funder of a new college scholarship program, the lottery could no longer be offered as a solution to the state's budgetary problems. In 1999 and 2000, the very time when the state was desperate for new revenues for its general fund, the lottery became irrelevant to that discussion.

*Internal Characteristics.* Internal characteristics of Tennessee politics tended to undermine efforts to legalize gambling at the end of the decade. To be sure, public opinion polls remained favorable to a lottery but less so than in the past.

Although several national lottery companies hired lobbyists to represent them in Nashville, none of them worked as effectively as gambling opponent Bobbie Patray. Patray says she "never lobbied the issue on a moral basis because the legislators to whom that matters are against it anyway and with legislators to whom that doesn't matter, I'm wasting my breath." Instead, she offered new arguments that would have broader political appeal and keep legislators from getting bored: arguments about the lottery's effect on bankruptcies one year, arguments about problem gambling among youths the year after that, and so on.

*Policy Entrepreneurs.* Lottery opponents were not the only ones developing new political strategies. After concluding that it would be difficult to obtain two-thirds support for the lottery in the Senate, Crutchfield developed a strategy to win the simple majorities in each house needed to set the wheels in motion for a constitutional convention. On the face of it, Crutchfield's strategy should have worked. As Senate majority leader, he was the most prestigious member of the legislature ever to take up the lottery cause. What's more, the lottery had seldom failed to win majority support in both the House and Senate.

What Crutchfield learned, however, was that Cohen was not about to cede the entrepreneurial spotlight to anyone on an issue that he had originated and pursued for more than fifteen years. Crutchfield also learned that constitutional conventions make Tennessee politicians nervous in ways that the resolution method of amending the constitution does not. For one thing, no one is quite sure that the delegates, however limited their charge, might not decide to propose controversial amendments on all sorts of subjects. For another, the constitution allows only one convention every six years, which would prevent the state from dealing with other compelling constitutional issues that might arise during that period. Most important to legislators, however, were the effects a convention might have on their own political fortunes. Because incumbent senators and representatives are constitutionally barred from participating in a convention, the delegate election process would expand the pool of potential legislative challengers.

## TENNESSEE CREATES A LOTTERY, 2000-2003

Tennessee's long history of resistance to legalized gambling finally came to an end in the early years of the twenty-first century. The crucial decisions were made in 2001, when the General Assembly approved a constitutional amendment to open the door to a lottery, and in 2002, when the voters approved the amendment by a strong majority. Opponents, conceding after the referendum that the people had spoken, abandoned their resistance to legislative enactment of a lottery in the 2003 session of the General Assembly.

The lottery amendment that the legislature placed on the 2002 ballot was long and complicated. Although it left intact the constitution's longstanding ban on "lotteries," it authorized the legislature to enact by statute a "state lottery" such as those "in operation in Georgia, Kentucky, and Virginia in 2000." The amendment made clear that the Georgia lottery was Tennessee's true model by providing that the "net proceeds" from the Tennessee lottery must "be allocated to provide financial assistance to citizens of this state to attend post-secondary educational institutions located within this state," with any remaining funds to be spent building "K–12 educational facilities" or on early-education and after-school programs.

In response to some charitable organizations' desire to resume sponsoring occasional fundraising events that involved gambling, the amendment also authorized a two-thirds majority of the General Assembly to permit any "501(c)(3)organization" to raise funds through a gambling-related "annual event." But it forbade "games of chance associated with casinos, including, but not limited to, slot machines, roulette wheels, and the like." Cohen wanted to attract support for his amendment by including fundraising opportunities for the state's many churches and charities, but he also wanted to preempt any charge that a state lottery would open the floodgates to casino gambling.

### The General Assembly Approves a Lottery Amendment, 2001

Because the General Assembly had approved Cohen's lottery amendment by simple majority votes in both houses during its 1999–2000 session, the amendment remained before the legislature when it reassembled in 2001. Cohen needed to secure the amendment's passage in the 2001–2002 General Assembly by a two-thirds majority of the House and Senate. As in the 1990s, approval by the House was all but certain and Senate approval was doubtful. Nonetheless, the early indications were that Cohen was closer to winning the needed twenty-two votes than at any time in the past.

Public support for the lottery had rebounded to a high level: by January 2001 a Mason-Dixon poll showed 68 percent of Tennesseans in favor and only 26 percent opposed. The voters' support for a lottery was accompanied by their adamant opposition to a new state income tax or any other effective measure to address the state's growing fiscal crisis. Although legislators realized that the lottery would do nothing to alleviate Tennessee's revenue shortfall—indeed, Cohen's amendment still provided that the proceeds from the lottery would be used to create a new spending program—they were convinced that the voters would never consider serious solutions until a lottery was actually up and running. "We need to get the lottery before the people to vote on it," said House Speaker Naifeh, "and then people will be more willing to look at the shortfalls of the revenues."[50]

Voters expressed their anti–income tax, pro-lottery sentiments in the 2000 legislative elections. Two lottery opponents in the state Senate were replaced by candidates pledged to support the lottery, one of them a pro-lottery Democrat and one a Republican whose conservative constituents' skepticism toward a lottery was overcome by their dread of an income tax. Cohen's amendment had received seventeen votes when it was voted on in 2000, five votes short of the twenty-two he would need in 2001. Two pro-lottery senators had been absent from that vote; adding them to the two new lottery supporters who just had been elected brought the amendment to twenty-one votes, one shy of the required two-thirds. The remaining vote seemed likely to come from Republican senator Bill Clabough, who had opposed the lottery in the past but now reported that his mail, much of it from anti–income tax constituents, was running 75 percent in favor.[51]

Cohen moved quickly in 2001 to bring the lottery amendment to a vote. As the main House sponsor of the amendment, Republican representative Chris Newton, said, "Steve is on a fast track to get this thing passed while campaign promises are still fresh in everybody's mind."[52] (Newton's district, like Senator Crutchfield's, was near the Georgia border.) With such a small margin of support in the Senate, Cohen could not afford to lose a single member of his coalition.

In Senate debate, Doug Henry, one of the few Democratic senators to oppose a lottery, raised the specter of another Rocky Top scandal, pointing to the amendment's provision that the legislature could grant charitable organizations the right to raise funds with "an annual event" that involved gambling. Henry also warned that the amendment might open the door to Indian casinos. Even though Tennessee has no federally recognized tribes and the amendment explicitly banned casino gambling, Henry claimed that a tribe might acquire land in Tennessee and declare that it had a right to operate a casino based on Tennessee's operation of a lottery and authorization of charitable games. At least one senator in Cohen's fragile coalition responded to Henry's arguments by publicly doubting that he could continue to support the lottery amendment. Cohen also had to deal with colleagues' concerns, prompted by a February 4, 2001, *New York Times* article about the Georgia lottery, that "an enormous transfer of money" would occur "from lottery players, who tend to live in the poorest counties of the state, to . . . college students, who come from the wealthiest counties." Lobbying on behalf of religious conservatives, Bobbie Patray fanned all of these doubts. It was lobbyists hired by Mississippi casinos to represent them in Nashville who planted the argument about Indian casinos with Henry, however.[53]

Cohen and other lottery proponents fought back fiercely. Cohen argued that for legislators to vote against the lottery was to serve Mississippi's interests, not Tennessee's—otherwise the casinos would not be fighting his amendment. To waverers, he urged that all he was asking them to do was turn the issue over to the voters. Cohen pointed to other, more favorable statements in the *Times* story about the Georgia lottery, namely, that it "had succeeded in one of its principal goals—keeping top students in the state" and also "had increased the enrollment of black students at four-year colleges around Georgia by 24 percent." He crowed that the Georgia lottery, in contrast to many other state lotteries, had increased its profits every year, reinforcing his argument that he had chosen wisely in modeling his proposal on Georgia's.[54]

On February 7, Cohen brought the lottery amendment to a final vote. "The issue is this," he declared. "Do you put this to a vote of the people?" Crutchfield, who had abandoned his earlier strategy for a constitutional convention in favor of Cohen's approach, said, "All over Chattanooga, I talk to people who tell me they are moving to the state of Georgia . . . to take advantage of the HOPE scholarship."[55] Every senator whose vote Cohen had counted on came through, and the amendment passed twenty-two to eleven. Although Republicans opposed the lottery by a vote of seven to eight, Cohen's Democratic colleagues supported it by fifteen to three.

One week later, the House affirmed the Senate's decision by a vote of eighty to fifteen. "We've got members who may not favor the lottery," said Speaker Naifeh, "but they favor giving Tennesseans the right to vote on it." As in the Senate, Democrats supported the amendment overwhelmingly (54 to 3), and even House Republicans favored it by twenty-six to twelve. Many Republican members in both houses—including Newton, the chief House sponsor—hastened to explain to their Christian conservative constituents that although they "favor giving the people the right to vote" on the issue in a referendum, they would personally vote *no*.[56]

### Why the General Assembly Approved the Lottery Amendment

Diffusion theory certainly helps to account for the General Assembly's approval of Cohen's lottery amendment. The continuing profitability of the Georgia lottery and its widely reported success in keeping that state's talented young people home for college affirmed that Cohen had chosen a politically appealing model for his lottery proposal. News stories continued to feature the many millions of dollars that Tennesseans were spending on beer, milk, and gasoline when they drove across the state line to play the Georgia, Kentucky, Missouri, and Virginia lotteries. The media also highlighted the seeming absurdity of requiring Tennessee-based charities, such as the St. Jude Children's

Research Hospital in Memphis, to go out of state to raffle off a new home or conduct other gambling-related fundraising events.

West Tennesseans' desire for casino gambling no longer complicated the effort to obtain a lottery. Their defeat in the 1994 legislative session discouraged Memphis-area legislators from pressing the issue any further. Also, because casino taxes in Mississippi go into the state's general fund, advocates of casino gambling could not point to a tangible benefit that Mississippi derived from its casinos that was as politically appealing as the college scholarships Georgia funded with its lottery. Indeed, when Mississippi casinos hired lobbyists in Nashville to oppose the Tennessee lottery, they played into Cohen's hands, rousing charges of "outside interference."

Chief among the internal characteristics that contributed to the lottery's passage was the 2000 election, which increased the ranks of lottery supporters in the Senate to within striking distance of a two-thirds majority. This result did not occur in a vacuum. The state's revenue crisis, joined with the popularity of the lottery and the unpopularity of Governor Sundquist's proposal for a new income tax, created a strong incentive for candidates seeking open seats in the legislature to feature support of the lottery in their campaigns. Because it would create a new spending program, the lottery would do nothing to solve or even meliorate Tennessee's fiscal situation. But many legislators who sought a more responsible solution believed that until a lottery was adopted and the voters saw that the state still needed revenue, the political climate for tax reform would not change. As for Rocky Top and the fears it aroused of gambling's pernicious effects on state government, each year fewer legislators and reporters were around who remembered the scandal.

Finally, in 2001 Cohen played the role of policy entrepreneur more adroitly than he ever had in the past. As noted earlier, Cohen's design of the politically appealing amendment was no small accomplishment. Placing it on a legislative fast track while the results of the 2000 election were fresh in everyone's mind was tactically astute, as was his emphasis on college scholarships and the "let the people decide" argument in wooing legislators who personally regarded the lottery as bad public policy. Cohen won Sundquist's support but, realizing that this was a politically mixed blessing in view of the governor's increasing unpopularity, did not cede leadership on the issue to him. Cohen was still capable of over-the-top attacks on those who disagreed with him (on one occasion, he described his efforts as "a battle against the dark forces"), but for the most part he honored his commitment "to be on my best behavior" during the 2001 legislative session.[57]

## The Voters Approve the Lottery Amendment, 2002

The campaign to approve the lottery referendum got off to a fast and strong start. Two days after the legislature voted to place the lottery on the November 2002 ballot, Cohen announced the formation of the Tennessee Student Scholarship Lottery Coalition (TSSLC) and showcased its bipartisan board of business, political, and educational leaders from across the state. He brought in political consultant Kevin Geddings, who had orchestrated Gov. Jim Hodges's successful campaign for a lottery in South Carolina, to run the TSSLC, then toured the state with Georgia State University professor Ross Rubenstein, who touted his research on the benefits of the Georgia lottery. At the same time, Cohen and Geddings darkly warned of a different kind of out-of-state influence on the Tennessee referendum: the millions of dollars they predicted Mississippi casino interests would spend to defeat the lottery.[58]

In forging his own campaign, Cohen reaped the benefit of his adroit design of the lottery amendment. The leaders of charitable organizations such as the Boys and Girls Clubs of Greater Knoxville spoke favorably about the amendment because it authorized the legislature to restore their right to hold annual fundraising events that involved raffles, cakewalks, bingo, and other forms of charitable gambling. Until the state Supreme Court made all such events illegal, the Knoxville group had raised $150,000 per year with its annual "Rubber Duck" race on the Tennessee River.[59] Fears that a lottery might open the door to casinos operated by Indian tribes were assuaged by Attorney Gen. Paul Summers, who assured the voters in an official opinion that the amendment's explicit ban on casino games would keep that door closed.[60] Several legislators reported that conservative constituents who in the past had opposed a lottery were now convinced that it offered the only painless solution to the state's budget problems, a perception that was no less politically potent for being inaccurate. Public opinion polls continued to show strong general support for a lottery. A May 2001 Mason-Dixon poll found 63 percent of voters planning to vote for the lottery amendment, nearly double the 32 percent who intended to vote against it.[61]

Opponents of the lottery were slower to mobilize. All of the state's predominantly white religious denominations announced their intention to help defeat the referendum, but for a time their efforts were divided between liberal and conservative churches. Nashville United Methodist minister Skip Armistead, speaking for a coalition of Presbyterian, Lutheran, and Methodist churches, declared the lottery a "social justice issue" because lottery gambling "preys on the poor."[62] The conservative Tennessee Baptist Convention, by far the largest denomination in the state with more than three thousand churches and 800,000 members, was more inclined to oppose the lottery as a morally dubious activity.

Realizing how diffuse and ineffective their efforts were in danger of becoming, representatives of fourteen liberal and conservative statewide religious organizations united to form a single umbrella body to oppose the referendum. Meeting in Nashville in conjunction with the annual convention of the National Coalition Against Legalized Gambling in September 2001, they organized the Gambling Free Tennessee Alliance (GFTA). The combination of GFTA's rollout and a coordinated strategy of antilottery sermons in Southern Baptist and United Methodist churches helped to narrow the gap on the lottery issue in an early October 2001 Tennessee Poll. Support for the lottery dropped to 55 percent, and opposition rose to 40 percent.[63]

Lottery opponents in the legislature added fuel to the anti-amendment fire. Republican representative Bill Dunn revived the charge that the amendment's provision for charitable gambling would invite the same kind of political corruption that bingo had in the Rocky Top scandal. "That's when the corruption comes in," he said, "when you have people [in the legislature] deciding who gets to run gambling operations and who doesn't." More important, or so it seemed at the time, the House defeated a Cohen-orchestrated proposal to place the lottery referendum at the top of the 2002 ballot instead of below the list of candidates for governor. Cohen's effort to change the ballot was sparked by the provision of the Tennessee constitution which requires that to pass, an amendment must receive a majority large enough to represent more than half of those voting for governor. In 1998, the most recent gubernatorial election year, more than 20 percent of voters who cast ballots for governor declined to vote in either of the two constitutional referenda. As a result, passing those referenda required a *yes* vote of 63 percent. To be sure, the lottery was more visible and controversial than the typical constitutional amendment. But Cohen was concerned that even with a smaller roll-off among voters, the votes of 55 percent or more of those casting ballots in the referendum might be needed to enact the amendment.[64]

The Tennessee constitution also requires that referenda on constitutional amendments be held in conjunction with a gubernatorial election. This aspect of the ballot was a source of concern for opponents of the lottery. The experience of other states, especially Alabama, persuaded them that if they had time to familiarize voters with their criticisms of lottery gambling over the course of a long campaign, they could reduce and perhaps eliminate the public's strong initial support for a lottery. But that strategy worked best when, as in Alabama, there was nothing else on the statewide ballot. It would be much harder to execute in an election that featured close, open-seat contests between Democrat Phil Bredesen and Republican Van Hilleary for governor and Democrat Bob Clement and Republican Lamar Alexander for U.S. senator. Campaign spending on these two elections by the candidates alone approached $30 million, more than twelve times the combined spending of GFTA and TSSLC on the lottery. The November 2002 ballot also was crowded with elections for U.S. representatives and for both houses of the state legislature.[65]

Drawing his own lesson from the defeat in Alabama, Cohen backed away from an early pledge to press the General Assembly to enact the enabling legislation for a new lottery before the referendum passed. His original thinking had been that with such a law in place, the Tennessee lottery could begin operating that much sooner. But Cohen realized that the Alabama legislature's decision to pass enabling legislation in advance of its state's referendum had alienated many groups who previously had thought they might share in the proceeds of a lottery. The absence of such legislation allowed Cohen to talk vaguely but expansively about the possibility of college scholarships for all students, whether meritorious or needy and whether at a public institution or a private one. Bredesen, a lottery supporter, said that if he were elected governor, he wanted the lottery to cover all the educational expenses of students planning careers in teaching, nursing, or social work. Other proponents predicted that the lottery would richly fund public school construction and after-school and early-education programs.[66]

GFTA's chances of defeating the lottery were weakened severely when its campaign plan was leaked to the press in April 2002. The plan eschewed traditional antilottery arguments as being politically ineffective. "A message centered around the lottery's injustice to the poor does not resonate with the voters," the plan said. "Under no circumstances should we make economic arguments." Instead, GFTA should "tap into" voters' existing "fears [of] corruption" and "distrust of politicians." In particular, "the objective is to make Steve Cohen the incarnation of the politician you cannot trust." Disdaining "stupid Republicans—political pragmatists who think being pro-lottery will endear them to voters later on but who are too stupid to realize that gambling is a Democratic issue," GFTA also would tie its efforts to Hilleary's campaign for governor. (For his part, Hilleary said he was personally against the lottery but did not intend to emphasize the issue and would not veto lottery legislation if the voters approved the amendment.) Prominent lottery opponents denounced GFTA's plan and testified to Cohen's honesty and sincerity, however much they disagreed with his views. Cohen charged GFTA with "singling out" the only Jewish member of the state senate, "a very non-Godly thing to do."[67]

In the aftermath of GFTA's self-inflicted political wound, support for the lottery in the July Mason-Dixon poll rose to 64 percent and opposition declined to 30 percent. GFTA continued to stumble. Its chairman, Nashville businessman Joe Rodgers, misread an attorney general's opinion and, in a televised debate, mistakenly accused Cohen of improperly using his Senate office to oppose the lottery. Although GFTA raised more than $1 million (little if any of it from Mississippi casinos), it allocated so much of its budget to consultants and other organizational expenses that it had little left to spend on television commercials. TSSLC, which raised only $231,000, managed to channel nearly 90 percent of its funds into ads.[68]

As Cohen stumped the state relentlessly, the reins of the antilottery campaign quietly passed from GFTA to the Tennessee Baptist Convention. In August, attractive brochures, a well-produced video, and well-crafted sample sermons were distributed to all Southern Baptist churches and preachers across the state. Dan Ireland, the Alabama Baptist minister who had campaigned so effectively to defeat his state's lottery referendum, was brought in to tour Tennessee, giving antilottery speeches and interviews. Methodist leaders also worked hard among their denomination's 1,300 churches and 300,000 members. Instead of targeting Cohen, opponents now focused on the dangers of the lottery itself, noting its reliance on the poor for ticket sales and the door it would open to compulsive gambling among adults and illegal gambling by young people.

Michael Gilstrap, GFTA's campaign director, began conceding defeat in September. "If I were to bet and take odds," he told the *Chattanooga Times Free Press* editorial board in a curious turn of phrase, "I think we're definitely not in good shape right now as a campaign." Yet October polls showed that the church-based strategy was working. Support for the lottery dropped to 53 percent, with the greatest decline occurring among regular churchgoers. Fearing that such a slim margin would be insufficient to meet the constitutional requirement for a majority of those voting for governor, Cohen began noting in public that "you can vote for the lottery and help it by not voting in the governor's race." Bredesen, who was locked in a tight race for governor with Hilleary, resented these remarks, however coy Cohen may have been about identifying rather than endorsing the strategy ("My vote is private," he said.) The worried Cohen also occasionally indulged in the sort of abrasive behavior that had caused him problems in the past. Crashing a press conference by Reverend Ireland outside the Memphis Public Library, Cohen jeered irrelevantly, "Blah, blah, blah. The Earth is not flat—that's a fact. No matter how many times they say it, the Earth is not flat."[69]

All of Cohen's fears were assuaged on election day when the lottery amendment passed by a majority of 894,137 (58 percent) to 638,452 (42 percent). Only 119,043 fewer voters cast ballots on the lottery than in the governor's election. In contrast, the other constitutional amendment on the ballot, which would have authorized city courts in Tennessee to assess fines greater than the prevailing constitutional limit of fifty dollars, passed by a 101,263-vote margin but fell well short of the 825,816 votes needed for enactment. The next morning, Cohen placed Senate Bill 1—a bill to create a lottery—in the legislative hopper and expressed his hope that "by Christmas Day 2003 we could have it up and running. We could have Santa Claus pick the first ticket." Although GFTA vice chairman Randy Tyree had said earlier that his organization might try to defeat the enabling legislation if the lottery amendment was approved narrowly, Gilstrap now conceded, "This thing passed with not just flying colors, but a resounding yes from the people of Tennessee."[70]

## Why the Voters Approved the Lottery Amendment

As diffusion theory would lead one to expect, the 2002 lottery campaign involved frequent invocations by both sides of the examples of other states. The most effective arguments by lottery advocates invoked Georgia as the model for what a Tennessee lottery could accomplish and as a drain on the incomes of lottery-playing Tennesseans. Opponents drew their confidence that the lottery could be defeated, their church-based strategy, and one of their most prominent public advocates, Rev. Dan Ireland, from neighboring Alabama, which had defeated a lottery referendum in 1999. Cohen brought in his own out-of-state strategist, Kevin Geddings, who had successfully managed the pro-lottery referendum campaign in South Carolina. Cohen also drew an important lesson from the Alabama defeat: do not pass the bill to create a lottery in advance of the referendum that authorizes the legislature to do so. As soon as the enabling legislation was enacted, he realized, many groups that may have hoped to benefit from the lottery would be disappointed and resentful. Cohen and Bredesen kept such hopes alive by trumpeting the many ways that the lottery might serve a broad array of beneficiaries.

In addition to the workings of interstate diffusion, a number of Tennessee's internal characteristics affected the referendum campaign. The state's recent fiscal crisis enhanced the desire of many voters, including some conservatives who ordinarily would have opposed a lottery, to embrace any source of revenue that did not involve new taxes. The fiscal crisis also undercut the argument of lottery opponents that the state should pay for a new college scholarship program out of the general fund. When Cohen and the editorial pages of the state's leading newspapers asked lottery opponents about their plan for educational opportunity, they had little to offer.

Some of Tennessee's internal characteristics, especially the strong effort to fight the lottery by the state's thousands of Southern Baptist, United Methodist, and other white churches, served to slow the lottery juggernaut. But few efforts were made to incorporate African American churches into this coalition of opposition, as lottery opponents had done in Alabama. Opponents who began the campaign trailing by nearly two-to-one in the polls also found that the state's crowded calendar of spirited statewide election contests in 2002 made it hard to get their message through to voters. Although all of the major party nominees in the open-seat contests for governor and senator took positions on the lottery, none of them featured the issue in their speeches or advertising. Spending on both sides of the referendum campaign constituted a tiny fraction of the amount spent by candidates touting their own virtues and their opponents' demerits.

Among the state's would-be policy entrepreneurs on the lottery issue, none excelled in the referendum campaign, but Cohen clearly outperformed his antilottery opponents. He successfully recruited an impressive bipartisan board to lend prestige to the lottery cause. His adroit design of the amendment gave charitable organizations as well as the parents of college-bound students a stake in the amendment's passage while reassuring doubtful voters that casinos would not enter the state through a constitutional crack opened by the lottery. To be sure, Cohen failed to rein in his occasionally abrasive style and rhetoric. But GFTA's leaders were astonishingly ineffective. Although they outspent their pro-lottery opponents by nearly five-to-one, most of the money was wasted on organizational expenses that did little to get their message out. Indeed, some funds were spent developing a campaign plan that accomplished something previously unknown in Tennessee politics: it made Cohen a sympathetic figure.

### The General Assembly Enacts Lottery Legislation, 2003–2004

The legal effect of the 2002 referendum was to clear the constitutional path for the General Assembly to create a lottery by legislation. The experience of neighboring Mississippi, whose voters passed a similar referendum in 1992 but whose legislature did not enact a lottery, suggests that the creation of a Tennessee lottery was no sure thing. A few lottery opponents, such as the Tennessee Baptist Convention, declared that the fight was not over.[71] Yet most were so dispirited by the results of the referendum that they abandoned the field, and even the Baptists did little more than send an antilottery letter to each member of the General Assembly.

The lack of active opposition did not ensure a smooth ride to passage. Indeed, so divided were lottery supporters about how revenues from a lottery should be allocated and who should run it that the road to legislative enactment was bumpy and, at times, uncertain. When the referendum passed in November 2002, Cohen predicted that a new lottery statute would become law in little more than three months—that is, by February 15. Instead, the fight lasted more than twice that long, until June 11, when Bredesen, the newly elected Democratic governor, signed the bills creating the lottery.

Cohen and his House cosponsor, Chris Newton, lost no time persuading House and Senate leaders to appoint a joint legislative committee on the implementation of the lottery, chaired by Cohen, in advance of the 2003 session. In mid-December 2002, members of the committee spent several days in Atlanta, seeking advice from lottery director Rebecca Paul and touring the offices of the Georgia lottery's main contractors, GTECH and Scientific Games.[72]

Few legislators questioned the joint committee's use of the Georgia lottery as the template for the new lottery in Tennessee. Yet serious doubts were raised by legislators and by groups representing minority voters about the merit basis on which Georgia's HOPE scholarships were awarded to college students. "The dumb and dumbest are going to be paying for the best and brightest's education," complained Sen. Jim Kyle, a white Democrat from Memphis. "That's a helluva policy." The Memphis chapter of the NAACP argued that every Tennessee student admitted to any state college should receive a scholarship regardless of their grades in high school. Rejecting this appeal, Cohen argued, "Lowering the GPA requirement . . . would dilute the power of the program's incentive and would be prohibitively expensive."[73]

Although he was in all other ways an uncritical admirer of Georgia's lottery, Cohen demanded a departure of his own from the Georgia model. Instead of a board appointed by the governor to oversee the lottery, he wanted one dominated by legislative appointees. Bredesen cited Georgia in insisting that the governor must appoint a majority of the board because, as chief executive of the state, he would be held accountable for how the lottery operated. Little love was lost between Cohen and the new governor. They had campaigned testily against each other in the 1994 Democratic gubernatorial primary (Bredesen won easily), and in 2002 Cohen had irritated Bredesen by publicly observing that voters could increase the lottery referendum's chances of passing by not voting in the gubernatorial election.

Other disputes revolved around which Georgia lottery the Tennessee lottery initially would be based on: the fully developed Georgia lottery of 2003, which offered scholarships to all students with a 3.0 GPA to attend any of the state's public or private colleges, or the Georgia lottery when it first began ten years earlier, which restricted the scholarships to students whose family income was below $66,000 and which gave much smaller awards to students attending private colleges. The relationship of lottery-funded scholarships to federal Pell Grants for minority students posed a similar issue. Only recently had Georgia begun awarding HOPE scholarships to Pell Grant recipients. Yet some in Tennessee, especially in the General Assembly's Black Caucus, insisted that the Tennessee lottery follow Georgia's current practice and allow Pell grantees to receive both scholarships simultaneously.

In preparation for the 2003 legislative session, Cohen and Newton worked with the joint committee and with a legislatively appointed Education Lottery Task Force, consisting of legislators and educators, to prepare two bills, one to implement the lottery and the other to create the lottery-funded scholarships. Confident of the House's support, Newton let the Senate take the lead.

The implementation bill was introduced on February 4, 2003, and received the joint committee's approval one week later. With one major exception—a lottery board dominated by legislative appointees—the bill followed the Georgia model for lottery operations. The Tennessee lottery would be run by a quasi-public corporation headed by a chief executive officer appointed by the board. All of the proceeds would go to education—college scholarships first, then K–12 school construction and after-school and early-education programs if any funds were left.

The scholarship bill, introduced soon after the implementation bill, was initially more controversial. Students who earned a 3.0 GPA in high school and scored nineteen or better on the ACT would receive an annual $4,000 scholarship if they enrolled in an in-state public institution and their family income was $100,000 or less. A student who met the merit requirement and had a family income below $36,000 would receive an extra $1,000 per year. A student whose GPA exceeded 3.75 and who earned at least a twenty-nine on the ACT would receive a full scholarship regardless of family income. Scholarships would be reduced by half for qualifying students who enrolled in an in-state private college or university. Smaller scholarships also were offered to any student who chose to attend a state community college or one of Tennessee's twenty-six technology centers.[74]

Criticisms of the proposed scholarship bill arose quickly from both Republican legislators and members of the Black Caucus. Although they attacked the bill for different reasons, their criticisms shared a common theme: the scholarships were insufficiently generous to their constituents. Because Cohen's main concern was to get the lottery up and running as soon as possible so that revenues for scholarships could begin to accumulate, he was inclined to accommodate every politically influential demand. Republicans wanted full scholarships for private as well as public college students; they also insisted that the family income ceiling on eligibility be lifted. The scholarship bill was changed to accommodate both demands. The Black Caucus, joined by several rural white legislators, wanted the merit standard lowered. As a result, the qualification for a scholarship was reduced from a 3.0 GPA and a nineteen on the ACT to a 3.0 GPA or a nineteen on the ACT, with half-scholarships awarded to students with a GPA of 2.75.[75]

One consequence of these decisions to broaden eligibility for the new scholarships was to reduce the standard award from $4,000 to $3,000. Another was to increase the estimated first-year cost of the scholarship program from $115 million to $177 million, crowding out any possibility that surplus revenues from the lottery would be available to fund other educational programs. In the end, the modified scholarship bill passed both houses easily: twenty-eight to four in the Senate on April 21 and seventy-six to twenty-one in the House on May 21.

Cohen's generally smooth handling of the scholarship bill was no predictor of the controversies he provoked on the implementation bill. Frustrated by the deliberate pace with which the Senate Government Operations Committee was considering implementation, Cohen agreed with a reporter's suggestion that committee chair Thelma Harper, an African American Democrat from Nashville, was "slow-walking" the bill. Harper took to the Senate floor to reply that "slavery is dead" and that her committee was "not going to be whipped with straps and made to do anything." When the bill was amended in a different committee to bar the purchase of lottery tickets with credit or debit cards, Cohen said, "That's like putting needles in kids' arms and pulling the money out." In the course of his disputes with Bredesen about the makeup of the lottery board and other issues, Cohen variously called the governor "arrogant," "Chicken Little," and "similar to [Tennessee's famously corrupt former governor] Ray Blanton in the matter of administrative arrogance and power." During conference committee deliberations, Cohen described House Democratic leader Kim McMillan as "paranoid," "without principle or honor," and a "chastising harpy."[76]

Having alienated so many of his fellow Democrats, Cohen was in no position to win his fight with Bredesen about who would appoint the board of the new state lottery corporation. Although both houses, acting at Cohen's insistence, had passed implementation bills granting the governor and the leaders of the House and Senate three appointments each to a nine-member board, neither house was willing to continue resisting Bredesen's demand that the governor be empowered to fill three seats on a five-member board. On May 29, Cohen astonished Bredesen and his colleagues by paying an early morning call at the governor's mansion and offering to support a seven-member board consisting entirely of gubernatorial appointees. Bredesen happily accepted Cohen's more-than-total capitulation and both houses passed the revised implementation bill later that day. The governor signed it and the scholarship bill on June 11. The Tennessee Education Lottery became law.

Bredesen quickly appointed the board of the new lottery corporation, which set about hiring a chief executive officer and awarding contracts to national gambling corporations to operate the lottery. Not surprisingly, board members took the well-worn path to Atlanta to visit with the Georgia lottery's Rebecca Paul and to tour the offices of Scientific Games and GTECH. Paul surprised Bredesen and the Tennessee lottery board a few weeks later by proposing an unprecedented arrangement in which the two states would operate their lotteries jointly. Tennessee would benefit, Paul argued, because it could begin selling tickets sooner if it merged its lottery with Georgia's than if it went its own way; both states would benefit by massing their negotiating power against GTECH and Scientific Games. In 2001 Paul had proposed a similar arrangement to the board of the new South Carolina lottery, which declined because "we wanted to maintain our independence."[77]

Critics of Paul's offer echoed South Carolina by arguing that Tennessee would always be the junior partner in any alliance with the larger and more established Georgia lottery. But before a full-scale debate could get underway, a number of other lottery supply companies suggested that they would sue to block any Tennessee-Georgia arrangement as violating Tennessee's competitive bidding requirement for procurement contracts. Fearing that lawsuits would delay indefinitely the sale of lottery tickets, the board reluctantly rejected Paul's proposal. But in a dramatic development, it persuaded Paul to leave Georgia and become CEO of the new Tennessee lottery. Throughout the implementation process, Cohen expressed his unhappiness that the board was not consulting him. "I'm so turned off to the whole process and the whole team up there," Cohen lamented. "I am just really turned off to all of it."[78]

Having dealt with the lottery in 2003, Bredesen and the General Assembly turned to charitable gambling in 2004. The same constitutional amendment that authorized the lottery also authorized 501(c)3 nonprofit organizations to hold an annual gambling-based fundraising event if two-thirds of both houses of the legislature approved. The enabling legislation that emerged in 2004 reflected legislators' eagerness to satisfy charitable groups in their constituencies and the governor's concern that a door not be opened to the sort of abuses that the state had witnessed in the past. Bredesen was especially concerned that professional operators not be allowed once again to run gambling halls in the name of charitable organizations, setting the stage for another Rocky Top–style scandal. The bill that the General Assembly passed and Bredesen signed in April 2004 allowed eligible groups to apply each year to hold a one-day event and instructed the secretary of state to compile all proper applications into an omnibus bill that would need to be passed each year by a two-thirds majority of the General Assembly. The new law was filled with provisions designed to prevent abuse. For example, only nonprofit groups that had been active for five years could apply; such groups could not offer bingo or casino-style games; they had to run the event themselves rather than contract with a professional operator; and they had to report any expenses above one hundred dollars.[79]

### Why the General Assembly Enacted the Lottery Legislation It Did

The most important internal characteristic of Tennessee that shaped the legislature's enactment of the lottery in 2003 and charitable gambling in 2004 was the change in the state constitution wrought by the previous year's referendum. Voters clearly expected the General Assembly to use its new constitutional power to enact a lottery speedily. To be sure, the latter action did not necessarily follow from the former: Mississippi voters had lifted their state's constitutional ban on lotteries, then watched passively as the legislature refused to create a lottery. But Tennessee did not, as Mississippi did, have casino gambling; indeed, the new amendment explicitly barred casinos. Equally important, Mississippi's amendment did not create a constituency for a lottery by designating who would benefit if one were enacted. In contrast, the Tennessee amendment whetted the appetites of parents and students for new lottery-funded college scholarships.

Nonetheless, victories like the one lottery advocates won at the polls in 2002 bring challenges of their own—in this case, the many ideas, interests, and egos that had to be accommodated if general agreement on the need for a lottery was to manifest itself in specific legislation. The burden fell on Cohen and, to a lesser extent, Representative Newton to face the formidable challenges of policy entrepreneurship. They met these challenges skillfully in the initial stages of legislative development, in part by persuading the leaders of their respective chambers to set the enactment process in motion by ap-pointing task forces in advance of the 2003 session, and in part by dividing the process into two tracks: an implementation bill and a scholarship bill. Enact-ment of either bill, they realized, would increase the pressure on legislators to enact both. But as the 2003 session deliberated well past the mid-February goal Cohen had set for placing lottery legislation on the books, his growing impatience burst every self-imposed restraint on his impatience toward col-leagues and Governor Bredesen. Matters degenerated to the point that if Cohen was for something, that was all some legislators needed to know to be against it. Newton showed much greater skill at accommodating the many voices who wanted their interests expressed in the new lottery legislation. In the end, Cohen capitulated to the governor on the appointment issue that divided them, and the two bills were passed.

As it had throughout the adoption process, the influence of the Georgia example affected Tennessee powerfully in writing the lottery laws. No one doubted that the Georgia lottery would provide the template for Tennessee. As a result, some important matters were entirely uncontroversial, such as the administration of a lottery by a quasi-public state corporation. Even the disputes that ignited the most controversy, especially the appointment of the lottery board and the eligibility criteria for scholarships, took the Georgia lottery as their point of departure.

As for charitable gambling, pressure on legislators was strong from non-profit groups that wanted to hold fundraising events as soon as possible. But

Tennessee's history of abuse and scandal in charitable gambling persuaded the General Assembly to accept all of the strict safeguards that Governor Bredesen insisted be built into enabling legislation.

## AFTER-POLITICS OF GAMBLING IN TENNESSEE

As in Georgia, most of the issues that have arisen in Tennessee since the launch of the lottery have involved how to spend the proceeds, which initially turned out to be even more substantial than expected. On January 20, 2005, for example, Rebecca Paul announced that in its first year the lottery generated $246 million for the state treasury, considerably more than was needed to fund the HOPE scholarship program. Cohen and Newton immediately insisted that the additional money be used to raise the amount of the scholarships. Governor Bredesen proposed instead to devote $25 million of lottery revenues to prekindergarten programs for at-risk four-year-olds. The General Assembly responded by doing both: increasing the lottery-funded scholarships by around 10 percent and approving Bredesen's prekindergarten proposal, but not before Cohen and Bredesen traded angry words in the news media. All sides realized that if lottery revenues did not continue to grow as expected, more difficult choices would have to be made in the future.[80]

Lottery revenues did grow, however. By January 2006, the end of its second full year of operation, more than sixty-thousand Tennessee students had received college scholarships. (About half lost them because of poor academic performance, but most of them stayed in school anyway.)[81] In May 2006 the General Assembly adopted a budget for the coming fiscal year that raised the amount of each scholarship by several hundred dollars and nearly doubled the amount allocated to prekindergarten education from $25 to $45 million.[82]

# SIX

# ARKANSAS

## Politics Gets Wacky

Ever since Arkansas's current constitution was enacted in 1874, it has included a ban on lotteries: "No lottery shall be authorized by this state, nor shall the sale of lottery tickets be allowed." To be sure, Arkansas is not gambling-free. Two state court decisions established the legal precedent that betting on horseracing and greyhound racing did not violate the prohibition on lotteries because they involve an element of skill.[1] Oaklawn Park, a thoroughbred racing facility in the central resort town of Hot Springs, opened in 1905. Until the cash-strapped state legislature voted to authorize (and tax) pari-mutuel wagering at the track in 1935, the gambling that took place there, although voluminous, was illegal. (So were Hot Springs's once-fabled casinos.) In 1956, concerned that a future court might reverse the state supreme court's 1949 decision validating horserace wagering, Oaklawn's owners successfully petitioned for a constitutional amendment confirming that betting on horses at the track is legal. The only other legal gambling facility in the state, Southland Greyhound Park in West Memphis, began operating in 1956. Southland never achieved explicit constitutional protection, but the court case distinguishing pari-mutuel racetrack betting from a lottery has stood unchallenged.

As in many southern states, efforts to legalize casinos and a lottery became a prominent feature of Arkansas politics during the latter part of the twentieth century, especially in the 1990s. None of these efforts has succeeded, although the scope of legal gambling at the state's two racetracks has gradually been broadened to encompass certain electronic gambling machines. In this chapter, we first chronicle the recent series of failed gambling legalization campaigns in Arkansas, then analyze the reasons for these failures in terms of the main elements of our theory of state policy innovation: diffusion, internal characteristics, and policy entrepreneurship.

## FAILED CAMPAIGNS TO LEGALIZE CASINO
## AND LOTTERY GAMBLING

Arkansas's modern resistance to most new forms of gambling is in some ways surprising, not just because of national and regional trends to the contrary but also because of the state's own history. Until the early 1960s, casino gambling enjoyed a long and lucrative run in Hot Springs. Illegal casinos were publicly condemned but privately winked at by Arkansas's political leaders and law enforcement officials. "I figured that as long as the residents of Hot Springs were satisfied with it [casino gambling] and were getting good from it, that I would let it alone," said Orval Faubus, who was governor from 1955 to 1967. In 1964, however, Faubus came under enormous pressure from the state's overwhelmingly Protestant religious organizations to close down the casinos. Reluctantly, on March 29, he ordered the state police to do so. Faubus was facing a tough challenge in his bid for reelection to a sixth two-year term from Winthrop Rockefeller, a wealthy Republican who opposed gambling.[2]

### The 1964 Campaign and 1967 Shutdown

No sooner were the Hot Springs casinos closed down than the city's mayor, chamber of commerce, and other business and political leaders turned for relief to the state's initiative process for amending the constitution, gathering nearly 75,000 signatures for a proposal to legalize ten casinos in Hot Springs and surrounding Garland County. The initiative process offers one of the two ways that the Arkansas constitution may be amended. If petitioners can get valid signatures for a proposed constitutional amendment equal to 10 percent of the turnout in the most recent gubernatorial election, the amendment will go on the ballot at the next general election and can be passed by a simple majority of those voting on it. Alternatively, the legislature may place, by a simple majority vote of both houses, as many as three proposed amendments on each general election ballot. Again, the voters' approval is required for enactment.

Outside of Hot Springs, organized support for the 1964 casino measure was meager. At the time, only Nevada allowed casino gambling and its casinos were widely perceived as crime-ridden. As election day neared, the *Arkansas Gazette* ran daily page-one excerpts from *Greenfelt Jungle,* a new book that chronicled the influence of organized crime in Nevada's casino industry.[3] On November 3, the casino amendment failed by 318,229 to 215,744, a nineteen-percentage-point margin of defeat.

Faubus was reelected in the same election and, shortly afterward, turned a blind eye when several Hot Springs casinos reopened as private clubs. In 1966 he retired as governor and Rockefeller was elected. Convinced that Rockefeller would not cast a veto, the General Assembly narrowly approved a bill in 1967 to legalize casino gambling in four of the Hot Springs clubs. Rockefeller vetoed it, provoking the bill's chief sponsor, Sen. Q. Byrum Hurst of Hot Springs, to declare that the governor had "perpetuated a fraud upon me . . . I feel that I have been misled, that the people of my country have been crucified." Soon after, Rockefeller sent in the state police not only to shut down the clubs but also to destroy their slot machines.[4]

### The 1984 Campaign

In 1984, seventeen years after the Rockefeller administration ended casino gambling in Hot Springs, a small group of local businessmen launched another petition drive to add a casino amendment to the state constitution. In advancing their proposal, which would have authorized seven large and ten small casinos in Hot Springs and Garland County, they were able to point to New Jersey's recent decision to legalize casino gambling as a strategy for reviving the economy of Atlantic City. Even though it was in faraway New Jersey, advocates argued, Atlantic City was a lot like Hot Springs: a once thriving resort town that had fallen on hard times because its cool summer breezes no longer held the same attraction for tourists whose homes were now air conditioned. In contrast to 1964, Hot Springs casino supporters also could cite Nevada's generally successful campaign to weed out organized crime from its casino industry, which by now was dominated by publicly traded corporations.

Arkansas voters found these new arguments unpersuasive. The 1984 amendment was defeated even more resoundingly than its predecessor: 561,825

(70 percent) to 236,625 (30 percent). One reason for the defeat was that, since the 1960s, Hot Springs had been trying to rebrand its tourist industry to attract families with children. Mayor Jim Randall opposed the 1984 casino measure, and none of the city's other political leaders endorsed it. Garland County voters disapproved the measure by a strong majority on election day.

Another reason voters rejected the amendment was that, statewide, nearly every political, business, law enforcement, and religious organization opposed it, including Gov. Bill Clinton. First Lady Hillary Clinton told a rally on the steps of the state capitol, "We are on the move in Arkansas. Why on earth would we want to give ourselves a burden we can't carry and an image we don't want?"[5]

Other opponents raised the specter of casino-spawned crime. "With casino gambling," charged U.S. attorney Asa Hutchinson, a Republican at the same rally, "you can say we have just given up on the drug battle." Opponents ran a television ad that, according to political scientists Diane Blair and Jay Barth, is "still quoted two decades later." The ad "showed a disheveled young father pleading, 'Baby needs a new pair of shoes!' as he bets—and loses—more of his family's money."[6]

Arkansas's first serious discussion of a state-run lottery also occurred in 1984. Doug Wood, a member of the state House of Representatives, began a petition drive to place a lottery amendment on the ballot but failed to secure the required number of signatures. Polls showed majority support for a lottery, and it was obvious that Missouri, which shares a border with twenty-nine Arkansas counties, was about to create one. In response to letters from constituents, Governor Clinton wrote, "While I certainly think that a state lottery would be preferable to legalized casino gambling, I still cannot support a state lottery" because "many people would be tempted to spend money for lottery tickets that should be spent for food, clothing, and shelter for themselves and their families." That said, he added to one letter in his own hand, "I have no objection to the people voting on this issue. If a majority wants a lottery, then we can have one but I would not vote for it." But religious opposition to an Arkansas lottery was strong and organized. After a difficult reelection bid in 1984, Wood declared that the lottery "is just too hot an issue for a political leader to propose." Running for reelection in 1986, Governor Clinton scorned a lottery as "easy money."[7]

Clinton softened his opposition to a lottery in 1989, saying that although he would "hate to see the state in the gambling business," he "would not oppose putting it on the ballot if the money went to education." Later that year, the state legislature considered placing a referendum on the 1990 general election ballot that would amend the state constitution to legalize charitable bingo and create a lottery with the revenues earmarked for education. But the legislative majority in favor of the lottery amendment collapsed when a committee tacked on a provision to repeal Amendment 44, a civil rights–era amendment to Arkansas' constitution that required state officials to uphold segregation. "If people vote against the lottery, it puts us in the position of affirming segregation," said state senator Nick Wilson. Religious leaders opposed to segregation, a lottery or, more commonly, to both also were outspoken.[8]

The legislature seriously considered a lottery for the last time in 1989. Since then, every organized campaign to legalize a lottery and other forms of gambling has arisen from the initiative process. The legislature's failure to act inspired Robert Walker, a research technician at the University of Arkansas, to organize Arkansas for a Legalized Lottery and use the petition process to try to place on the 1990 ballot a lottery amendment, with the proceeds earmarked for education. Walker had launched a similar campaign in 1988, but that effort was so poorly conceived that Walker himself admitted it was "a poor amendment [that] . . . I'm not comfortable with because of the issues that have come up."[9]

Walker's 1990 petition gained strength from news reports of polls showing strong support for a lottery in Arkansas and of new or imminent lotteries in several southern and border states, including Kentucky, Florida, Georgia, and three of Arkansas's neighbors: Texas, Louisiana, and Missouri.[10] His group succeeded in meeting the 10 percent signature requirement (68,855 at the time) to place the amendment on the November ballot. But opponents, led by W. H. "Buddy" Sutton, a prominent Little Rock attorney and Baptist layman, sued to have the initiative declared invalid. Sutton argued that the amendment's ballot title (the brief description of the amendment that voters would see on the ballot) was "deceptive and misleading." For example, he pointed out that the ballot title failed to disclose that the proposed amendment would create a new state commission to run the lottery and that it actually named four of the five commissioners, one of whom had recently died.

Two weeks before the November 6, 1990, general election, Sutton revealed the results of an investigation showing that many of the signatures on the qualifying petitions for Walker's lottery amendment—including one purporting to be from the incoming speaker of the state House of Representatives—had been forged. Walker, who was not implicated in the forgeries, announced that he would vote against his own amendment on election day. He never had to. On October 26, the state supreme court, by a four-to-three majority, struck the measure from the ballot on the grounds that the ballot title was deceptive and misleading.

### The 1994 Campaign

After a three-year hiatus in the politics of gambling in Arkansas, three new proposals for gambling amendments to the state constitution emerged in early 1994. Advocates of all three emphasized again that Arkansas was increasingly surrounded by gambling states. Lotteries operated in Louisiana, Texas, Oklahoma, and Missouri, and casinos had been legalized in Mississippi, Missouri, and Louisiana. All of these states were drawing customers from Arkansas.

Two of the new proposals came through the initiative process and were designed to remove the constitutional ban on lotteries. The Oaklawn Park horseracing track in Hot Springs and the Southland Greyhound Park in West Memphis teamed up to form the Arkansas First Committee, with Craig Douglass, a Little Rock lawyer, as executive director. Arkansas First began a petition drive to place on the November 1994 ballot a measure to create a state-run lottery with the revenues earmarked for law enforcement and education; to legalize charitable bingo (Arkansas was one of only four states that forbade it); and, most important, to authorize casino gambling at two sites, Oaklawn and Southland.

The alliance between the two tracks was based primarily on their fears that the budding casino industry in Tunica, Mississippi—only a short drive from Southland and just two hours by car from Oaklawn—would divert customers and profits from both tracks. The first Tunica casino had opened in October 1992, six months after Oaklawn concluded a well-attended, financially successful season. The following year, both tracks experienced significant declines in attendance and wagering. By 1994 six Tunica casinos were in operation, accelerating the Arkansas tracks' downward trend. Decline fed on itself: the tracks had to reduce their purses, which made it harder for them to attract the kind of racers that generate attendance and wagering. Eric Jackson, the general manager of Oaklawn, says that he "saw what was happening with the casinos in Mississippi and realized that if we were going to have any chance of competing we were going to need to be able to offer a similar product." Southland's management reached the same conclusion after the legislature denied its 1993 request to install video gambling machines.[11]

The second 1994 initiative to legalize gambling proposed to authorize one casino site, which would be located near West Memphis but not at Southland. Mike Wilson, an Arkansas farming magnate and mayor of the small town of Wilson, established the Committee to Promote Arkansas in an effort to gather signatures for this constitutional amendment. Wilson envisioned a vast resort—complete with restaurants, hotels, and golf courses—that would draw on Little Rock and, especially, nearby Memphis as feeder markets. In a classic exercise of distributive politics, Wilson's measure also provided that each county in the state would receive, for law enforcement purposes, a percentage of the tax revenues the state derived from the casino resort. Even antigambling lobbyist Larry Page, a Southern Baptist activist who served as the executive director of the Christian Civic Action Committee, admits that the "general consensus was that Mike Wilson had the best casino proposal for Arkansas."[12]

The third 1994 proposal to legalize gambling came from the Arkansas legislature. Acting on its authority to propose no more than three constitutional amendments every two years, the legislature decided to put on the ballot an amendment to legalize charitable bingo. The measure included an explicit ban on casinos and lotteries.

Opposition to the Oaklawn-Southland and Wilson casino proposals emerged immediately from two groups not commonly found on the same side: conservative Christians and the public interest group Common Cause. Larry Page of the Christian Civic Action Committee and Scott Trotter, who was executive director of the Arkansas chapter of Common Cause, made it clear within a week of the casino proposals' unveiling that they would fight the measures at every stage of the legalization process.

The sponsors of casino gambling, aware of the battle to come, worked shrewdly to build momentum for their proposed amendments. Using out-of-state professional signature-gathering firms, the Oaklawn-Southland and

Wilson proposals attained enough signatures to be certified for the November ballot. In addition, Wilson met with Michael Rose, the chairman of the Memphis-based Promus Corporation, which at the time was the parent company of Harrah's Casinos, and formed a partnership to run the new casino resort if the amendment passed. Promus funneled more than $3.2 million into the campaign to pass Wilson's constitutional initiative.

Any momentum that may have been gained by the sponsors of the two casino amendments proved to be short-lived, however. Polls conducted in October by the *Arkansas Gazette* found that 51 percent of Arkansans opposed the Oaklawn-Southland proposal and 55 percent opposed Wilson's proposal. A mere 42 and 38 percent, respectively, supported the proposals. The only gambling measure that had the support of a plurality (48 percent in favor, 42 percent opposed) of Arkansans was the legislature's proposal for a charitable bingo amendment.[13]

In the end, litigation displaced campaigning as the main arena of political conflict in 1994, and the voters never had a chance to vote on any of the three proposed gambling amendments. Bill Walmsley, the president of the Arkansas Thoroughbred Breeders and Horsemen's Association, filed suit against the legislature's proposal to legalize charitable bingo while forbidding lotteries and casinos. Walmsley's group wanted Oaklawn to have a casino because of the added purses the track would be able to offer with its new revenues. The Arkansas constitution complicated this effort, however, because it provides that if two proposed amendments contain contradictory provisions and both pass, only the amendment that receives the most votes will take effect. The Horsemen's Association feared that the charitable bingo amendment would pass by a larger margin than would the Oaklawn-Southland amendment, and that a ban on casino gambling thus become part of the constitution. Walmsley's legal argument against the bingo amendment was that the secretary of state, who is responsible for overseeing the initiative process, did not follow the correct procedures for getting it on the ballot.

Meanwhile, the Christian Civic Action Committee and Common Cause filed suit against the Arkansas First Committee's proposal for casinos at Oaklawn and Southland. Their lawsuit alleged that the ballot title was not adequately descriptive. The two groups filed a similar ballot title lawsuit against the Wilson-Promus proposal to bring a casino resort to West Memphis.

On October 14, the Arkansas supreme court removed two of the three amendments from the November ballot. The legislature's charitable bingo amendment was removed by a six-to-one vote on the grounds that the secretary of state did not publish its full text in state newspapers six months before the election, as required by the state constitution. The Oaklawn-Southland casino amendment was removed by a four-to-three vote because the ballot title did not state explicitly that it would allow casino gambling.

Finally, on October 20 the Arkansas supreme court removed the Wilson and Harrah's–sponsored proposal for a casino resort in West Memphis. In a five-to-two vote, the court ruled that the ballot title was incomplete. Together, these decisions eliminated any chance that Arkansas would expand legalized gambling in 1994.

### The 1996 Campaign

By 1996, Arkansans were crossing the border in greater numbers than ever to play high-stakes bingo on Indian reservations in Oklahoma, to buy lottery tickets in Texas and Missouri, and to gamble in Mississippi, Missouri, and Louisiana casinos. With support from a coalition of Hot Springs business and political leaders, an Oaklawn-dominated group called the Arkansas' Future Committee announced in January that it would try once again to place a constitutional amendment on the November ballot. The amendment would allow Oaklawn to open a casino in Hot Springs, pending voter approval in a subsequent local referendum. In an effort to broaden its political appeal, the amendment also would create a state lottery, with the proceeds earmarked for education and law enforcement, and would legalize charitable bingo. Finally, hoping to attract the interest of national casino corporations, the amendment authorized two more casinos in Hot Springs.[14]

Oaklawn's motive was economic survival: from 1983 to 1996, its average daily attendance had fallen from 23,000 to 13,000 and its daily handle from $3.0 million to $1.4 million. "The Arkansas [gambling] dollar is flying out of Arkansas, literally flying," said Oaklawn's St. Louis–based owner, Charles Cella. Legislative measures designed to shore up racing—Sunday meets, simulcast wagering, and a dramatic reduction of the state's pari-mutuel tax from 5.5 to 2.5 percent—had been inadequate, especially to the challenge posed by the Mississippi casinos. Answering skeptics who doubted that the prospects for voter approval of Hot Springs casinos were better in 1996 than they had been in 1964 or 1984, Arkansas' Future Committee executive director Craig Douglass said, "There was not so negative an impact on the state then as we're experiencing now with lotteries and casinos in surrounding states."[15]

Mike Wilson, whose own casino legalization amendment, like Oaklawn's, had been struck from the ballot in 1994, also revived his campaign to place a casino measure before the voters. Wilson modified his previous proposal to include a lottery and charitable bingo and to allow eight casinos instead of one, with most of the proceeds to the state used to create a college scholarship program like the HOPE scholars program funded by the Georgia lottery. A third proposed amendment, sponsored by an out-of-state company called Lottery Systems would have allowed the company to own and operate untaxed video gambling machines in Arkansas. The amendment also proposed to legalize charitable bingo and create a state lottery with the proceeds earmarked for education, law enforcement, prescription drugs for seniors, and shelters for abused women and children.

Larry Page of the Christian Civic Action Committee made clear that he would once again vigorously oppose all of these gambling amendments. "It's time for some smash-mouth football," he declared. "They need to strap on their chinstraps because we're ready to play." In addition, as a way of getting off the defensive and carrying the fight to gambling proponents, Page announced a petition drive to place an amendment on the ballot which would abolish pari-mutuel wagering where it already existed in the state. That proposal "was meant to send a signal to Oaklawn that if they kept going, we would come after them," says Page. "We weren't really trying to get the tracks out. We live in peaceful coexistence with the tracks."[16]

Page adopted a two-pronged strategy to defeat the gambling amendments: he used pastors and other local church leaders to rally conservative Christian voters who were morally opposed to gambling, and he appealed to moderate voters by making social and economic arguments about the crime, bankruptcies, and gambling disorders that casinos would spawn. Page also criticized the amendments on "good-government" grounds: "I carried around a card to remind myself of the three points I wanted to make again and again. First, this was going to be an unregulated monopoly. Second, they [the casino corporations] were getting a preferred tax rate on net rather than gross income.

Third, we'd have a lottery that can't ever be changed." Scott Trotter of Common Cause gave the opposition a nonsectarian public face while offering a battery of similar arguments.[17]

Notably, too, outgoing Democratic governor Jim Guy Tucker and incoming Republican governor Mike Huckabee expressed their opposition to casino gambling. Huckabee, the former president of the Arkansas Baptist Convention, had been elected lieutenant governor in a 1993 special election in which gambling was an issue. His Democratic opponent, Nate Coulter, had argued, "We've got a lot of our poor folks who are going across the border paying those dollars to other states. If we were living in a perfect world, I would be opposed to casinos and lotteries. We're not living in a perfect world, our neighbors are doing it. If it's going to happen, I think we ought not to let our citizens give their dollars to other states."[18]

Gambling proponents, overlooking Coulter's defeat in the election, adopted his focus on the money Arkansans were losing in surrounding states. They took advantage of news reports about the opening of a second casino in Coahoma County, Mississippi, directly across the Mississippi River from Helena, Arkansas, and about studies that showed a recent decline of in-state tourism by Arkansans, whom the proponents claimed were taking their vacation dollars to adjacent casino states. When Page compared his underfunded opposition campaign to David fighting Goliath, Oaklawn casino advocate Craig Douglass rejoined, "Arkansas is David and the surrounding states are Goliath." A month before the election, Arkansas television stations began airing antigambling commercials paid for by Mississippi casino interests under the misleading name Arkansas Wins Committee. "We thought that having a couple additional casino licenses up for grabs in Hot Springs would cause some companies that owned Tunica casinos to see a stake in our amendment passing," says Eric Jackson of Oaklawn. "Clearly we were wrong."[19]

As had happened in 1994, a host of lawsuits challenging the various proposed amendments were filed in the weeks before the November election. Some of these suits were brought by gambling opponents and others by sponsors of one gambling amendment against another gambling amendment. Supporters of the Oaklawn casino amendment, for example, sued to have Lottery Systems' video gambling amendment removed from the ballot. Page's group, deciding to concentrate its efforts on defeating the proposals for new forms of gambling, actually petitioned to have its own anti-pari-mutuel betting amendment removed. The state supreme court, citing a variety of irregularities in the wording of ballot titles and the gathering of signatures on petitions, sustained most of these challenges. By late October, the only gambling proposal left on the ballot was the Oaklawn amendment.

The closing days of the 1996 campaign were dominated by exchanges of funding-related charges by the rival camps. Craig Douglass, Eric Jackson, and other Oaklawn advocates focused on the $1.2 million that Mississippi casinos were pouring into the state to oppose casino legalization. "Mississippi is interfering with an Arkansas election," said Douglass. "Arkansas voters should be mad as hell."[20] Opponents of the amendment charged that Oaklawn's $5 million contribution to the Arkansas' Future Committee—the group's only funding source—represented a hypocritical effort to enhance an out-of-state track owner's profits in the name of protecting Arkansas against out-of-state gambling interests.

Statewide polls never showed a plurality in favor of any of the 1996 gambling proposals—the four-point margin by which the Oaklawn proposal trailed in a mid-October poll was the closest a measure ever came. On election day, 61 percent of Arkansas voters cast their ballots against the amendment, providing a nearly 200,000-vote margin of defeat. Citing the "extraordinary" costs of waging an initiative campaign, Oaklawn manager Eric Jackson says, "We'll never do it again. We simply cannot go through this again."[21]

### The 2000 Campaign

Not everyone shared Jackson's pessimistic assessment that no casino legalization campaign could succeed in Arkansas. In July 1997, Donald Nicholas of Walnut Ridge, Arkansas, and Jim Harris of Dallas, Texas, formed the Arkansas Casino Corporation (ACC) and launched a new campaign for casino gambling. Taking their cues from the sponsors of several earlier casino amendments, Nicholas and Harris included a state-run lottery and charitable bingo in their proposal in hopes of broadening its appeal.

ACC's amendment, like the 1996 Oaklawn proposal, proposed to grant its corporate sponsor constitutional authority to conduct casino gambling. Specifically, the amendment awarded ACC the exclusive right to operate a casino in each of six counties—Sebastian, Pulaski, Garland, Miller, Crittenden, and Boone. These counties were strategically chosen. Garland includes Hot Springs and Pulaski includes the state's capital and largest city, Little Rock. Boone, Crittenden, Miller, and Sebastian counties are located on the northern, eastern, southern, and western borders of the state, respectively, and thus would be convenient to gamblers from Missouri, Tennessee, Mississippi, Louisiana, Texas, and Oklahoma. All six are "wet" counties, which meant that the corporation would be able to offer alcoholic beverages in its casinos.

Nicholas and Harris thought they had learned important lessons from Oaklawn's mistakes in 1994 and 1996. The real secret to a successful bid for casinos in Arkansas, they believed, was to assure the voters that most of the profits from casino gambling would remain in the state. Their plan was to have ACC sell large amounts of stock to Arkansans, who would then accumulate wealth from the state's new industry.

Few voters and even fewer investors responded to this appeal. (Harris was, after all, a Texan.) The sponsors of the ACC amendment failed to get enough signatures to win a place on the ballot in 1998. In preparation for the 2000 election, they contracted with the Nevada-based National Voter Outreach, a signature-gathering firm, to obtain the required 70,701 valid signatures. The amendment provided that ACC would pay 15 percent of the net revenues from its six casinos as a special gambling tax but "shall not otherwise be regulated by the Gaming Commission" or the state legislature. These tax revenues, along with 45 percent of total lottery revenues, would pay for the elimination of the state sales tax on groceries and fund Georgia-style HOPE scholarships for Arkansas' college students.

Although ACC was able to obtain the required number of signatures and survive legal challenges to its place on the November 2000 ballot, its casino legalization campaign was no more successful than the failed campaigns of the past.[22] For one thing, news accounts pointed out that a small group of non-Arkansans were the primary sponsors of the effort. Not only was Harris a Texan but so was Bob Buckholz, the other major ACC stockholder and the largest contributor to the initiative's campaign committee. Buckholz contributed 98 percent of the approximately $400,000 eventually spent by ACC.

In addition, Larry Page successfully mobilized many of the 2,500 churches in his statewide organization (now called the Arkansas Faith and Ethics Council) to oppose the measure. The amendment's out-of-state sponsorship was grist for Page's mill, as was the casino monopoly that it granted ACC. "Even people who favor casino gambling oppose an unregulated monopoly," he noted. When Scott Trotter of Common Cause spoke to audiences, he would hold up a thick stack of papers that contained Mississippi's casino regulations, then hold up a blank sheet of paper, which represented the lack of authority the Arkansas Gaming Commission and the state legislature would have to regulate ACC if the company was granted the constitutional right to operate casinos.[23]

Finally, as in 1990, scandal and, in the view of Governor Huckabee, "sleaze" was attached to the ACC proposal at its most critical hour. On October 18, barely two weeks before the voters went to the polls, the Arkansas Securities Commission filed criminal charges against Buckholz and Harris, accusing them of selling stock without a license, selling unregistered stock, and providing false information about their company in order to make it appear viable. Prosecuter Larry Jegley called the casino backers "a bunch of skunks."[24]

The combination of all these factors caused the Arkansas Casino Corporation to cancel the television ad campaign it had planned to run during the final days of the election. Poll results in late September had estimated that 51 percent of Arkansans intended to vote against the ACC amendment, a fourteen-point margin over the 37 percent who said they favored it. By early November, after the scandal broke and ACC stopped advertising, opposition had risen to 60 percent. On election day, Arkansas voters defeated Amendment 5 by a twenty-eight-point margin: 234,986 for and 420,740 against.

### Legislative Efforts to Expand Gambling, 2000-2005

One change in Arkansas' gambling policy did occur in 2000, quietly and by statute. In January 2000, the state legislature authorized Oaklawn and Southland to open video gambling rooms filled with "Instant Racing" machines. In playing the machines, gamblers bet on races that already have been run, with all identifying marks removed from the horses and jockeys. Because they are given limited handicapping information before placing their bets, the electronic games are considered games of skill and thus are not barred by the state constitution.

Encouraged by this success, and dispirited by the failure of the expensive initiative campaigns they had waged for casino gambling, the racetracks continued to pursue a legislative strategy. In 2001, the legislature considered permitting Oaklawn and Southland to begin taking bets by telephone and over the Internet. More important, in 2003 the two tracks secured the support of the Arkansas Chamber of Commerce and its manufacturing arm, Associated Industries of Arkansas, for a bill allowing them to expand their offerings of "electronic games of skill" to include games such as video poker and video blackjack. Southland estimated that the new Tennessee lottery, which the state's voters approved in 2002, would reduce the amount bet at the West Memphis track by around 10 percent when tickets began to be sold in early 2004. As a way of evening the score, said the video gambling bill's House sponsor, Rep. Steve Jones of Marion, most of the money gambled on new electronic machines at Southland would come from Memphis, more than making up for the expected loss.[25]

Although the games-of-skill bill cleared committees in both the House and Senate, opposition from antigambling groups kept it from being enacted in 2003. Page, as executive director of the religiously conservative Arkansas Faith and Ethics Council, cited court decisions from other states in arguing strenuously that "calling these virtual slot machines games of skill is nothing more than a subterfuge." In addition, Mississippi casino interests anonymously funded a half-million-dollar media campaign against the bill through a dummy organization called Arkansans for the 21st Century. "It seems like I filed that bill on a Thursday and they had radio ads running on Friday," said Sen. Terry Smith of Hot Springs, who sponsored the measure in the Senate. In April, the House rejected the bill by thirty-seven to fifty-seven, and Smith kept it from coming to the Senate floor because he did not have the votes to pass it. When the Mississippi casinos' role was revealed after the legislative session, Jones said he would reintroduce the bill. "This shows that there are interests in other states trying to control certain interests in our state."[26]

Out-of-state efforts backfired during the long lead-up to the 2005 legislative session. In December 2003, the Mississippi casinos–funded Arkansans for the 21st Century ran radio and television ads urging voters to call a toll-free number and express their opposition to gambling. The group transferred the calls to the legislature, tying up the House and Senate switchboards for days and infuriating legislative leaders such as President Pro Tempore Jim Hill, who threatened to have the calls transferred back to the home of the group's leader. A year later, Tom McPherson, a vice president for governmental affairs with Boyd Gaming, which owns casinos in Mississippi, made the rounds in Little Rock in hopes of heading off any new move to expand electronic gambling at Oaklawn and Southland, publicly arguing that such a move would be bad for his company as well as for Arkansas.[27]

The maladroitness of the Mississippi casinos' campaign was more than matched by the shrewdness of the Arkansas tracks. In March 2005, in the space of three days, the bill opposed by Boyd Gaming was introduced in the Senate, endorsed on a voice vote by the City, County, and Local Affairs Committee, and approved on the floor by a vote of eighteen to fourteen. Sen. Bob Johnson of Bigelow, the bill's new sponsor, made it more politically palatable by removing any explicit mention of video poker, as well as by making approval from the voters in the tracks' home communities a condition of implementation. Remarkably, though, the bill (which Johnson admitted had essentially been written by representatives of Oaklawn and Southland) empowered each track to set the date of its local referendum and, if the voters rejected the measure, to schedule subsequent referenda until one passed. The bill also allowed each track to decide whether its referendum would include voters from the entire county in which the track was located or just voters in the city. Page, who later confessed to being "not very savvy" on the bill because he thought the new gambling machines would be "more akin to the Instant Racing machines than anything else," mounted no campaign in opposition.[28] When Governor Huckabee declined to take a stand against the bill, the House passed it by fifty-seven to thirty-eight.[29]

Oaklawn and Southland both decided that they wanted their referenda held in November 2005, and each insisted, after doing some polling, that only voters in Hot Springs and West Memphis, not those in surrounding Garland and Crittenden counties, be allowed to participate. Southland spent more than $800,000 and Oaklawn more than $300,000 to urge voters in their home cities to vote *yes*. Both tracks touted the additional jobs that electronic gambling would generate, the money they planned to donate to local charities, and the additional revenue the state would derive from the 18 percent tax on profits from the new games allowed by the new law.[30] Page's Arkansas Faith and Ethics Council and the Mississippi casinos chose to sit out the campaign (as did Governor Huckabee), and local church groups were able to raise only a few thousand dollars in opposition.[31] On election day, the voters of West

Memphis approved electronic gambling at Southland handily, by 64 to 36 percent. In Hot Springs, the margin of approval was only 89 votes out of 9,401 cast, less than one percentage point.

The politics of electronic gambling's creation spawned an after-politics of continuing controversy. The bill authorizing the new forms of gambling defined "electronic games of skill" as "games played through any electronic device or machine that afford[s] an opportunity for the exercise of skill or judgment where the outcome is not completely controlled by chance alone." It also required that each machine pay back at least 83 percent of the money wagered on it "over the expected life time of the electronic game." This made the machines seem more like games of chance than games of skill, which presumably could have widely ranging payback rates depending on the skill of the players. Finally, the bill assigned the state Racing Commission responsibility to evaluate specific gambling devices before approving them for use by the tracks.

Lawsuits and other implementation problems briefly delayed the tracks' installation of the machines. A month after the Hot Springs and West Memphis referenda were approved, the conservative, Little Rock–based Family Council Action Committee filed suit to have the entire law declared unconstitutional on the grounds that allowing Southland and Oaklawn to determine the time and eligible electorate for the gambling referenda was an improper delegation of legislative authority. Although judges in both cities rejected the committee's arguments in May 2006, it decided to appeal its case to the state supreme court. In addition, the Racing Commission decided in July 2006 that it lacked statutory authority to license or enforce pending clarification from the state legislature, which took three months to act.[32] Any games it eventually licenses may be challenged in court by the Family Council Action Committee or by Page's group on the grounds that no machine can be a game of skill if it offers gamblers the same rate of return whether it is played "skillfully" or not.[33] Nonetheless, Oaklawn and Southland proceeded on the assumption that they would be able to offer gamblers 900 to 1,000 new machines by November 2006. Southland even dropped *Greyhound* from its name, becoming Southland Park.[34]

One group that took notice of the November 2005 referenda authorizing electronic gambling machines at the Arkansas tracks was the Oklahoma-based Keetowah Band of Cherokee Indians. Although Arkansas contains no tribal reservation lands at all, businessman Bennie Westphal deeded ten acres of land he owned in downtown Fort Smith to the Keetowah Band to build a casino in which Westphal would have an interest. (Fort Smith sits across the Arkansas River from eastern Oklahoma, which has two nearby tribal gambling halls.) According to the federal Indian Gaming Regulatory Act of 1988, under certain circumstances a tribe with land in a gambling state that the federal government has taken in trust may operate a casino. In March 2006, the Keetowahs asked the federal Bureau of Indian Affairs to accept the donated land in trust for the tribe so that it could do so. Governor Huckabee, Sen. Mark Pryor, Rep. John Boozman (who represents Fort Smith in Congress), and Fort Smith mayor Ray Baker all expressed strong opposition. The number of federal and state hurdles Westphal and the Keetowahs would have to clear to get a casino in the face of such opposition is formidable.[35]

As for the lottery, it has remained on the state's political agenda for years but has made little progress toward adoption. Although it became a minor issue in the 2002 gubernatorial election, neither Huckabee, running for reelection, nor state treasurer Jimmie Lou Fisher, his Democratic opponent, championed the lottery. Huckabee reiterated his oft-stated position that lotteries are "a cruel hoax on poor people . . . the people most likely to buy the tickets and least able to afford them." Fisher only said that she would be open to changing the constitution "if the people of this state want a lottery" even though personally she was "very much opposed."[36]

A month after Huckabee was reelected, the state supreme court ruled that Arkansas's system of school funding was unconstitutionally inequitable, igniting a debate about how to raise the estimated $450 to $900 million that might be needed each year to meet the court's insistence on equitable funding. Lottery advocates such as Skip Rutherford, who was the former chair of the Little Rock school board, pointed to the estimated $47 million in revenues that a lottery would generate as a good place to begin. At the start of the 2003 legislative session, Rep. Barbara King, a Democrat from Helena, introduced a constitutional amendment authorizing the General Assembly to create a lottery for education. "With all the surrounding states having casinos or lotteries," she argued, "it's time for the state of Arkansas to have the debate."

King pointed out that the voters had never had a chance to vote on a lottery amendment that was not harnessed to a casino proposal.[37]

Although King's amendment was the subject of committee hearings, it had to compete with dozens of other proposed constitutional amendments whose advocates were seeking one of the three available places on the 2004 ballot, as well as with a wacky proposal by a fellow legislator to have the state treasurer buy a lottery ticket each week in every other state's lottery. In addition, public support for a lottery was soft and inert. "I don't see anybody championing it," said Rep. Jodie Mahoney.[38] An August 2002 statewide poll showed a lottery leading by 52 to 45 percent, far below the level of support lottery referenda usually need in the early stages of a campaign if they are ultimately to pass.[39]

Rep. Vivian Flowers, a Democrat from Pine Bluff, revived the lottery issue in 2005 by pairing it with a proposal to remove the ban on charitable bingo. In late 2004 some prosecutors had begun enforcing the bingo prohibition even against previously winked-at local organizations like the American Veterans Post No. 62 in Pocahontas. On February 28, 2005, prompted by the public backlash against these efforts at strict enforcement, the House State Agencies and Local Affairs Committee came within one vote of including Flowers's lottery-bingo amendment on the short list from which the legislature would choose which three constitutional amendments to place on the 2006 ballot.

Seizing the political moment, Rep. Shirley Borhauer, a Republican from Bella Vista, proposed a lottery-free amendment that would allow bingo and raffles to be conducted by charitable organizations. Borhauer, who had moved to Arkansas from Illinois in 1987, noted that the bingo games conducted by her Roman Catholic church in Chicago had served as "a social event for a lot of older ladies." Although Larry Page did not support Borhauer's proposal, he was relieved to see Flowers's lottery amendment defeated and later speculated that legalizing bingo might even reduce interest in legalizing other forms of gambling, especially casinos and a lottery.[40] In April 2005, both houses of the legislature voted overwhelmingly to place the charitable bingo amendment on the 2006 ballot. Antigambling groups decided not to fight it. Al Page observed, "We cannot conduct a typical gambling campaign with charitable bingo. We can't talk about organized crime and corruption and prostitution."[41] In the November election, the bingo amendment passed easily.

Two threads run through the history of gambling politics in Arkansas. One is that proposals to legalize casinos and a lottery by amending the state constitution keep rising to the top of the state's political agenda. The other is that these proposals invariably have failed. In explaining the Arkansas experience all three elements of our theory of state policy innovation are useful: interstate diffusion, the internal characteristics of the state, and policy entrepreneurship. The same is true in explaining how the established gambling enterprises in the state, the Oaklawn horse track and the Southland dog track, have recently adapted their strategies for expanding gambling by pursuing a course of incremental legislative and local change.

### Diffusion

Arkansas lies in the heart of the Mississippi River Valley, where the spread of commercial casinos from state to state during the 1990s was most prominent. Unlike neighboring Missouri, Louisiana, and Mississippi, however, Arkansas has consistently rejected casino gambling. It also has retained its constitutional ban on lotteries. Diffusion theory accounts in large part for the frequency with which casinos and lotteries have been considered in Arkansas. As gambling opponent Larry Page says, "Gambling in Mississippi and other states has driven the whole process of gambling proposals in Arkansas."[42]

Robert Walker's 1990 push for a lottery occurred at a time when several other southern states adopted or were considering lotteries to help address state revenue problems. Although the failure of Walker's lottery proposal is better explained by Arkansas's internal characteristics than by interstate diffusion, its emergence on the state's policy agenda was directly attributable to the new and popular lotteries in Florida and Virginia and the obvious momentum for creating lotteries in Texas, Louisiana, and Georgia. The same can be said about Rep. Barbara King's sponsorship of a lottery in 2003, shortly after Tennessee voters had approved a lottery referendum.

The policies of other states also contributed directly to the 1994 and 1996 campaigns to expand casino gambling in which the Oaklawn track played such a prominent role. By 1994 the Mississippi casinos had begun to drain business from Arkansas's racing industry and, by 1996, were substantially hurting it. Thus the owners of Oaklawn (and, in 1994, the Southland dog track) tried to alter the state constitution so that they could build casinos on their properties and better compete for the region's gambling dollars. Similarly, Mike Wilson's 1994 and 1996 pushes for casino gambling in eastern Arkansas were attempts to capitalize on neighboring Tennessee's gambling policy, which at the time prevented Memphians from gambling legally in any way in their own state. The seeming popularity of lotteries in other southern states prompted casino advocates during the 1990s to attach state-run lotteries to almost all of their proposed constitutional amendments.

The Arkansas Casino Corporation's 2000 push for casinos also stemmed from the actions of other states. By the late 1990s, the revival of tourism on Mississippi's Gulf Coast made at least a few investors think that Hot Springs's waning tourism could be jump-started by the presence of casinos. Likewise, the apparent economic success of the new tourism industry in Tunica, Mississippi, persuaded some that certain Arkansas counties bordering on neighboring states could generate casino-based tourism for themselves. The geographic location of the counties that would have had commercial casinos if the 2000 initiative had passed (most of them situated on the state border) illustrates the degree to which its sponsors were trying to follow the Mississippi model.

Although the internal characteristics of Arkansas explain best why all of these casino amendments failed, a variant of diffusion theory offers an additional partial explanation of at least one proposal's failure. In the introduction, we defined antidiffusion as efforts by actors in one state or political jurisdiction to forestall adverse consequences for themselves by preventing another state or jurisdiction from enacting a policy. Under the label of the Arkansas Wins Committee, the Mississippi casino industry's advertising campaign against the 1996 Oaklawn-sponsored proposal for casinos and a lottery provides a textbook example of antidiffusion. As Oaklawn's Eric Jackson recalls, "Nineteen ninety-six showed us how hard it is to get casinos in a state that is next to a state that already has casinos and will fight to keep out any competition . . . Mississippi killed us. They demolished us. They dropped nuclear bombs on us. We went down like the Titanic." Scott Trotter's assessment seems more accurate. "The initiative would have been defeated but they [Mississippi casino interests] added to the margin."[43] Antidiffusion also describes the Mississippi casinos' campaign to rouse public opinion against allowing expanded video gambling at Oaklawn and Southland in 2003, acting in the guise of the misleadingly named Arkansans for the 21st Century in order to cover their activities.

### Internal Characteristics

In addition to the examples and influence of other states' recently enacted gambling policies, several of Arkansas's internal characteristics have strongly affected the politics of gambling there. Working in favor of legalization—and thus helping to explain why the issue is a recurring one—is the state's historical legacy of gambling. The history of Hot Springs in particular is intertwined with what is to some the romantic image of bootleg casinos, where flappers drank bathtub gin and Al Capone (and, a generation later, the mother of future president Bill Clinton) placed bets into the wee hours of the morning. For more than half a century, pari-mutuel betting has been legal at Oaklawn and Southland. In recent years the economic vitality of the racing industry has declined nearly everywhere, as has the appeal to vacationers of older resort towns like Hot Springs.[44] To the extent that gambling is a part of the state's traditions and economy which Arkansans want to preserve, proponents of legalization have been able to draw on these historical and economic factors in politically advantageous ways.

Most of Arkansas's internal characteristics, however, have been adverse to campaigns to legalize casinos or create a lottery. For one thing, nearly all of these campaigns have urged the passage of blatantly flawed proposals. Some of the flaws have involved procedural aspects of the constitutional amendment process, such as the accuracy of ballot titles and the regularity of petition gathering, as judged by the state supreme court. Other flaws have been more substantive, especially from a political standpoint. The 1990 lottery proposal was joined to the proposed repeal of an anti–civil rights provision of the constitution in a way that tied one controversial issue, the lottery, to another, racial segregation. Casino legalization amendments in 1994 and 2000 would have enshrined certain private companies in the state constitution as the exclusive owners of casinos.

Even the seemingly astute strategy of combining casino legalization in a single measure with more popular proposals for charitable bingo and a lottery may have backfired. A September 1996 poll found, for example, that Arkansans supported a lottery by 51 to 39 percent and were divided evenly (45 to 45 percent) on casinos. But when asked about the combined casino-lottery measure that was on the November ballot, they said they opposed it by 50 to 45 percent.[45] Adding the lottery to the casino measure apparently attracted no new support for casinos, but it did arouse additional opposition from those voters who had not made up their minds about casinos but were certain they did not want a lottery.

Finally, several provisions of the Arkansas constitution help explain why campaigns to legalize new forms of gambling by amending the constitution have been both prominent and unsuccessful features of the state's politics. Arkansas is unusual among southern states in including a user-friendly initiative process in its constitution. (Mississippi's, in contrast, is extremely difficult to use, and none of the other southern states besides Florida allows initiatives at all.) As a result, casino legalization proposals not only appear frequently on the Arkansas ballot but also, because initiative campaigns are costly, are usually designed to fill the pockets of those who sponsor them. In the latest of these failed efforts, Texas businessman Michael Wasserman launched but then abandoned a 2006 campaign to allow him to operate casinos in seven counties around the state while also creating a state lottery.[46]

Politically, however, the presence of the initiative process has impeded efforts to legalize casino and lottery gambling in Arkansas. To be sure, the ease with which the constitution can be amended by initiative has offered gambling advocates the opportunity to get their proposals before the voters by gathering signatures on petitions. But this same ease has channeled the energies and resources of gambling supporters into the initiative process and enabled the state legislature to stand aside from these controversial issues. Legislators in Arkansas need not fear being accused, as legislators in other southern states have been, of refusing to "let the people decide" gambling issues by not placing them on the ballot. What the people have been allowed to decide in Arkansas, however, usually has involved poorly designed initiatives marked by none of the craftsmanship that the legislative process usually affords. And in several cases these initiatives have been struck from the ballot by the state supreme court before the voters could register their choices.

Another reason that the legislature has not played an active role on gambling amendments is also constitutional in origin. The Arkansas constitution is unusually detailed: it is the tenth longest state constitution in the country. As Common Cause's Scott Trotter points out, "The constitution requires that many simple matters be dealt with through constitutional amendments." But the constitution also allows the legislature to refer only three proposed amendments to the voters every two years. "In most years, there are pressing needs that require amendments," says Trotter, "such as school funding or property tax reform." The need for such measures makes even legislators who support gambling reluctant to devote one of their three referrals to that issue.[47]

### Policy Entrepreneurship

In Arkansas, politically flawed proposals to amend the state constitution typically have been matched with politically flawed advocates. For example, Oaklawn and Southland's claims during the 1990s that they were local industries in need of state protection were belied by both tracks' out-of-state ownership. In 2000, the Arkansas Casino Corporation's appeal for support to Arkansas investors was undermined by evidence that the corporation's main owners were Texans, one of whom was indicted for securities fraud. Most important, none of the gambling-legalization campaigns has been led or even supported by a prominent state political leader. Every governor since the 1960s, including Bill Clinton, has discouraged the General Assembly from adopting casino and lottery amendments and urged the people of his state to vote against the proposed constitutional amendments that made it to the statewide ballot. Not until January 2006, when former Clinton administration official Bill Halter announced his candidacy for the Democratic nomination, did a gubernatorial candidate support even a lottery, and Halter dropped out of the race two months after he entered it and announced he was running for lieutenant governor.

In contrast, the opposition to casino and lottery amendments in Arkansas has been politically astute and effective. Larry Page and, when he was active in Common Cause, Scott Trotter have been articulate, energetic, and experienced antigambling campaigners. The alliance on this issue that they forged between the groups they represent—the conservative Faith and Ethics Council and the secular, generally liberal Common Cause—was a broad and appealing one. Voters who respond to moral and religious opposition to gambling have been guided by Page's organization. Voters put off by such arguments, rather than being driven to support gambling, took their cues from Common Cause.

Oaklawn and Southland's fortunes improved in the 2000s when, abandoning the constitutional amendment process, they embraced a legislative strategy. The tracks realized that electronic "games of skill" could offer many of the same attractions to gamblers as casino-style slot machines without falling afoul of the state constitution's ban on games of chance. Simple legislation, not a constitutional amendment, was enough to secure this more modest goal. Although the tracks' initial attempt to win legislative permission to offer these games foundered in 2003 in the face of the covert antidiffusionary campaign of the Mississippi casino industry, they adroitly turned the tables in 2005 when the casinos overplayed their hand and lobbied publicly against the tracks. A political backlash against Mississippi's intervention in Arkansas' affairs occurred, helping to persuade the legislature to pass the games-of-skill bill and the Mississippi casinos to stay out of the ensuing referendum campaigns in Hot Springs and West Memphis. Oaklawn and Southland also were adroit in framing the issue for legislators in terms of letting the voters of those two cities decide whether to allow more gambling in their communities. This appeal was especially effective when the tracks emphasized the jobs that would be lost if they could not expand their offerings and the jobs that would be gained if they could.

# SEVEN

# LOUISIANA

## The Place Where "Gaming" Isn't "Gambling"

Legalized gambling has deeper historical roots in Louisiana than in any other southern state. It is hard to imagine, say, Alabama or South Carolina adopting "*Laissez les bon temps rouler*" as its unofficial state motto. From 1699 to 1803, during Louisiana's century of Spanish and French rule, gambling of every kind was legal and pervasive. In 1810, seven years after the Louisiana Purchase brought the territory into the United States, New Orleans had more gambling halls than New York, Philadelphia, Boston, and Baltimore combined. Even when the federal government banned gambling in the Louisiana Territory in 1812, New Orleans received a special exemption. After becoming a state, Louisiana vacillated between legalizing casinos in New Orleans (six "temples of chance" were authorized in 1823) and banning them altogether. But casino gambling's legal status was a matter of indifference in the city. In 1840, five years after the legislature voted to outlaw casinos, New Orleans still had an estimated five hundred gambling halls. After the Civil War, the revenue-starved legislature legalized casinos again and taxed them each $5,000 per year.

The postbellum state legislature also authorized the privately owned Louisiana Lottery Company to conduct a lottery in return for donating $40,000 per year to New Orleans's Charity Hospital. The Louisiana lottery thrived by selling more than 90 percent of its tickets outside the state. In 1890 ticket sales totaled $28 million, more than half a billion in current dollars. The other states, tired of seeing their unlucky citizens' money flow to Louisiana, responded by pressuring Congress to close the U.S. postal system to lottery sales and advertising. As historian John Samuel Ezell has noted, critics "derided the Louisiana firm's claims of being a mere defensive measure against the Havana Lottery or a public benefactor protecting an 'infant industry' from the 'pauper labor' of Cuba."[1] Critics also charged that despite the prominent role played by P. G. T. Beauregard and Jubal Early, two widely admired Confederate generals, in "supervising" the drawings, the Louisiana lottery had a corrupting influence on politics and society. Congress finally destroyed the lottery during the 1890s by purging the mails of "letters, newspapers and circulars" relating to lottery gambling and by barring all lottery activity from interstate commerce.

Although legal pari-mutuel betting on horse races at New Orleans' Fair Grounds racetrack flourished in Louisiana beginning in the 1920s, racing was not enough to slake the public's appetite for gambling. Casinos operated illegally under the aegis of organized crime in New Orleans and adjacent Jefferson and St. Bernard parishes. In 1928 Gov. Huey P. Long, the dominant political figure in the state, ordered warrantless raids of several of these casinos by armed National Guard soldiers.[2] But after reaching a secret agreement with New York mobster Frank Costello to allow Costello's organization to move slot machines into the New Orleans area, illegal gambling once again flourished.[3] "Ninety-five percent of the people in this grand and glorious old city and its environs love to gamble," Long told reporters. "If they have got to gamble, I am in favor of letting the majority rule. I'm tired of using my police to close up every little gambling hole in New Orleans."[4]

In the early 1950s, the combination of nationally televised hearings by Sen. Estes Kefauver's Select Committee to Investigate Organized Crime in Interstate Commerce, which dramatized the involvement of New Orleans' Marcello crime family in the city's gambling operations, and the anti-Long governor Robert Kennon's appointment of Francis Grevemberg, a crusading state police superintendent, led Louisiana to crack down on illegal gambling in a serious, sustained way.[5] Within a few years, most gambling facilities were closed. But by the mid-1970s, according to the Louisiana state police's senior intelligence analyst, illegal gambling had revived again to become a quarter-billion dollar industry, the third largest in the state.

Through the 1970s, with petroleum prices spiking and severance taxes from oil and gas supplying half of the state government's revenue needs, political interest in extending legalized gambling beyond racetrack betting and charitable bingo was slight. In 1972 Louisiana elected a governor, Democrat Edwin Edwards, who, as the journalist Tyler Bridges observed, "loved to take gambling junkets to Las Vegas but saw no need to bring gambling to the Bayou State."[6] Indeed, in 1974 Edwards successfully pressed for the adoption of a new state constitution. The document solemnly enjoined that "gambling shall be defined by and suppressed by the legislature."

## LOUISIANA AGAIN EMBRACES LEGALIZED GAMBLING, 1986–1992

In 1979, after serving eight years as governor, Edwards bumped up against the state constitution's ban on more than two consecutive gubernatorial terms. By the time he was returned to office in 1983, oil and gas prices and, with them, the state's "one-crop economy," had collapsed.[7] Edwards's new term was dominated by federal charges that during the four years he was out of office he had accepted $1.9 million in bribes from hospital companies in return for actions he promised to take when, as expected, he resumed the governorship after sitting out a term. Prosecutors alleged that Edwards had needed the money to pay off gambling debts to Nevada casinos. His 1985 trial ended in a hung jury.

Edwards began 1986 by announcing that he would call a special session of the legislature to address the state's desperate fiscal condition by creating a state-sponsored lottery and legalizing land- and water-based commercial casinos in and around New Orleans. Reactions to the governor's plan varied widely. An editorial in the *Baton Rouge Advocate* questioned whether Louisiana wanted to be known around the country as the state where a governor famous for high-stakes gambling addressed ongoing budgetary problems by fostering gambling as an industry. The Greater New Orleans Hotel-Motel Association, on the other hand, supported Edwards's proposal in hopes of filling empty rooms with tourists. Teachers' organizations around the state supported the lottery but remained silent on casinos. Economists and budget experts endorsed casino gambling as a way to create new jobs but said little about the lottery.

Resistance in the legislature to Edwards's gambling initiatives, along with a January 1986 poll that placed the governor's unfavorability rating at 57 percent, convinced him to rescind the call for a special session. During the regular legislative session, antigambling representatives in the state's House of Representatives voted to table Edwards's lottery-casino bill by a vote of fifty-three to thirty-three. The timing of the governor's proposal was part of the problem.

Rep. John Hainkel, a New Orleans Republican, and Senate president Sam Nunez, a Democrat from Chalmette, agreed that "a lottery and possibly limited casino gambling could be passed but not in the current political climate in view of Edwards' legal problems."[8] Nor, in the mid-1980s, was Edwards able to point to any other lottery or casino states in the South as successful examples of what he expected legalized gambling to accomplish in Louisiana. Gambling legalization "will come to pass," said the governor. "I just happen to be a little bit ahead of my time, as is generally the case."[9] Instead of creating a lottery or authorizing casinos, the legislature defied the Democratic governor and balanced the budget by cutting spending nearly 15 percent and suspending several exemptions to the sales tax.

In November 1986, however, it became clear that the legislature's fiscal remedies, draconian as they were, would be insufficient to meet Louisiana's revenue crisis and that another session was needed to deal with the expected $269 million budget shortfall. Edwards, still suffering from low public approval ratings, called a special session and proposed a state lottery to bring the budget into balance. Eleven days into the session, the House again voted down the lottery bill, but by a considerably narrower margin of fifty-five to fifty.

Edwards's bid for reelection in 1987 was unsuccessful. After finishing second with 28 percent of the vote in the state's all-parties primary, he dropped out of the race, ceding the runoff to Charles E. "Buddy" Roemer III. Roemer was a four-term conservative Democratic congressman from Bossier City, in the northwest corner of the state. Although he had run against Edwards as an opponent of casinos and a lottery, opposition to gambling was not the basis of his victory. The state's economy was in a trough: Louisiana's 14 percent unemployment rate was the highest in the nation, and the budget was now $750 million in deficit. Because Edwards dropped out after the primary, Roemer was elected with only 33 percent of the vote. Edwards's decision spared Roemer the uncertainty of a runoff election, but it also denied him the opportunity to take office with the endorsement of a majority of the electorate.

### Lottery

Louisiana's desperate need for revenue and economic development dominated Roemer's term as governor. He spent 1988, his first year in office, getting the state's finances in order by laying off state employees, reducing spending on social programs, and securing a "temporary" sales tax increase from the legislature, among other measures. Riding what he thought was a wave of public support, Roemer moved quickly to place his tax reform plan on the ballot in April 1989. The plan proposed to reduce business taxes enough to attract new employers, even though that meant raising property and personal income taxes to make up the difference.

As Roemer campaigned around the state, he frequently ran into an unexpected objection to his tax plan. Florida and Virginia, the first two southern states to create lotteries, had recently begun selling tickets. "I was talking about tax reform," Roemer recalls. "But people were telling me, 'Buddy, check your numbers. We don't need tax reform because a lottery will take care of everything.'"[10] Raymond "La La" LaLonde, a Democratic state representative from the small southwest Louisiana town of Sunset, remembers hearing similar sentiments from his constituents. "At that time the lottery was floating around several states and my people said, 'Y'all, don't raise taxes. Pass a lottery,'" says LaLonde. "They thought that would be the panacea."[11] Not surprisingly, perhaps, an electorate accustomed to an oil-and-gas-financed state government that provided public services while taxing them lightly embraced what they regarded as a painless solution. Roemer's tax reform plan was voted down decisively, 55 percent to 45 percent.

The conclusion state legislators drew from the defeat of tax reform and the continuing fiscal crisis was that the state should enact a lottery. LaLonde, who was an influential member of the Administration of Criminal Justice committee, sponsored the lottery bill in the House. Although he knew that a lottery would not solve Louisiana's revenue problems, he saw it as a way to keep a certain amount of money in the state and to attract some additional money from out of state. "People were taking thousands of dollars in orders for lottery tickets and going to Florida," he recalls. "A lot of Louisiana money was going to Florida that would stay here if we had our own lottery. And Florida's experience convinced me that if we were the first state in the Gulf South to have a lottery, people from states on our border like Mississippi and Arkansas would be buying our tickets."[12]

An April 1990 poll showed that 67 percent of voters supported a lottery. But legislators knew that in a state where, because of the Kefauver hearings and the Edwards prosecution, gambling was still associated with corruption, much of that support would evaporate unless they could ensure that a lottery would operate honestly. Once again, the example of another state was politically crucial. LaLonde brought officials of the new Kentucky lottery before his committee "to get their pointers on what to do and what not to do. The best idea we got was to take it out of politics by having an independent board of directors run the lottery and contract out the operations."[13]

Because the state constitution included an explicit ban on lotteries, three things had to happen in order for Louisiana to enact one. First, a two-thirds majority of both the House and Senate had to pass a constitutional amendment removing the ban. Second, the amendment would have to be approved by the voters in a referendum. Third, the legislature would have to pass enabling legislation to create the lottery.

Matters proceeded briskly during the 1990 legislative session. On June 13, both houses passed a lottery amendment, the Senate by twenty-seven to eleven and the House by seventy-two to thirty-three. The Senate's version dedicated the revenues from any lottery the legislature might create to catastrophic health insurance, higher education, and local governments. The House's bill provided that the revenues simply would go into the state's general fund. Once again, LaLonde and his colleagues were drawing on the experience of another southern state. "The Florida people told us, 'Don't earmark the money for education because that creates a false sense that the schools problem has been solved.' They said that Florida had not been able to pass a local referendum for education since the lottery was enacted."[14] The Senate accepted the House bill, and within a few weeks both houses approved the version that would go before the voters on the October 6 ballot.

In all of these votes, the division in the legislature was more along regional than partisan lines: heavily Catholic and African American south Louisiana and New Orleans against heavily white and Baptist north Louisiana. (The lottery amendment's Senate sponsor, Ken Hollis, was a Republican from Metairie.) Historically, observe political scientists David Landry and Joseph Parker, "A generally more tolerant attitude prevails throughout South Louisiana. The sale of alcoholic beverages on Sundays has never been an issue there, and gambling has never been an issue there, although it [was] illegal by state statute."[15]

Responding to constituent opinion, several legislators said that although they personally opposed a lottery, they wanted to let the people decide the matter in a referendum. Democratic representative Rodney Alexander of Quitman, for example, declared, "I'm not for the lottery. I'm just for putting it out there for the people to decide." Governor Roemer said he hoped "voters will take a hard look at it. It's not a good deal." Nonetheless, he remained neutral as the legislature debated the lottery amendment.

The amendment that appeared on the November 1990 ballot repealed the constitutional ban on lotteries and provided that any lottery the legislature created would be run by a state-owned corporation. Rather than being earmarked, the proceeds from the lottery could be used by the state "for any purpose." The legislature also passed enabling legislation explicitly based on the example of the Kentucky lottery in advance of the referendum. Politically, LaLonde said, "You can't ask people to vote for something like this without telling them how it will work." The lottery law, which would take effect only if the referendum passed, provided that the lottery corporation would be run by a nine-member board appointed by the governor and confirmed by the Senate, and that the board would hire a president who in turn would hire a staff and run the lottery like a corporation.

Ken Ward, a Christian conservative leader in Baton Rouge, helped organize the Coalition Against Legalizing a Lottery in Louisiana (CALL) to mobilize opposition among voters. CALL's efforts met with little success. "The lottery seemed so innocent to most people," Ward recalls. "You know what they say—you 'play' the lottery. Some of our own people even supported it. Their attitude was, 'Let poor people pay some of their own way—I'm paying a ton of taxes.' The pastors didn't prepare their people."[16] After a desultory campaign, the lottery amendment passed by 826,746 (69.2 percent) to 368,360 (30.8 percent). The first ticket was sold in September 1991.

### Riverboat Casinos

Approval of the lottery encouraged supporters of casino gambling to think that their time also had come. They figured that if one of Edwards's failed 1986 gambling initiatives had succeeded in the new political climate, perhaps the other could as well. And, in the case of casino legalization, advocates had new arguments to make. By 1991, three states along the Mississippi River had authorized riverboat casinos, including neighboring Mississippi. With full-blown casino gambling available in nearby Gulf Coast cities like Biloxi and

Gulfport, casino supporters warned, New Orleans's tourism business would suffer greatly. Just as bad, Louisianans drawn by the lure of Mississippi casinos would leave behind millions of dollars each year in that state's casinos, restaurants, and hotels. "We are losing our competitive edge," argued Democratic representative Francis Heitmeier, the main sponsor of riverboat casino legislation in the House.[17] Finally, the enactment of the lottery amendment meant that casino-style games of chance no longer faced the same constitutional bar that had forbidden lotteries. Until the constitution was changed to remove the lottery ban, slot machines and other casino games that require no skill from the players had been legally classed with lotteries as illegal games of chance. Now they were free from that constitutional ban. As for the constitution's remaining hurdle—the provision that the legislature is charged to "suppress gambling"—that could be gotten around, casino advocates ingeniously (and ingenuously) argued, by characterizing casinos as being engaged in "gaming."

Heitmeier's bill called for the creation of a state board appointed by the governor to award licenses for fifteen riverboat casinos. To attract the support of other legislators, the gambling boats would float on rivers and lakes throughout the state. To defuse the opposition of gambling opponents such as Ken Ward, they would be limited in number. "We Christian conservatives thought that limiting the number of casinos limited the harm," Ward recalls.[18]

In order to evoke the romantic Mark Twain imagery of antebellum riverboat gamblers, Heitmeier required that the casino boats be designed to resemble nineteenth-century paddle wheelers and actually cruise. At the same time, to make the law more attractive to gamblers who like to come and go as they please (and thus to enhance its appeal to casino corporations seeking their business), Heitmeier included a provision stating that even though each floating casino must take three-hour cruises, ninety minutes of gambling time on each cruise could be devoted to boarding and debarking. What's more, the casino boat could avoid cruising altogether if its captain was concerned about dangerous river currents or other safety issues. Casinos located in Shreveport–Bossier City on the perennially low Red River were exempted from ever having to sail. Finally, the state would tax the casinos' profits at a rate of 18.5 percent.

In contrast to the lottery, Governor Roemer lent his support to riverboat casinos. To a large extent, he had his eye on what other states were doing.

"Mississippi's experience figured very heavily in what we did," he recalls. "I mean, with 26 percent of their gamblers driving over from Louisiana, *hello*. And we knew that Louisiana would be irresistible as a magnet to the major national casino corporations. We were going to beat Mississippi." Further, Roemer says, "we knew that with our two hundred mile border with Texas, we could do to Texas what Mississippi had been doing to us in terms of drawing out-of-state people who enjoy that form of activity."[19] Among the fifteen casinos would be five in Shreveport–Bossier City, four in Lake Charles, three in New Orleans, and two in Baton Rouge. The casino boats in Shreveport–Bossier City, which is in northwest Louisiana, and Lake Charles, in the southwest part of the state, were well situated to draw gamblers from two of Texas's largest cities, Dallas and Houston, respectively.

Roemer also regarded casinos as an engine for economic development within his still-suffering state. "I looked at casinos as a jobs issue," he says. "My idea was that casinos would provide jobs for people who other businesses regarded as unemployable." He was drawn to the idea that the casinos would be on actual riverboats. "Where do you think those boats would be built? In Louisiana shipyards. We'd be building an industry and putting people to work. We knew that if our shipyards built fifteen good boats for Louisiana, casinos in other states would order their boats from us. That's economic development."[20] Another benefit Roemer anticipated from the casinos was that "on our western border they'll take tourist money from Texas, and in New Orleans from all over the world."[21]

With little time remaining in the 1991 legislative session, the House approved riverboat "gaming" on July 10 by a vote of sixty to thirty-six. The Senate added its endorsement the following day, voting twenty-two to ten. A week later, on July 18, Roemer signed the bill into law and declared, "This follows what Mississippi, Illinois, and Iowa have done. We are the tourist center of the Mississippi Valley, and we should have it."[22]

### Video Poker

Although the legislature's decision to legalize video poker coincided with its vote in favor of riverboat casinos, video poker received much less public and media attention. The debate on casino legalization overshadowed the video poker issue. So did the 1991 gubernatorial election, which featured Roemer running for a second term after switching to the Republican Party, Edwin Edwards seeking to return to office for a fourth term, and former Ku Klux Klan leader David Duke mounting a serious challenge to both.

Since the late 1980s, illegal video poker machines had become a prominent and highly profitable feature of Louisiana's bars and restaurants. The choice confronting the state was whether to crack down on video gambling or to legalize, tax, and regulate it. Democratic representative Charles Emile "Peppi" Bruneau Jr. of New Orleans offered a bill embodying the latter approach. "These machines are a fact of life," said Bruneau, who estimated that 18,000 of them were operating in the state. "They are there from Caddo Parish to Plaquemines Parish and from the Delta to Cameron Parish, and at all points in between."[23] Bruneau's bill, which sailed through the House, allowed any bar or restaurant with a Class-A liquor license to operate three video gambling machines. The machines would be regulated by the state police and taxed by the state government at a rate of 22.5 percent, one fourth of which would go to the local governments where they were located.

Late-developing opposition from the Louisiana Coalition of Charitable Gaming Organizations, whose members operated bingo games in churches and veterans' halls, made the video poker bill more controversial in the Senate. Sen. Gerry Hinton, a Slidell Republican and an opponent of the bill, offered to change his vote if truck-stop owners were also allowed to offer video poker. "I've got a friend of mine, a constituent of mine named Fred Goodson," said Hinton. "He's a God-fearing Baptist like me. He owns the biggest truck stop in the state, and . . . he ought to have the same right to put in those machines, just like bars do."[24] Written in haste, Hinton's amendment allowed truck stops to operate as many as fifty machines each but offered no definition of a truck stop. Needing Hinton's vote to get the bill out of committee and, in the rush of late session business, not exploring the consequences of his amendment, video poker supporters accepted it. The video poker bill passed the Senate twenty to seventeen, and the next night, which was the last night of the legislative session, the House approved the Senate version with little discussion. As LaLonde recalls, "Neither we nor the public had any awareness that this was a significant issue."[25]

Roemer, who had vetoed a more modest video poker bill in 1990, let the new version become law without his signature. "The state police told me that if video poker was legal we could reduce the number of machines from 18,000 to 8,000 and tax and regulate them," he recalls.[26]

### New Orleans' Land-Based Casino

Between July 1991, when the legislature passed the video poker and riverboat casino bills, and October 1991, when the first round of voting in the gubernatorial election between Roemer, Edwards, and Duke occurred, gambling took a back seat in Louisiana politics. Duke focused his campaign on opposition to affirmative action and other racially charged issues, while Roemer emphasized "good government" concerns, such as honesty and fiscal austerity. Edwards, however, realizing that he needed a strong turnout in New Orleans to get into the runoff election, called for new legislation authorizing a land-based casino in the city. He argued that casino gambling would help ignite an economic recovery in New Orleans by generating 25,000 jobs.

Edwards's strategy succeeded: he finished first in the primary with 34 percent of the vote. Duke's appeal to frustrated working-class white voters earned him 32 percent, while Governor Roemer finished third with 27 percent and was eliminated from the November runoff ballot. Roemer's popularity had waned for several reasons, including the continuing economic recession, his inability to pass his tax-reform package, and his change of parties.

The challenge for Edwards and Duke during the four-week runoff campaign was to win a majority of Roemer's mostly conservative supporters. Sensing that he was hemorrhaging support among voters concerned about corruption and crime, Edwards abandoned his call for a land-based casino and pledged not to push for one if elected. This strategy, joined with widespread revulsion at Duke's thinly disguised racism, worked: most Roemer supporters reluctantly got on board with Edwards. Their lack of enthusiasm was evidenced by bumper stickers declaring: "Vote for the Lizard, not the Wizard" and "Vote for the Crook. It's Important." Edwards won his fourth term as governor with 61 percent of the vote.[27]

In early 1992, Edwards publicly kept his promise not to seek a land-based casino in New Orleans. The idea advanced, however, because other politicians latched onto the issue. Sidney Barthelemy, the mayor of New Orleans, and several members of the city's legislative delegation began pushing the state legislature to authorize a downtown New Orleans casino as an economic development measure for their distressed city. Casino industry leaders such as Steve Wynn and Donald Trump showed serious interest in building a New Orleans casino, and Christopher Hemmeter, a Hawaii resort developer, offered a specific proposal to build the world's largest casino in the city.

On March 30, Edwards reentered the discussion during his opening address to the 1992 legislative session. "I do not have a bill to create one," he said, referring to a land-based casino. "I'm not pushing for one." But, he added, "It is one thing the city of New Orleans should be given an opportunity to do in order to attract tourists, create jobs, stimulate the city and provide $250 million in revenue for the people of this state without them having to pay additional taxes."[28] Edwards's speech, joined with the New Orleans legislative delegation's own efforts, placed the campaign for a land-based casino at the top of the legislature's agenda.

Representative LaLonde, who had been instrumental in helping to legalize other forms of gambling in Louisiana, offered to author the 1992 New Orleans casino bill. Sherman Copelin Jr., a Democratic state representative from New Orleans and, as speaker pro tempore, the House's second-ranking member, agreed to help shepherd it through the chamber. Another influential Democratic legislator, Don Kelly of Natchitoches, served as the bill's chief strategist in the Senate. Governor Edwards, for his part, quietly eliminated two potential roadblocks to land-based casino legislation. In mid-May, he met with the New Orleans delegation and insisted that it unite behind a single bill. He also met with riverboat casino firms, who were frustrated by the delay in obtaining licenses for floating casinos from the governor's appointed board, and offered them a quid pro quo. He would expedite licensing in return for their support of a land-based casino in New Orleans.[29]

LaLonde's bill, which the New Orleans delegation agreed to endorse, called for a single freestanding casino at the Rivergate site on the edge of the city's French Quarter. In exchange for a monopoly on land-based casino gambling in New Orleans, the casino would pay the state an annual tax amounting to 18.5 percent of its gross revenues or $100 million, whichever amount was greater. At the insistence of French Quarter hotel and restaurant owners, the bill barred the new casino from operating any hotels or full-service restaurants, a restriction imposed on no other casino in the country.

Although Kelly succeeded in gaining strong support for the bill in the

Senate, which passed it twenty-three to sixteen on May 20, whip counts showed a far closer division in the House. On June 3, the eve of the vote, forty-four representatives were found to favor the bill, and forty-four to oppose it. Seventeen said they were undecided. Religious opponents of gambling and other antigambling activists had organized to fight the bill, staging a well-attended rally at the Rivergate site to charge that a land-based casino would revive organized crime in the city. In addition, Mayor Barthelemy had turned against the bill because it provided that the taxes on the casino would go to the state rather than to his city. In Edwards's view, the only way to win the support of legislators outside New Orleans was to assure them that their constituents would benefit from the $250 million in annual tax revenues that he estimated the casino would generate. But on June 4, the House voted forty-three to fifty-eight against the land-based casino bill.

Edwards did not take this apparent defeat lying down. During the weekend after the House vote, he devoted the full force of his persuasive powers to reversing the outcome. He made phone call after phone call to legislators who had voted against the casino bill, as well as hosting a series of one-on-one meetings at the governor's mansion. The governor of Louisiana has much more control over patronage, contracts, and projects than most state governors do. Tyler Bridges, the journalist who most closely covered gambling issues in Louisiana, is convinced that Edwards traded road construction projects, hospital additions, patronage jobs, and other government benefits for votes in support of the casino bill.[30]

On June 8, Edwards told Barthelemy that the casino bill had the fifty-three votes it needed, with or without the mayor's support. Speaker of the House John Alario, a longtime ally of Edwards, called up the bill for another vote on June 11. Alario's practice was to conduct House votes in a way that allowed members to balance the sometimes competing pressures from their constituents and from important political leaders such as the governor. The speaker would order the chamber's electronic voting machines open, ask after five seconds if members were finished voting, ask after another five seconds if members were finished voting, then call for the machines to be closed and the clerk to announce the outcome. This process allowed reluctant supporters of a bill to vote *aye,* see if their vote was decisive or not, then change their vote at the last second if it made no difference to the outcome.

Alario had noticed that some initial supporters of the casino bill changed their *ayes* to *nays* during the June 4 vote. On June 11, he announced that the voting machines were open, watched the tally of *aye* votes rise to fifty-six before dropping to fifty-four, and then, just as he began to ask, "Are you finished voting?" cut the machines off. The clerk announced the outcome: fifty-three for the casino bill, forty-two against. An opponent of the bill yelled from the back of the chamber, "This is a Huey Long vote!" The *New Orleans Times-Picayune* editorialized the next day that "a Machiavellian governor, abetted by the top legislative leadership, recklessly manipulated a legislative majority into approving casino gambling." Edwards was unfazed. A week later he signed the land-based New Orleans casino bill into law with a flourish, declaring, "With the stroke of a pen, we've taken the largest step toward economic development and the creation of jobs undertaken in Louisiana in the last twenty-five years."[31]

## WHY LOUISIANA LEGALIZED GAMBLING

As in other states, no single theory of state policy innovation comprehends the politics of gambling in Louisiana. In explaining how Louisiana became the southern state with the broadest array of legalized gambling in the South, we draw on our entire theoretical apparatus: interstate diffusion, the internal characteristics of Louisiana, and policy entrepreneurship by certain important leaders.

### Diffusion

The example of other southern states that chose to legalize lotteries and casinos, as well as the threat some of these states' innovations seemed to pose to Louisiana's economy, played an extremely important part in Louisiana's rapid adoption of both forms of gambling during the early 1990s. When the ardently progambling governor, Edwin Edwards, tried to enact gambling legislation in 1986, a time when the South was free of lotteries and casinos, he failed. By 1991, however, Florida and Virginia had begun operating lotteries and Georgia was poised to do so. Serious efforts also were under way to establish lotteries in all three of the states that share a border with Louisiana: Mississippi, Arkansas, and Texas. The Mississippi legislature had just voted to legalize casino gambling, opening the door to full-scale commercial casinos along the Gulf Coast.

Responding to this wave of gambling legalization efforts among the southern states, Louisiana changed its own policies. In an act of what we call *anticipatory diffusion,* Louisiana instituted a lottery before Texas, Mississippi, or Arkansas could do so, thereby attracting players and revenues from these states. (As it happened, only Texas actually followed through by creating its own lottery.) In a more traditional act of diffusion, Louisiana based the organization and operations of its new lottery on the example of Kentucky, a state whose lottery legislators admired. They copied almost word-for-word the law and regulations of the Kentucky lottery.

Ironically, a governor who was much less supportive of gambling than Edwards, Buddy Roemer, signed not only the lottery bill but also a bill to legalize casino gambling on several of his state's lakes and rivers. Louisiana's adoption of water-based casinos was a policy innovation that "incrementally diffused" across state lines. With good intentions but ill effects, Louisiana altered the policy toward riverboat casinos that it borrowed from Mississippi. Mississippi had confined casinos to certain counties but within those counties it allowed the market to decide how many casinos actually would operate. In a misguided effort to reassure casino opponents that gambling boats would not pop up everywhere, the Louisiana legislature limited the number of riverboat casinos licenses in the state to fifteen. As we will see, in making these licenses a scarce and highly valuable commodity that could only be obtained from the state government, Louisiana invited political corruption in a way that Mississippi did not.

As for video poker, one reason the legislature voted to legalize it during its 1991 session was that it had just legalized riverboat casino gambling. Video poker proponents were able to argue that the legislature should not provide economic opportunities for out-of-state casino corporations without doing something for truck-stop, bar, and restaurant owners who lived in Louisiana.

### Internal Characteristics

The unusually deep, oil bust–rooted economic recession that Louisiana experienced in the 1980s and early 1990s permeated the politics of gambling there. Louisianans had grown accustomed to a state government so rich in severance tax revenues from the oil and gas industry that taxes on individuals could remain low. When recession hit, most of the state's leaders realized that the only politically acceptable way to continue funding the government was to find new sources of revenue that did not burden their constituents, at least not overtly. (Political leaders who did not realize this, such as Governor Roemer, found themselves out of a job when they sought reelection.) Gambling in all its major forms—a lottery, riverboat casinos, video poker, and a land-based casino—suddenly became appealing as a legal and taxable phenomenon in a way that it had not been before. The state could profit from activities in which no one was forced to participate, enjoying a seemingly painless form of revenue enhancement. As an added benefit, casinos in particular seemed like a potentially rich source of employment for workers left jobless by the recession.

Cultural and historical factors also help explain the enactment of legalized gambling in Louisiana. During the previous two centuries, the state had at times been the regional, even the national center of casino and lottery gambling. The policy innovations of the late twentieth century marked a reclaiming of that heritage. If gambling was going to be legalized in the South anyway, some state politicians argued, why should tradition-rich Louisiana allow Mississippi to be the region's casino capital? Why let Texas make money by selling lottery tickets to players from the home state of the once-famous Louisiana lottery? Louisiana also views itself as the "tourism center of the Mississippi Valley," as Roemer puts it.[32] Thus, it seemed to many Louisiana lawmakers that if casino gambling were to become a tourist attraction anywhere in the region, it ought to be an attraction in their state as well, especially in tourism-dependent New Orleans.

In contrast to the experience of most southern states, Louisiana's constitution played only a small role in the policy innovation process concerning gambling. To be sure, the explicit constitutional ban on lotteries meant that an amendment had to be enacted to clear the way for the legislature to create a lottery. But the amendment process in Louisiana is not especially arduous. That the legislature could circumvent the constitutional requirement to "suppress gambling" by calling what goes on in casinos and video poker parlors *gaming* more truly indicates the near irrelevance of the document, especially since the state supreme court chose to overlook the subterfuge. One can imagine circumstances—say, if the popularity of gambling proposals had been less, or if historical and cultural forces conducive to gambling had been weaker, or if the recession had not been so severe—in which the constitution could have been used by opponents to slow or forestall gambling. Indeed, that is what happened in 1986. But the political climate in Louisiana in the early 1990s was already primed for gambling in too many ways for the constitution to provide an effective deterrent to gambling legislation.

### Policy Entrepreneurship

Governor Edwards served as an effective policy entrepreneur for lottery and casino gambling in Louisiana, as did some members of the state legislature. Edwards's original push to legalize casinos and create a lottery in the mid-1980s placed the issue high on the state's policy agenda. A handful of progambling legislators, such as Representative LaLonde, Representative Heitmeier, and Senator Kelly, kept these proposals alive after Edwards lost the 1987 election. As Edwards's successor Buddy Roemer conceded, one important reason that his own tax-reform referendum was defeated in 1989 was that many voters had come to regard gambling as a painless solution to the state revenue crisis. Thus, when the revenue situation spiraled steeply downward, the political ground had already been prepared for gambling's legislative supporters to bring forward Edwards-style lottery and casino bills even in Edwards's absence, both as a fiscal remedy and, in the case of casinos, as a strategy for economic development. Although Roemer signed the lottery and riverboat casino bills and let video poker become law without his signature, he was less a policy entrepreneur than a policy enabler—a bystander who refused either to campaign for gambling or campaign against it.

As for the land-based casino in New Orleans, Edwards deserves nearly all the credit. He placed it on the agenda during his 1991 comeback campaign for governor, then lobbied tenaciously and effectively after he was elected to see it passed into law the following year.

## THE FEVERISH AFTER-POLITICS OF GAMBLING LEGALIZATION IN LOUISIANA

Louisiana rapidly became a casino and video poker state without the voters ever having a direct say in the matter. Unlike the lottery, no state or local referendum ratified casino or video poker legalization. Nor was any gubernatorial candidate elected on a progambling platform. Roemer ran as an opponent of gambling in 1987 and, although he was elected on that basis, signed the riverboat casino bill and let video poker become legal without his signature. Edwards promised not to seek a land-based casino in New Orleans when he ran in 1991, then fought hard for the land-based casino bill that became law in 1992.

Not surprisingly, public opinion polls revealed that considerable opposition to these new forms of gambling remained after they became legal.[33] The state had been transformed into a gambling Mecca without the voters ever being directly consulted. All four candidates for governor in 1995—Republicans Roemer and state senator Mike Foster and the two Democratic contenders, state treasurer Mary Landrieu and U.S. representative Cleo Fields—tried to outdo each other in the fervency of their opposition to gambling. Roemer, whom Landrieu labeled "the father of gambling in this state," promised to make video poker "dead, gone, kaput."[34] Fields had worked hard behind the scenes to steer seats on the riverboat casino commission to his friends, but as a candidate for governor he publicly spurned campaign contributions from gambling interests.[35] Foster, who had voted for land- and water-based casinos in the Senate, promised the electorate "one up or down vote" on gambling—a binding statewide referendum on whether to keep casinos and video poker legal in Louisiana or to expel them from the state. With active support from Christian conservatives (his other campaign mantra was "I'm a Christian and a gun owner"), Foster was elected.

As we have seen in other states, when the political process through which controversial policies are enacted is truncated, a complex after-politics is likely to ensue. In Louisiana, the after-politics of riverboat casinos, the land-based casino, and video poker followed this pattern. In this regard, the new state lottery, which was enacted at about the same time as these other new forms of gambling, is the exception that demonstrates the rule. Of all Louisiana's recent policy innovations concerning gambling, only the lottery was supported by a large majority of voters after it became law. It is no coincidence that only the lottery had been brought before them as part of the enactment process.

### Riverboat Casinos

The bill authorizing fifteen floating casinos on Louisiana rivers and lakes was slow to be implemented. It became law in the midst of the 1991 gubernatorial election. Distracted by the campaign and, after the first round of voting in October, dismayed by his defeat, Governor Roemer did not appoint anyone to the new Riverboat Gaming Commission, which was responsible for deciding who would get the casino licenses. Roemer's successor Edwin Edwards stacked the commission with political supporters when he took office in 1992, then charged them not to act until license seekers and their supporters in the legislature dropped their opposition to his bill for a land casino in New Orleans. By spring 1993, when the commission finally began to award licenses, casinos in Mississippi were up and running. Their success in a state not thought to be particularly receptive to casino gambling inspired forty-three casino companies to apply for the fifteen licenses in traditionally gambling-friendly Louisiana. The bidders' attitude, said commission chair Kenneth Pickering, was, "If you can do that in Tunica or Bay St. Louis, [Mississippi,] man, imagine what can you do in New Orleans."[36]

Louisiana's decision to keep the number of available riverboat licenses below the market demand invited corruption, and Edwards and some of the casino applicants accepted the invitation. The governor took a strong interest in who got the licenses. In March 1993, the commission awarded the first eight, seven of them to applicants with close ties to Edwards. (The eighth had the united support of city officials in Baton Rouge.) Three months later, commissioners awarded the remaining seven, again to applicants supported either by Edwards or, with his approval, by one of his chief lieutenants in the legislature. Two recipients later pleaded guilty to paying Edwards bribes as part of their effort to obtain licenses. All four of Edwards's children secured contracts to supply goods or services to one or more of the new casinos. Edwards, along with his son Stephen, was convicted in 2000 of these and other actions related to the awarding of riverboat casino licenses. The former governor was sentenced to ten years in prison and is not scheduled for release until July 2011.[37]

Despite the corrupt nature of its after-politics, Louisiana's floating casinos generally have been successful, especially those in the western cities of Shreveport–Bossier City and Lake Charles, which draw many of their customers from Texas. In binding referenda held in 1996, residents of each of the six casino parishes voted to keep them. Voters in the state's other thirty-eight parishes with navigable waters were asked in nonbinding referenda if they would like casinos of their own, and in twenty-three parishes a majority said yes. A 1999 scholarly study of the water-based casinos commissioned by the legislature concluded that the casinos' economic benefits outweighed their social and regulatory costs by a margin of two-to-one, with a net benefit to the state economy of a half-billion dollars per year.

In 2001, the revenue-starved legislature, desperate to fulfill a long overdue promise to raise public school teachers' pay, authorized the casino boats to remain permanently docked as compensation for raising their tax rate from 18.5 to 21.5 percent. By 2004, riverboat casinos were providing nearly as much revenue for the state treasury—$335 million per year—as all the other forms of legalized gambling combined. In 2005, Governor Foster's strongly (and, in contrast to Foster, sincerely) antigambling successor, Democrat Kathleen Blanco, proposed raising the riverboats' tax rate to 32.5 percent to fund a proposed salary hike for teachers. This time, however, the Casino Association of Louisiana organized to beat back the increase. "At 32.5 percent," said Wayne Duty, the association's executive director, "that's a 'close-the-boats' level of taxation."[38]

Hurricane Katrina had a mixed effect on casino gambling in Louisiana. Although the same flooding that devastated much of New Orleans when the levees broke on August 29, 2005, shut down the city's three floating casinos and the land-based casino, it did not damage them severely. All reopened within a few months, attracting business from construction and other workers who were in town to rebuild the city, which helped to make up for their reduced customer base among tourists and local residents. In the meantime, riverboat casinos in cities rich with hurricane evacuees, such as Baton Rouge, did record business. Overall, Louisiana riverboats took in $171.8 million in October 2005, down only 4 percent from the previous October. In November 2005, they actually did 9 percent better than in November 2004, and continued to do better well into 2006.[39] In the short term, at least, Louisiana casinos also benefited from the more severe damage that Katrina did to competing casinos along Mississippi's Gulf Coast.

### The New Orleans Land-Based Casino

The after-politics of the newly authorized land-based casino in New Orleans was complicated by the overlapping jurisdictions of the city and state governments. The Rivergate site of the casino, adjacent to the French Quarter, belonged to the city. Four bidders competed for the right to use the site, and on November 5, 1992, Mayor Sidney Barthelmy announced that the city would lease it to a partnership formed by developer Christopher Hemmeter and Caesars Palace, a Las Vegas–based casino corporation.[40]

Deciding which bidder would get the license to operate the casino, however, was the province of the state land casino board created for this purpose by the 1992 statute and appointed by Edwards. The governor encouraged two of the losing bidders for the Rivergate site—Harrah's Entertainment, a national casino corporation, and Jazzville, a local group of investors, many of them friends of Edwards—to team up as Harrah's Jazz and petition for the operating license.[41] They took the advice, and in August 1993 the state board awarded them the license. Edwards then pressured Harrah's Jazz to cut Hemmeter in on the deal so that it would have use of the site.[42]

In bidding for the casino license, Harrah's Jazz had agreed to pay the state an amount no less than the minimum annual tax of $100 million required by the 1992 law. It planned to economize by converting an existing building at Rivergate into a casino, at an estimated cost of $327 million. As a condition of transferring the lease from Hemmeter to Harrah's Jazz, however, Mayor Barthelmy added to the company's financial burden in several ways. Impatient to begin reaping the revenues that the new casino would generate for the city treasury, the mayor demanded that Harrah's Jazz open a temporary casino while the permanent facility was being built. Finally, hoping to revive the city's marginal Treme neighborhood, he also insisted that the temporary casino occupy aging Municipal Auditorium. Taken together, Barthelmy's demands helped nearly to triple Harrah Jazz's projected construction costs to around $850 million.

Certain that its monopoly on land-based casino gambling in New Orleans justified all of these costs, Harrah's Jazz still hoped to make money when it opened the doors of its temporary casino in May 1995. But tourists and other gamblers stayed away from the reputedly sketchy Treme site. "Hotel clerks routinely warned guests that it was a good place to go for anyone who wanted to gamble with his life," wrote *Times Picayune* columnist James Gill. The temporary casino took in two-thirds less money than Harrah's had projected.[43] Six months after the opening, Harrah's Jazz declared bankruptcy, shut down the temporary casino, and halted construction on the permanent casino.

During the next several years, Harrah's and the state government engaged in a long, politically charged negotiation designed to bring into being the permanent

New Orleans casino. Harrah's insisted that the $100 million minimum annual payment to the state and the ban on casino-operated restaurants made it impossible to compete with nearby riverboat casinos, which were de facto dockside facilities because they nearly always found excuses not to sail. The city strongly supported Harrah's in its efforts to win these concessions. In a 1996 referendum, 66 percent of New Orleans voters endorsed the casino, and Marc Morial, Barthelmy's successor as mayor, lobbied the legislature extensively on its behalf. So did the avowedly antigambling Governor Foster, who feared not getting any revenue at all if the land-based casino never opened.

After coming out of bankruptcy, Harrah's New Orleans Casino opened at the Rivergate site on Canal Street in October 1999. It did so in the firm expectation that Foster would persuade the legislature to reduce its minimum tax burden by half. But the legislature refused to act, and in January 2001 the casino declared bankruptcy once again. Desperate for new funds to finance pay raises for teachers, the legislature reconsidered. It agreed to reduce Harrah's minimum state tax payment to $50 million in the casino's first year and $60 million in subsequent years. Harrah's also was freed from the original legislative ban on operating restaurants. By 2004, Harrah's arguably had become the leading tourist attraction in Louisiana, attracting 6.6 million customers and taking in $300.2 million.[44] Although Hurricane Katrina shut down the casino for six months, it reopened in time for Mardi Gras in February 2006 and by May was taking in 8 percent more revenue than it had the previous year.[45]

### Video Poker

The after-politics of legalizing video poker was even more contentious than the after-politics of casino legalization. When the casino laws were passed, the public had little trouble envisioning what fifteen gambling boats and one land-based casino would look like. But the video poker bill was sold as a measure to allow local bars and restaurants to offer a small number of machines (no more than three) to their customers. The amendment to the bill that allowed truck stops to house as many as fifty gambling machines was enacted at the last minute and with virtually no public discussion or floor debate. The absence from the amendment of any definition of *truck stop* went completely unremarked at the time. So did the consequences of assigning to the state police the responsibility to license the manufacturers of the video gambling machines, the operators of the machines, and the brokers who bought the machines from the manufacturer and leased them to the operators—with no accompanying increase in the police force's budget or personnel.

One result of the hasty enactment of the video poker law in 1991 was the rapid and massive spread of poker machines around the state, far beyond what the public or most legislators had anticipated. No sooner did the law take effect than hundreds of license applications flooded in to the small state police division charged to evaluate them. Nominal truck stops with only one or two fuel pumps were created for the purpose of operating video poker parlors. When the license-granting process proceeded slowly, Governor Edwards placed enormous pressure on the state police to issue conditional licenses to truck stops and other applicants immediately. After the lieutenant in charge of the video gaming division, Riley Blackwelder, insisted on investigating certain applicants first, Edwards had him transferred. During video poker's first decade, the number of truck stops in Louisiana (many of them unfrequented by trucks) rose from 19 to 121.[46]

A second result of legalizing video poker so carelessly was more corruption. Taking advantage of Louisiana's loose regulatory climate for video poker, the Gambino crime family of New York moved in, teaming up with the remnants of New Orleans's notorious Marcello organization. One reason the mob-backed companies the gangsters created were licensed so easily was that they hired a close friend of Edwards, Aaron Mintz, to be their public face in Louisiana. In 1995, the Federal Bureau of Investigation (FBI) busted the mob operation and secured convictions against twenty-one individuals, including Mintz and members of both crime families. That same year, in a separate scandal, the FBI caught video poker truck-stop owner Fred Goodson (the same "God-fearing Baptist" who in 1991 had persuaded Senator Hinton to add the truck stop loophole to the video poker bill) bribing Senate Judiciary B committee chair Larry Bankston to bury a bill authorizing local referenda in which voters could decide whether to expel video poker from their parishes. Polls showed 90 to 95 percent public support for the bill, which the House had already passed, with 60 to 70 percent saying they would vote against video poker if given the chance. Bankston and Goodson were later convicted and sentenced to prison for their crimes.

As noted earlier, Mike Foster, who had voted for casino legalization as a state senator, nonetheless rode the antigambling tide in the state from obscurity to election as governor in 1995. But Foster let his campaign promise of a statewide referendum on whether to abolish video poker and casino gambling throughout Louisiana fall by the wayside after he was elected. Reluctant to jeopardize the extensive revenues the state derived from casinos and video poker, Foster played a clever game. He insisted that the legislature pass a constitutional amendment to forbid video and casino gambling, when all that was needed to accomplish that end was simple legislation. The amendment required a two-thirds vote of both the House and Senate to get on the ballot. A legislative ban would have taken only a simple majority of legislators and no referendum. Opponents of gambling were furious. "We didn't need a [constitutional] amendment to put gambling in," said antigambling activist C. B. Forgotston. "So why do we need one to take it out?"[47]

When, not surprisingly, Foster's antigambling amendment failed in the legislature, he endorsed a measure to hold local referenda in all sixty-four parishes on whether to expel video poker. (This was the same measure that placed riverboat casinos on the ballot in some parishes.) The measure required that the referenda coincide with the November 1996 presidential election, the date favored by gambling lobbyists because turnout would be at its highest, especially among lower-income voters who were expected to support gambling. And even in parishes that voted against video poker, the measure provided that the machines would remain legal for another three years. In April 1996, the House, by a vote of eighty-eight to fifteen, and the Senate, by thirty-three to six, approved Foster's local referenda measure.

Although the opinions of Christian conservatives and other opponents of gambling about Foster ranged from disappointment to anger, they worked hard to prevail in the November 1996 referenda. Foster continued to muddy the political waters. He taped a television commercial lambasting gambling as "not good for our state," but he also praised video poker operators as small business owners working hard to scratch out a living. ("I've never thought of him as anti-gambling," said John Georges, a major distributor of poker machines.)[48] Officials in parish governments, which had grown as dependent on tax revenues from video poker as the state government, joined with truck-stop owners and other operators and distributors of poker machines to fight against the referenda.

On election day, thirty-three parishes voted to ban video poker and thirty-one to keep it. Reflecting the state's long-standing political and cultural division, nearly all of the anti–video poker parishes were in heavily Baptist north Louisiana, while nearly all the pro–video poker parishes were in mostly Catholic south Louisiana. Because video poker was a smaller presence in the counties that voted to expel it than in those that voted to keep it, only around one-third of the approximately 15,000 machines in the state were shut down when the ban finally took effect in 1999.[49] By 2005, the number of machines had crept back to nearly 15,000 and the number of video poker truck stops had expanded from 88 after the 1999 parish referenda to 155. Video poker taxes added $172.2 million dollars to the revenue-starved state treasury in fiscal year 2005, taking the steam out of any further political efforts to reduce the industry's presence in the state.[50]

## Lottery

The lottery that Louisiana created in 1990 resembled other modern state lotteries much more than it did the Louisiana lottery of the 1800s. From the beginning the new lottery was state owned. By all accounts, it has been free of corruption and inappropriate political influence. In contrast to Louisiana's idiosyncratic approach to authorizing casino gambling and video poker, it designed its lottery on the model of other successful state lotteries, especially Kentucky's.

Louisiana's lottery has continued to be influenced by other state lotteries, for better and for worse. The launch of the Texas lottery in mid-1992 helped reduce the revenues the state of Louisiana received from its own lottery from $167 million in the first year to little more than $100 million in ensuing years.[51] The Louisiana lottery not only lost customers from Texas, who now could stay home to play a lottery, but also lost customers in Louisiana, who were attracted to the bigger prizes that the Texas lottery's much larger population base sustained. Louisiana also was influenced by Georgia, which pioneered the idea of dedicating lottery funds to new merit-based college scholarships. In the course of creating its own Georgia-inspired merit scholarship program in 1997, the legislature eventually decided not to fund it from the lottery. But in 2003, it approved a constitutional amendment to dedicate lottery revenues to public education instead of continuing to place the revenues in the state's general fund. Voters approved the amendment in October 2003 by a vote of 64 to 36 percent.

As much as anything else, the Louisiana lottery has been affected by the state's embrace of other forms of gambling. "When the lottery kicked off," said lottery corporation president Bonnie Fussell, " . . . we were the only game in town. But now, of course, Louisiana is inundated with gaming."[52] Nonetheless, the lottery remains popular in Louisiana. No serious effort has been made to repeal it.

## GAMBLING BEGETS GAMBLING:
## TRIBAL CASINOS AND RACINOS

Remarkably, Louisiana's constitution still contains the provision that reminds the legislature of its duty to define and suppress gambling. This admonition did not prevent the state's elected officials from legalizing "gaming" in the form of casino gambling and video poker. Nor did it chasten voters, who in parish referenda endorsed casino gambling where it already existed, and retained video poker (again, where it already existed) in nearly half the state's parishes. By the mid-1990s, gambling interests were pumping more money into legislative candidates' campaign treasuries than the state's next four industries combined, including the long dominant oil and gas industry. By 2002, Louisiana had tied much-larger California as the state with the most gambling lobbyists working to influence its legislature.

All of Louisiana's decisions to legalize various forms of gambling and to keep them legal were made intentionally. But state policy innovations made with eyes open sometimes beget further innovations that are unintentional and unexpected. In Louisiana's case, gambling in the form of a lottery, casinos, and video poker begat gambling in the form of tribal casinos and racinos, or casino-style slot machine facilities at racetracks. For legal reasons, in the case of tribal casinos, and for political reasons, in the case of racinos, policy makers in Louisiana had little or no choice but to authorize these new forms of gambling once the lottery, casinos, and video poker parlors were operating. The result was that Louisiana ended up with three of the five tribal casinos in the entire South, and became the first and only state in the region with racinos.

Tribal casino gambling in Louisiana began in 1993. Under the terms of the federal Indian Gaming Regulatory Act (IGRA) of 1988, Louisiana's decision to legalize casino gambling required it to allow Native American tribes whose sovereign lands are within the state's borders to open casinos of their own, free from taxation and most forms of regulation by the state government. Convinced that he would be sued by tribes invoking IGRA if he did not accommodate them, Governor Roemer signed compacts with the Chitimacha Tribe, the Louisiana Coushatta Tribe, and the Tunica-Biloxi Tribe to clear the way for casinos on their lands. Two of the three tribes negotiated contracts to operate their casinos with Grand Casino, a national casino corporation, and the other signed with Royal Management, a similar firm.

The legal climate surrounding tribal casinos changed in 1996 when the U.S. Supreme Court ruled that the Eleventh Amendment to the Constitution immunizes state governments from lawsuits by Indian tribes.[53] Governors realized that their negotiating positions were much stronger when new tribes sought casino compacts because their states could not be sued for failing to grant the compacts. Although IGRA still did not allow states to tax tribal casinos, some governors now negotiated "contributions" from the tribes to their state treasuries as part of the compact-granting process. In 2002, Governor Foster negotiated a new compact with the Jena Band of Choctaw Indians to open a casino on a site even closer to Texas than the Louisiana Coushatta Tribe's southwestern Louisiana casino. In return, the Jena Band agreed to contribute 15.5 percent of the casino's revenues to the state treasury.

Outside the public gaze, the Coushattas hired Washington lobbyist Jack Abramoff and his associate Michael Scanlon, first to help the tribe renegotiate its casino compact with Governor Foster and then to try to thwart the Jena Band's plan for a casino. In all, the Louisiana Coushattas paid about $32 million to Scanlon's Capitol Campaign Strategies firm, with Abramoff secretly receiving around one-third of it in the form of kickbacks from Scanlon.[54] Abramoff urged the Louisiana Coushattas to make campaign contributions to a large number of influential members of Congress. Consequently, thirty-three representatives and senators, including Speaker of the House Dennis Hastert and Senate Democratic leader Harry Reid, sent letters to Secretary of the Interior Gale Norton urging her to reject Louisiana's compact with the Jena Band. The Interior Department did so, ruling that the Jenas' negotiated 15.5 percent contribution to the state treasury was an illegal tax in all but name.[55] The department also reminded Foster and his successor, Governor Blanco, that federal law, however attenuated, still required Louisiana to continue negotiating seriously with the Jena Band toward a compact.[56]

In a separate effort on behalf of the Louisiana Coushattas, Abramoff advised the tribe to secretly finance an organizing drive by political consultant Ralph Reed, the former director of the Christian Coalition, against the Ysleta Del Sur Pueblo, or Tigua, tribe of Texas. The Tiguas, who owned the Speaking Rock casino near El Paso, were waging a public campaign to dissuade Texas attorney general John Cornyn from shutting down their casino as illegal under Texas law. The Louisiana Coushattas hired Reed, aware that if the Tiguas were forced out of the casino business, the Alabama Coushattas, a tribe whose casino in east Texas competed with the Louisiana Coushattas' facility, would be forced out of business, too. Reed, claiming to "have over 50 pastors mobilized, with a total membership in those churches of over 40,000," mobilized antigambling Christians to flood Cornyn's office with messages of support—none of which were necessary, since Cornyn had no intention of flinching. After Cornyn forced the Tiguas' and the Alabama Coushattas' casinos to close, Abramoff then signed the Tiguas to a separate deal by promising that he and Scanlon would get the casino reopened. They failed but not before taking $4.2 million of the tribe's money.[57] Payback against Reed came when the Alabama Coushattas filed a fraud and racketeering lawsuit against him in federal court less than a week before the July 18, 2006, Georgia primary, in which Reed was seeking the Republican nomination for lieutenant governor. Reed, the early favorite, was defeated.[58]

Although no law required Louisiana to grant its racetracks the right to open large slot machine parlors, political necessity did. Louisiana's four tracks—Louisiana Downs in Bossier City, Evangeline Downs in Lafayette, Delta Downs in Vinton, and the Fair Grounds in New Orleans—had existed long before lottery, casino, and video poker gambling became legal in the early 1990s. They were woven into the fabric of the state's traditions and in some cases were mainstays of their local economies. When a large portion of the tracks' customers were lost to the other, newly legal forms of gambling, the same state government whose decisions had unintentionally threatened their ability to stay in business had little choice but to come to their aid. Citing the example of tracks in other states that had survived by opening slot machine parlors (diffusion again), Louisiana's tracks petitioned the state government to grant them that privilege. In 1997, state senator Don Cravins of Lafayette introduced a bill to allow three of the tracks to become racinos, leaving out only the Fair Grounds for fear of jeopardizing the legal monopoly on land-based casino gambling assigned to Harrah's in New Orleans. "In my area, it's a bread-and-butter issue," Cravins told his sympathetic colleagues. "It's an issue that feeds families."[59]

After Governor Foster said he would allow the racino bill to become law, both houses of the legislature passed it during their 1997 session. The three long-dormant racetracks came to life, as did the Fair Grounds in the early 2000s when Harrah's waived its monopoly on land-based slot machines in New Orleans in the course to trying to persuade the state to dramatically reduce its $100 million minimum annual tax. National casino corporations bought all four tracks, and applications were filed with the racing commission to build three new ones around the state. In all cases, the new owners regarded horse-racing as the price they had to pay to open a large new slot-machine casino.

# WHY THE SOUTH JOINED
# THE GAMBLING NATION

At the start of the final decade of the twentieth century, the United States was well on its way to becoming a gambling nation, with the South the last pocket of resistance. In 1960, not a single state had a lottery. By 1990, thirty-four of the forty states outside the South—85 percent of them—were lottery states.[1] Of the eleven southern states, only two (18 percent) had state lotteries, Virginia and Florida. Nationwide, four states allowed commercial casino gambling: Nevada, New Jersey, Iowa, and Illinois. None of them were in the South.

Even as southern state governments resisted the spread of lottery and casino gambling occurring elsewhere in the country during the 1970s and 1980s, the South was pursuing another distinctive political course. Once the nation's most Democratic region (the term *Solid South* was coined to describe its unflagging devotion to the Democratic Party), the South was in the process of becoming a GOP stronghold. In 1972 Richard Nixon became the first Republican presidential candidate since Reconstruction to win a majority of the South's electoral votes. With the exception of Georgia Democrat Jimmy Carter's victory in 1976, the Republicans have won the South in every presidential election that followed. The number of Republican U.S. senators in the twenty-two member southern delegation rose from none as recently as 1960 to seven in 1988. Similar gains occurred in the House of Representatives, where the Republican ranks grew from 7 percent of southern members in 1960 to 34 percent in 1988.[2]

Republican success in gubernatorial elections during the 1970s and 1980s followed this trend—the number of Republican governors in the South rose from none in 1960 to three in 1972 to five in 1988. In the late 1980s, Southern Democrats knew they still enjoyed an advantage among voters on one important state political issue—education—but they also were aware that improving schools costs money and that any time Democrats proposed to raise taxes they risked playing into the Republicans' hands.

Ray Mabus of Mississippi was the first southern Democratic governor to seize on the idea of funding educational improvements through a state lottery as a way of beating back the rising Republican tide.[3] In 1990 Mabus urged the legislature and people of his state to repeal Mississippi's constitutional ban on lotteries and open the door to a new source of funding for schools. Ironically, although Mabus was successful in opening that door, the legislature never went through it to pass a law creating a lottery. Instead, Mabus's highly visible campaign to repeal the lottery ban served (unintentionally) to distract public attention from the quiet efforts underway in the legislature, led by Rep. Sonny Merideth, to legalize casino gambling. Mississippi remains a lottery-free state, but it has become the leading casino center in the nation's heartland.

At about the time that Mabus was pursuing a lottery in Mississippi, a Democratic candidate for governor of Georgia, Zell Miller, also seized on the issue as a way of funding educational improvements without raising taxes. To some extent, Miller was inspired by Democrat Wallace Wilkinson's lottery-based election as governor of Kentucky, a border state, in 1987. Miller's innovation was to promise to use a large share of the proceeds from a lottery to fund an entirely new college scholarship program for Georgia's students.

Miller's election in 1990, his reelection in 1994, and the great popularity of his HOPE scholarship program inspired ambitious Democrats in other southern states. In 1998 Jim Hodges was elected governor of South Carolina and Don Siegelman was elected governor of Alabama by running Georgia-style "education lottery" campaigns. (Part of the issue's appeal to voters in both states was that they were already crossing the border to play the Georgia lottery.) Although Siegelman was unable to persuade Alabamians to approve a constitutional amendment authorizing a state lottery, Hodges was successful in South Carolina. Meanwhile, in Tennessee, Steve Cohen, a Democratic state senator who had been promoting a lottery since the mid-1980s, finally succeeded in 2002 after adapting his proposal so that it promised Tennesseans the same kind of scholarship program that Miller had brought to Georgia.

Arkansas is the only southern state besides Alabama with neither casinos nor a lottery.[4] No prominent state leader in Arkansas has ever championed casino or lottery gambling, leaving the fight to business owners eager to open casinos and willing to support a lottery in hopes (so far futile) of broadening their base of public support. Louisiana, on the other hand, is the only southern state, and one of only nine in the country, that has embraced both a lottery and casinos. Two Democratic governors, Edwin Edwards (enthusiastically) and Buddy Roemer (grudgingly), facilitated the state's adoption of these forms of gambling in the early 1990s, along with several Democratic state legislators, notably, representatives Raymond LaLonde and Francis Heitmeier and Sen. Don Kelly

By 2006, the South had joined the gambling nation. Two of the eleven southern states allowed commercial casino gambling, an almost identical proportion to the nine of forty states with commercial casinos outside the South. Seven southern states had lotteries, a 64 percent rate of lottery adoption not drastically below the 88 percent rate in the rest of the country. In addition, the South is dotted with the same other forms of gambling that dot the rest of the country: video poker, racetracks, bingo, and tribal casinos.

Summarizing what has happened with the politics of gambling in the South in recent years is one thing. Explaining why it happened is the greater challenge. In trying to meet this challenge we have relied on the insights of other scholars of state policy innovation. We also have added some insights of our own that emerged from our case studies of gambling in seven southern states and that may be of use to scholars trying to explain other innovations in public policy in other states and regions.

## LEGALIZED GAMBLING AS POLICY INNOVATION

Scholars who study why states create new public policies typically rely on some combination of three explanations, all of which are by now familiar to readers of this book. First, *diffusion* theory holds that states facing a common problem look to each other for successful solutions, gazing especially hard at states that are nearby and similar enough to seem comparable. Second, *internal characteristics* theory focuses on qualities of the state itself which shape its approach to new ideas, characteristics that may be economic, political, or social in nature but that, taken in combination, affect the state's willingness to adopt a new policy. Third, *policy entrepreneurship* theory emphasizes the essential work of the individual or individuals in a state who ardently and skillfully champion a new public policy in ways that are crucial to its adoption.

Most scholars of state policy innovation draw eclectically from all of these theories, and we are no exception. Diffusion, internal characteristics, and policy entrepreneurship have proven essential to us in explaining what southern states have done in adopting or sometimes rejecting proposals to legalize new forms of gambling in recent years. But each of these theories, taken on its own terms, also has shown its limits, which we have attempted to overcome by broadening state policy innovation theories to include new elements.

### Diffusion

Diffusion theory explains a great deal about the spread of casinos and lotteries around the South in the 1990s and 2000s. Mississippi was influenced by the examples of Iowa and Illinois, two fellow Mississippi River Valley states, in its decision to legalize water-based casino gambling. Iowa's experience showed Mississippi law makers that casinos could thrive in the nation's heartland, and Illinois showed the importance of allowing casinos to operate around the clock and without betting limits. Mississippi's example, in turn, helped inspire neighboring Louisiana to legalize riverboat casino gambling.

Meanwhile, Georgia was learning from adjacent Florida the good lesson that a lottery could raise money for education and the bad lesson that allowing that money to be deposited in the state's general fund would encourage the legislature simply to substitute lottery money for money it would have spent anyway. Applying both lessons, Democrat governor Zell Miller insisted that the lottery he wanted Georgia to create should fund an entirely new education program from an entirely new account. The popularity of the Georgia lottery and the HOPE scholarship program inspired two of Georgia's neighbors, South Carolina and, eventually, Tennessee, to adopt similar lotteries of their own.

Tennessee's slowness in creating a lottery (it was the first southern state to seriously consider the idea but among the last actually to do so) illustrates one of the gaps in diffusion theory that this study hopes to fill. The politics of gambling in Tennessee was immobilized for nearly a decade, not because of an absence of appealing examples from nearby states but because of an excess of appealing examples. By the mid-1990s, west Tennesseans' desire for casinos like the ones in neighboring Mississippi and Missouri clashed with east and middle Tennesseans' desire for a lottery like the ones in neighboring Georgia, Kentucky, and Virginia. Tennessee experienced *diffusion overload*. Too many examples of popular new gambling policies from nearby states long kept it from adopting any of them.

A second addition to diffusion theory that arises from our study is *anticipatory diffusion*, which occurs when a state adopts a policy because it thinks an adjacent state is about to do so, thus seizing the advantage of going first. One reason that Mississippi moved so quickly to legalize casino gambling was that state lawmakers were convinced that Louisiana would otherwise beat them to the punch. Similarly, Louisiana made its decision to create a lottery on the assumption that all of the states with which it shares a border—Mississippi, Texas, and Arkansas—were about to become lottery states. Even though only Texas actually did so, the expectation that Louisiana was about to start leaking dollars through all of its borders as its people crossed the state line to play other states' lotteries strongly influenced Louisiana policy makers who were making the decision.

*Antidiffusion* is a third addition to diffusion theory. It explains what the beneficiaries of a policy in one state sometimes do to thwart efforts to adopt the same policy in another state. For example, Mississippi's commercial casino interests fought fiercely to defeat proposals to legalize casino gambling in neighboring Arkansas. Similarly, the Mississippi Band of Choctaw Indians, which operates a successful tribal casino resort, lobbied to prevent the Poarch Creek Indians in adjacent Alabama from opening a casino of their own. Even within Mississippi, Tunica County casinos funded anticasino referendum campaigns in adjacent DeSoto County because casinos in the latter, being closer to Memphis, would have drained away much of Tunica's business. Antidiffusion campaigns such as these tend to be covert. When they become public, as happened when Mississippi casinos hired a Nashville lobbyist to oppose a lottery in Tennessee, state pride against the outside interloper becomes a powerful visceral argument for a policy's proponents.

State pride also helps to account for a fourth addition to diffusion theory— *incremental diffusion*. As Gov. Don Siegelman discovered in Alabama, urging his state simply to clone Georgia's lottery unwittingly sent voters the message that Georgia was better than Alabama and that Alabama had nothing to contribute to the design of its own lottery. This was not a message that Alabamians, tired of hearing about how great Atlanta is compared to Birmingham and of (occasionally) losing to the Georgia Bulldogs in football, wanted to hear. In contrast, when Tennessee adopted a Georgia-style lottery, it included an additional element authorizing charitable gambling under strict conditions.

Changing a policy, of course, does not necessarily improve it. Louisiana followed Mississippi in legalizing casino gambling but made its own mark by limiting the number of casinos in the state instead of letting the market decide, as in Mississippi, how many there would be. The decision to make casino licenses a scarce resource turned out to be an invitation to corruption by casino companies seeking licenses and the state officials awarding them.

### Internal Characteristics

Most of the internal characteristics that scholars have found to influence state policy innovation have helped shape the politics of gambling in the South as well. A state government's need for revenue has been a crucial economic characteristic affecting gambling legalization: the greater the need, the more likely the state is to authorize gambling as a new funding source. A related political characteristic has been the rising Republican tide in the South, which has made it difficult for Democrats to raise taxes to support social programs without playing into the GOP's hands. The high concentration of Southern Baptist and other antigambling Protestant churches is a social characteristic of southern states that long impeded the spread of gambling in the region.

What we found especially interesting, however, was the influence of a characteristic that generally has been overlooked in the state policy innovation literature: state constitutions. The prominence of southern state constitutions in the politics of gambling has been mostly due to the presence in every state's charter of a prohibition on lotteries. Because state courts typically interpreted this prohibition to extend to all games of chance played for money, southern constitutions effectively barred not just state lotteries but also the chance-based games from which casinos derive their profits, especially slot machines. Thus, in most states casinos could not be authorized or a lottery created until the constitution was changed in a way that allowed gambling to be made legal, clearing the path for the legislature to decide whether to authorize it by law.

The constitutional amendment processes in the seven states discussed in this book range widely. Alabama's constitution is the easiest one in the country to amend, requiring a three-fifths vote by the legislature, followed by majority approval of those voting on it in a referendum. Not surprisingly the Alabama constitution has more amendments than any other state constitution. Tennessee, in contrast, has amended its constitution at a slower rate than any of the other forty-nine states because its amendment process is so arduous. Amending the Tennessee constitution means securing the approval of the legislature twice, first by a simple majority and then, following an intervening general election, by a two-thirds majority. After that the amendment must be approved not just by a majority of those voting on it in a referendum but also by a number equal to a majority of those voting for governor, which is often much larger.

Four other states—Georgia, Mississippi, Louisiana, and South Carolina—have an amendment process that is neither as easy as Alabama's nor as difficult as Tennessee's. In these states, a two-thirds majority of the legislature and a simple majority of those voting in a referendum are sufficient to enact an amendment. The remaining state, Arkansas, has a constitution that does not fit easily into any category. In one sense, it is easier to amend than all the others, requiring only a simple majority of the legislature and a simple majority of those voting in a referendum. But Arkansas also restricts the number of amendments that the legislature may place on the ballot to three per election while requiring that many ordinary matters be dealt with through constitutional amendments. To add to the complexity, Arkansas allows amendments to be placed on the ballot though the initiative process—that is, by petition—but judicial scrutiny makes it difficult for initiatives to qualify.

State constitutions also have affected the politics of gambling in the various southern states in ways more subtle than simply making legalization easier or harder depending on the difficulty of the amendment process. In Arkansas, for example, legislators usually fill up their allotted three amendments with urgent, albeit minor, matters and, even when they do not, they are able to pass the buck on controversial issues such as gambling by deferring to the initiative process. As such, the Arkansas constitution offers an open invitation to the sort of poorly crafted, even wacky ballot measures that have brought legalized gambling to the voters in such unpalatable forms. The Mississippi constitution requires that revenue bills secure a three-fifths legislative majority for passage rather than the simple majority that is sufficient to pass other bills. As a result, once Mississippi removed its constitutional ban on lotteries, the legislature was able to legalize casino gambling with fewer votes than the bill to create a lottery received (a majority but not three-fifths). Unlike the proposed lottery law, the casino measure was not defined as a revenue bill because the anticipated tax revenues were so small. In South Carolina, the state supreme court interpreted the constitution to mean that a scheduled referendum on video poker was unconstitutional because it entailed a constitutionally impermissible delegation of the legislative power to the people. The result was that video poker became instantly illegal.

### Policy Entrepreneurship

Our study of the politics of gambling in the South confirms the vital role that other scholars have assigned to policy entrepreneurs in the innovation process, but with a twist. Most studies conceive of policy entrepreneurship as a rather bloodless activity in which policy experts in one state get good ideas from their peers in other states and bring them home for adoption. We found not experts seeking good policy but politicians seeking good issues to be at the heart of gambling politics.

In most instances, gambling legalization was the solution arrived at by a Democratic politician seeking to balance the need to satisfy the party's core constituencies, especially public employees and minorities, with new spending programs against the competing need not to alienate increasingly Republican, middle-class, white voters with new taxes. Typically, a Democratic candidate for governor in a southern state embraced an "education lottery" as a way of performing this balancing act. In the 1990s and early 2000s, a period when the GOP was gaining strength in the South, the education lottery strategy was one of the few that worked for Democrats in statewide elections. Interestingly, the one state in our study in which no prominent Democratic politician has championed a lottery is Arkansas, by most reckonings the southern state that has succumbed least to the region's Republican trend.

Not all of gambling's policy entrepreneurs have been Democratic governors. The most effective advocates of casino legalization in the South have been Democratic legislators, especially in Mississippi and Louisiana. Making casino gambling legal in these two states was more a matter of behind-the-scenes legislative maneuvering than of public advocacy. Indeed, no southern politician has run a successful gubernatorial campaign by advocating casino gambling, even those governors, such as Louisiana's Edwin Edwards and Buddy Roemer, who ended up supporting casinos after they took office.

As in the business world, policy entrepreneurs vary widely in skill. Among those who not only developed but also executed brilliant strategies for legalizing gambling in their states were Rep. Sonny Merideth of Mississippi, Rep. Raymond LaLonde of Louisiana, Gov. Zell Miller of Georgia, and Gov. Jim Hodges of South Carolina. In contrast, Gov. Don Siegelman of Alabama proved an ardent but inept champion of a lottery amendment in his state—it failed to be enacted even though Alabama has the easiest constitution in the country to amend. Sen. Steve Cohen, the father of Tennessee's lottery, offers a more complex case. Tennessee would not have a lottery had it not been for Cohen's persistence. On the other hand, Tennessee would have had a lottery much sooner had it not been for Cohen's abrasiveness.

Distressingly, some of the most effective policy entrepreneurs have been advocates of video poker who managed to make or keep it legal, at least for a time, through legislative slight of hand. In several southern states, for example, video poker lobbyists and their agents in the legislature snuck their form of gambling into the law through bills designed to allow children's restaurants to offer small prizes to kids who win arcade games—the so-called "Chuck E. Cheese" laws. In others, they duped legislators into thinking they were passing one bill when they actually were passing another that indirectly authorized video poker. In still other states, video poker became legal through a vote taken in the frenzied final minutes of a legislative session, essentially under the cover of darkness. No southern state has legalized video poker with its eyes open. Just as entrepreneurs can be skillful or not, they also can be above board or not.

### After-Politics

Nearly all scholarly studies of state policy innovation end when the newly adopted policy begins—that is, before it is actually put into effect. But a state's decision to create a lottery or legalize casinos does not always mark the end of the story. Instead, such a decision often sets in motion a series of subsequent controversies about how and where the new form of gambling will operate, who will share in the proceeds, how it will be implemented, and even whether it was wrongly adopted in the first place.

Three sets of circumstances presage such a period of after-politics. The first, and happiest, is when the benefits of a policy far exceed what anyone expected at the time it was adopted. Georgia's decision to create a lottery, for example, has triggered an ongoing debate about how the larger-than-expected revenues should be distributed. The same has occurred in Mississippi, where the revenue stream flowing from casino taxes into the state treasury has wildly exceeded anyone's expectations.

Second, a policy may be adopted with little public debate but with great consequence for the lives of the people, as casino legalization was in Mississippi and video poker was in Louisiana, South Carolina, and elsewhere. The absence of debate at the time of adoption keeps the new policy from being woven into the fabric of accepted state policies. In these cases, debate denied is merely debate postponed.

Finally, a policy may be poorly designed, with consequences that only become apparent when it is implemented. For example, Louisiana's riverboat casino bill triggered an after-politics that extended even to the trial, conviction, and sentencing of a former governor who took an improperly active role in assigning casino licenses.

### FINAL THOUGHT

What's going to happen next in the politics of gambling in the South?

Asking the question is easy; answering it is difficult. The trend line for gambling legalization in the South and the nation has been upward for the last two decades, and perhaps it will continue that way. It isn't hard to imagine scenarios in which, for example, Alabama creates a lottery or Arkansas legalizes casinos. On the other hand, upward trend lines have a way of eventually bending down. A familiar axiom among social scientists is that "all interesting relationships are curvilinear"—that is, they are true only up to a point. As we showed in the introductory chapter, twice before in our history, Americans, including southerners, have embraced legalized gambling for a time, only to turn against it. What scholars call gambling's third wave—the one we have been in—could recede just as the first two did. We do not know and can't wait to find out.[5]

# NOTES

## Introduction

1. The historical survey that follows draws heavily on John Lyman Mason and Michael Nelson, *Governing Gambling* (New York: Century Foundation Press / Brookings Institution, 2001), chaps. 2–3; Patrick A. Pierce and Donald E. Miller, *Gambling Politics: State Governments and the Business of Betting* (Boulder, Colo.: Lynne Rienner, 2004), chap. 2; Ronald M. Pavalko, *Risky Business: America's Fascination with Gambling* (Belmont, Calif.: Wadsworth, 2000), chap. 3; and John Samuel Ezell, *Fortune's Merry Wheel: The Lottery in America* (Cambridge, Mass.: Harvard University Press, 1960).

2. Quoted in John J. Dinan, *The American State Constitutional Tradition* (Lawrence: University Press of Kansas, 2006), 251.

3. Because this book studies policy innovations by state governments, its focus is on lotteries and commercial casinos. Tribal casino gambling is discussed to the extent that it involves state governments or affects state policy making. Tribal casinos are the subject of Mason and Nelson, *Governing Gambling*, chap. 4.

4. Calculated from data in Steven Andrew Light and Kathryn R. L. Rand, *Indian Gaming and Tribal Sovereignty: The Casino Compromise* (Lawrence: University Press of Kansas, 2005), 163–68. The eighteen facilities, most of them bingo halls, are in Alabama (Poarch Band of Creek Indians, 3), Florida (Miccosukee Tribal Indians of Florida, 1; Seminole Tribe, 5), Louisiana (Chitimacha Tribe of Louisiana, 1; Coushatta Tribe of Louisiana, 1; Tunica-Biloxi Tribe of Louisiana, 1), Mississippi (Mississippi Band of Choctaw Indians, 2), North Carolina (Eastern Band of Cherokee Indians, 2), South Carolina (Catawba Indian Nation, 1), and Texas (Kickapoo Traditional Tribe of Texas, 1).

5. Charles T. Clotfelter and Philip J. Cook, *Selling Hope: State Lotteries in America* (Cambridge, Mass.: Harvard University Press, 1989).

6. Ibid., chap. 8.

7. Frances Stokes Berry and William D. Berry, "State Lottery Adoptions as Policy Innovation: An Event History Analysis," *American Political Science Review* 63 (Sept. 1969): 880–99.

8. Pierce and Miller, *Gambling Politics*, 62, also argue that low-tax states are more likely to adopt a lottery than higher-tax states. John E. Filer, Donald L. Moak, and Barry Uze reach the opposite conclusion in "Why Some States Adopt Lotteries and Some Don't," *Public Finance Quarterly* 16 (July 1988): 259–83.

9. Berry and Berry, "State Lottery Adoptions."

10. Pierce and Miller, *Gambling Politics*, 39.

11. John Dombrink and William N. Thompson, *The Last Resort: Success and Failure in Campaigns for Casinos* (Reno: University of Nevada Press, 1990). The important political factors they list are: "political environment," such as the economy and the state's prior experience with gambling; "political elite and active interests," including the stance of public officials and business interests on casinos; "campaign sponsorship," such as the credibility and financial commitment of casino advocates; and "campaign issue dominance," notably, the ability of casino supporters to frame the issue as one of economic development rather than of crime, morality, or quality of life.

12. Pierce and Miller, *Gambling Politics*, chaps. 5–6. The quoted phrases appear on pages 172 and 94, respectively.

13. Berry and Berry's study of lotteries ended in 1986, Cook and Clotfelter's in 1988, and Pierce and Miller's in 1990. See Cook and Clotfelter, *Selling Hope;* Berry and Berry, "State Lottery Adoptions"; and Pierce and Miller, *Gambling Politics*. Dombrink and Thompson's study of casinos ended in 1989 (*The Last Resort*).

14. Jack L. Walker, "The Diffusion of Innovation Among the American States," *American Political Science Review* 63 (Sept. 1969): 880–99.

15. See Scott P. Hays, "Controversy and Reinvention in the Diffusion of State Policy Innovation," *Political Research Quarterly* 49:13–632; and Henry R. Glick and Scott P. Hays, "Innovation and Reinvention in State Policy Innovation: Theory and the Evolution of Living Will Laws," *Journal of Politics* 53:835–50. See also Michael Nelson and John Lyman Mason, "The Politics of Gambling in the South," *Political Science Quarterly* 104 (Winter 2003–4): 645–69.

16. Everett M. Rogers, *Diffusion of Innovations,* 4th ed. (New York: Free Press, 1995), 178.

17. Virginia Gray, "Competition, Emulation, and Policy Innovation," in *New Perspectives on American Politics,* ed. Lawrence C. Dodd and Calvin Jillson (Washington, D.C.: CQ Press, 1994), 230–48.

18. In *Gambling Politics,* Pierce and Miller say more likely, but their conclusion is not supported in the southern states by this study.

19. John W. Kingdon, *Agendas, Alternatives, and Public Policies* (Boston: Little, Brown, 1984).

20. Michael Mintrom, "Policy Entrepreneurs and the Diffusion of Innovation," *American Journal of Political Science* 41 (July 1997): 738–70.

21. J. David Woodard, *The New Southern Politics* (Boulder, Colo.: Lynne Rienner, 2006), chap. 8.

22. Graham T. Allison, *Essence of Decision: Explaining the Cuban Missile Crisis* (Boston: Little, Brown, 1971); Robert A. Dahl, *Who Governs?: Democracy and Power in an American City* (New Haven, Conn.: Yale University Press, 1961; Herbert Kaufman, *The Forest Ranger: A Study in Administrative Behavior* (Baltimore: Johns Hopkins University Press, 1960); and Jeffrey L. Pressman and Aaron B. Wildavsky, *Implementation: How Great Expectations in Washington Are Dashed in Oakland* (Berkeley and Los Angeles: University of California Press, 1973).

23. Sidney Verba, "Some Dilemmas in Comparative Research," *World Politics* 20 (1967): 111–27; Arend Lijphart, "Comparative Politics and the Comparative Method," *American Political Science Review* 65 (Sept. 1971): 682–93; Harry Eckstein, "Case Study and Theory in Political Science," in

*Handbook of Political Science,* vol. 7, ed. F. I. Greenstein and N. W. Polsby (Reading, Mass.: Addison-Wesley, 1975), 79–137.

24. John Gerring, "What Is a Case Study and What Is It Good For?" *American Political Science Review* 98 (May 2004): 341–54.

25. In terms of the phases and execution of our research, we employ the case study method as outlined by Alexander L. George, "Case Studies and Theory Development: The Method of Structured, Focused Comparison," in *Diplomacy: New Approaches in History, Theory, and Policy,* ed. Paul Gordon Lauren (New York: Free Press, 1979), 54–57.

26. Gerring, "What Is a Case Study and What Is It Good For?" 348.

## Chapter 1

1. Joint Committee on Performance Evaluation and Expenditure Review, Mississippi Legislature, *A Report on the Adequacy of the Mississippi Gaming Commission's Regulation of Legalized Gambling in Mississippi* (Sept. 11, 1996), 1.

2. "Mississippi," *USA Today,* Jan. 8, 1990.

3. Peter J. Boyer, "Gone with the Surge," *New Yorker,* Sept. 26, 2005, 76–86.

4. Dave Palermo, "The Day Gambling Died," *Biloxi Sun-Herald,* Aug. 23, 1998. Although "never the same," gambling continued in various Gulf Coast establishments long after Kefauver and his committee left. See Deanne Stephens Newer and Greg O'Brien, "Mississippi's Oldest Pastime," in *Resorting to Casinos: The Mississippi Gambling Industry,* ed. Denise von Herrmann (Jackson: University Press of Mississippi, 2006), 11–25.

5. Benjamin Schwarz and Christina Schwarz, "Mississippi Monte Carlo," *Atlantic Monthly* (Jan. 1996), 67–82.

6. Thomas B. Shepherd III and Cheryn L. Netz, "Mississippi," in *International Casino Law,* 3d ed., ed. Anthony N. Cabot, William N. Thompson, Andrew Tottenham, and Carl G. Braunlich (Reno, Nev.: Institute for the Study of Gambling and Commercial Gaming, 1999), 72–91.

7. IGRA's enactment went virtually unnoticed: it received only four mentions in the Lexis-Nexis newspaper database in the year it was passed. Matthew Continetti, *The K Street Gang: The Rise and Fall of the Republican Machine* (New York: Doubleday, 2006), 141.

8. Interview with H. L. "Sonny" Merideth, former representative, Mississippi Legislature, Nov. 1999.

9. Interview with Charlie Williams, representative, Mississippi legislature, Sept. 20, 1999.

10. Interview with Paul Jones, Nov. 5, 1999.

11. Interview with Charlie Williams, Sept. 20, 1999.

12. Ronald Smothers, "Riverboat Gambling Gets a Chance in Mississippi," *New York Times,* Dec. 4, 1990.

13. The model for this procedure was the 1966 repeal of Mississippi's prohibition on the sale of alcoholic beverages, in which the adoption of a local-option approach had secured an otherwise-unobtainable majority for passage.

14. John Branston, "Against All Odds," *Memphis,* Sept. 1997, 34.

15. National Gambling Impact Study Commission, *Final Report* (Washington, D.C.: U.S. Government Printing Office, 1999), chap. 3.

16. Terry R. Cassreino, "Fluke Ignites Phenomenon," *Biloxi Sun Herald*, Mar. 19, 2000.

17. Ibid.; Boyer, "Gone with the Surge"; interview with Ray Mabus, Nov. 5, 1999.

18. Daniel Smith explains the conditions in which legislators will vote contrary to their district's preferences as expressed in statewide ballot measures. Daniel A. Smith, "Homeward Bound?: Micro-level Legislative Responsiveness to Ballot Initiatives," *State Politics and Policy Quarterly* 1 (Spring 2001): 50–61.

19. Paul Barton, "Geography May Doom Mississippi Lottery Law," *Memphis Commercial Appeal*, Jan. 10, 1993.

20. Paul Barton, "Fordice Trumpets Miss. Job Growth," *Memphis Commercial Appeal*, Dec. 28, 1992; Barton, "Geography May Doom Mississippi Lottery Law," *Memphis Commercial Appeal*, Jan. 10, 1993.

21. Terry R. Cassreino, "State Lottery No Closer to Reality," *Biloxi Sun-Herald*, Aug. 21, 2000; Lora Hines, "Odds Against Miss. Lottery," *Jackson Clarion-Ledger*, Jan. 26, 2004.

22. Richard McGowan, "Lotteries and State Government: A Consistent Partner or a Stepping Stone for More Gambling," Testimony before the National Gambling Impact Study Commission, Mar. 17, 1998, p. 2. A copy of this testimony was given to the authors.

23. See, e.g., Charles T. Clotfelter and Philip J. Cook, *Selling Hope: State Lotteries in America* (Cambridge, Mass.: Harvard University Press, 1989).

24. See, notably, John Dombrink and William N. Thompson, *The Last Resort: Success and Failure in Campaigns for Casinos* (Reno: University of Nevada Press, 1990).

25. Louisiana enacted a lottery in 1990. Tennessee did not do so until 2003. See chapters 7 and 5 in this book.

26. Branston, "Against All Odds," 34.

27. In practice, only the Tunica and Gulf Coast casinos have attracted extensive out-of-state business. Denise von Herrmann, "Were Casinos a Solution for State Economic Growth?" in *Resorting to Casinos*, ed. Von Herrmann, 67–80. Interview with Merideth, Nov. 4, 1999.

28. Reed Branson, "Judge Slaps Ban on Miss. Bingo," *Memphis Commercial Appeal*, Apr. 28, 1990.

29. Myra Humphries, "Court Rules Bingo Legal in Mississippi, Calls for Controls," *Memphis Commercial Appeal*, Dec. 22, 1990; Tom Charlier, "Track Tried To Halt OK for Casinos," *Memphis Commercial Appeal*, Oct. 18, 1992.

30. Associated Press State and Local Wire, "Mississippi Casinos Have Lobbyist Fighting Video Gaming for Dog Tracks," LexisNexis, Apr. 9, 1999; Richard Locker, "Casino Lobbyists Fight Lottery, *Memphis Commercial Appeal*, Feb. 7, 2001.

31. Interview with Paul Jones, Nov. 5, 1999.

32. Reed Branson, "Issaquena Says Yes to Riverboat Gambling," *Memphis Commercial Appeal*, Mar. 27, 1991.

33. William C. Baynes, "Rose Says Rival Backs Casino Foes in DeSoto," *Memphis Commercial Appeal*, Nov. 1, 1992; Laurel Campbell, "Tunica Casinos Have High Stakes in DeSoto Vote," *Memphis Commercial Appeal*, Nov. 2, 1996.

34. Joint Committee on Performance Evaluation and Expenditure Review, *Report on the Adequacy of the Mississippi Gaming Commission's Regulation of Legalized Gambling in Mississippi*. Goodman's book is *The Luck Business: The Devastating Consequences and Broken Promises of America's Gambling Explosion* (New York: Free Press, 1995).

35. Bartholomew Sullivan, "Gaming Regulators Prefer a Light Touch," *Memphis Commercial Appeal*, Oct. 20, 1997; Reed Branson, "Gambling Regulators in Miss. Defend Task as Boosters," *Memphis Commercial Appeal*, Aug. 16, 1996; Gina Holland, "State's Casinos See Bright Future," *Biloxi Sun-Herald*, Sept. 10, 1999; Dave Palermo, "Casinos to Examine Free-Drinks Policy," *Biloxi Sun-Herald*, Oct. 26, 2000; Joint Committee on Performance Evaluation and Expenditure Review, Mississippi Legislature, *A Management Review of the Mississippi Gaming Commission*.

36. In 2006, for example, Mississippi Gaming Commission chair Jerry St. Pé declared, "We have a duty and a responsibility to honor our partnership with the private gaming industry. Tom Wilemon, "Choctaw Casino Debated," *Biloxi Sun-Herald*, May 19, 2006.

37. Geoff Pender, "Bill Would Shift Control of Casinos' Tax Bills," *Biloxi Sun-Herald*, Mar. 12, 2004.

38. Reed Branson, "Gambling: Miss. Casinos Bet on Unity to Sway Laws," *Memphis Commercial Appeal*, Sept. 10, 1997.

39. Interview with Gary Burhop, vice president, Harrah's Entertainment, Mar. 25, 1999; Dave Palermo, "Casinos Ask Santa for Favorable Legislation," *Biloxi Sun-Herald*, Dec. 24, 2000.

40. Lisa Monti, "Anti-Gambling Group Wants Vote to Go Statewide," *Biloxi Sun-Herald*, July 5, 1998.

41. African American legislators, fearing the laws that a white majority of Mississippi voters might enact, lobbied hard to make the initiative process difficult to employ. According to Black Caucus leader George Flagg, "It would be so hard to use, it isn't any good." Paul Barton, "Miss. To Weigh New Voters Powers," *Memphis Commercial Appeal*, Oct. 28, 1992. The residency requirement for petition gatherers was added by constitutional amendment in 1998.

42. Bartholomew Sullivan, "3 in Gov. Race Say Gaming 'Here to Stay,'" *Memphis Commercial Appeal*, Feb. 10, 1999; Dave Palermo, "Official: Ban Would Chill Wall Street," *Biloxi Sun-Herald*, Aug. 5, 1998; Terry R. Cassreino, "Fordice Opposes Gambling Ban," *Biloxi Sun-Herald*, July 23, 1998.

43. Kim Masters Evans, *Gambling: What's at Stake?* (Farmington Hills, Mich.: Gale Group, 2003), 55; Oliver Staley, "Tunica Hears a Distant Shuffle," *Memphis Commercial Appeal*, Aug. 21, 2004.

44. Staley, "Tunica Hears a Distant Shuffle"; Edward Walsh, "Two Sides of Casinos' Coin," *Washington Post*, July 12, 1998.

45. "Miss. Senate Rejects Compromise Casino-Sitting Bill," *Memphis Commercial Appeal*, Mar. 31, 1993; Sarah C. Campbell, "Lawmakers Not Keen on New Casinos for Miss.," *Memphis Commercial Appeal*, Jan. 2, 1994; Jack Elliott Jr., "High Court Reverses Casino Ruling," *Biloxi Sun-Herald*, Nov. 2, 2001.

46. Reed Branson, "Miss. Forces New Casinos to Make Big Land Investment," *Memphis Commercial Appeal*, Jan. 22, 1999.

47. Terry R. Cassreino, "Casino Education Bill Falls," *Biloxi Sun-Herald*, Jan. 14, 1999; Oliver Staley, "Casino-Business Classes Urged," *Memphis Commercial Appeal*, Apr. 12, 2004.

48. "Casino Management Courses Still Set for USM Gulf Coast," *Biloxi Sun-Herald,* Sept. 26, 2005.

49. Oliver Staley, "Gulf Casinos in Eye of Storm Recovery," *Memphis Commercial Appeal,* Sept. 28, 2005; Staley, "Casinos on Hold," *Memphis Commercial Appeal,* Sept. 29, 2005; Staley, "Katrina Aftermath Raises Storm of Discussion over Mississippi Casinos," *Memphis Commercial Appeal,* Sept. 14, 2005; Keith O'Brien, "Gulf Coast Casinos Six Feet Over," *Boston Globe,* Feb. 26, 2006.

50. Denise von Hermann, *Gaming in Mississippi: The Present and the Future,* report prepared for the Mississippi Gulf Coast Economic Development Commission by the University of Southern Mississippi-Gulf Coast, Mar. 15, 2002; Associated Press State and Local Wire, "Barbour Says Raising Miss. Casino Tax Foolish," LexisNexis, May 4, 2006.

51. The Mississippi Choctaws are often singled out for praise of their "exemplary tribal economic diversification." Steven Andrew Light and Kathryn R. L. Rand, *Indian Gaming and Tribal Sovereignty: The Casino Compromise* (Lawrence: University Press of Kansas, 2005), 103.

52. Dave Palermo, "Gaming Money Flows to Elections," *Biloxi Sun-Herald,* Sept. 24, 2000.

53. U.S. Senate, Committee on Indian Affairs, *"Gimme Five"—Investigation of Tribal Lobbying Matters: Final Report* (June 22, 2006), part 1, chap. 1.

54. The ties between Reed, Abramoff, and Americans for Tax Reform head Grover Norquist were forged during Abramoff's chairmanship of College Republicans during the mid-1980s. Continetti, *The K Street Gang,* chap. 1.

55. A U.S. Senate hearing in June 2005 revealed, however, that Abramoff and his associate, Michael Scanlon, withheld for themselves as much as $6.5 million of the $7.7 million they received from the Choctaws. Susan Schmidt and James V. Grimaldi, "Panel Says Abramoff Laundered Tribal Funds," *Washington Post,* June 23, 2005.

56. U.S. Senate, Committee on Indian Affairs, *"Gimme Five."*

## Chapter 2

1. Interview with Jack Black, president, Old Hickory House, July 8, 1999. Jack Black was one of the original seventeen investors in Atlanta International Racing.

2. Although pari-mutuel betting was never allowed in Georgia, automobile racing at the Henry County facility, now called the Atlanta Motor Speedway, grew in popularity.

3. UPI Regional News, "Gambling Raid Nets Arrest and Evidence," LexisNexis, Nov. 9, 1983.

4. Interview with Bill Shipp, editor, *Bill Shipp's Georgia,* June 8, 1999.

5. W. Lowry Anderson, "Zell Miller Affirms Gaming Stance," *Christian Index,* Jan. 16, 1975.

6. John J. Dinan, *The American State Constitutional Tradition* (Lawrence: University Press of Kansas, 2006), chap. 2, p. 44; Zell Miller, *A National Party No More: The Conscience of a Conservative Democrat* (Atlanta: Stroud and Hall Publishing, 2003), 40.

7. The chairman of the Industry Committee was Sonny Watson, an outspoken proponent of the lottery and an ally of Miller. The do-not-pass recommendation destroyed any realistic chance of the lottery bill passing because the General Assembly almost always accepts such recommendations.

8. Deborah Scroggins, "Lottery Helps Voters Define Candidates," *Atlanta Journal and Constitution*, June 17, 1990; Jim Barber, "Lottery's Luck Runs Out," UPI Regional News, LexisNexis, Feb. 1, 1990.

9. UPI Regional News, "Two Arrested for Allegedly Selling Florida Lottery Tickets," LexisNexis, Aug. 20, 1990

10. Al Cross, "Wilkinson Camp Holds Fund-raiser for Georgian," *Courier-Journal*, Dec. 6, 1989; "Miller Says His Gamble on Lottery Proposal Will Pay Off on Election Day," *Atlanta Constitution*, Jan. 20, 1990.

11. Miller, *A National Party No More*, 42; Charles Walston, "Top Contender Has Political Connections," *Atlanta Constitution*, Mar. 23, 1993.

12. Betsy White, "Educators May Oppose Lottery," *Atlanta Constitution*, June 29, 1990.

13. Polls showed that support for a lottery for education ran between 70 and 75 percent of the electorate. Bill Shipp, "Why I Believe Zell Miller Will Be Georgia's Next Governor," *Bill Shipp's Georgia*, Apr. 23, 1990.

14. Michael Barone and Grant Ujifosa, *The Almanac of American Politics 1992* (Washington, D.C.: National Journal, 1992), 296; Charles Walston, "Lottery a Sure Thing for Some," *Atlanta Journal*, Jan. 27, 1991.

15. Bill Shipp, "Zell's Attack Campaign Indicates He's Still Fearful of Johnny's Sting," *Bill Ship's Georgia*, Oct. 15, 1990.

16. Barone and Ujifosa, *Almanac of American Politics 1992*, 296; Charles Walston, "Miller Gambles on Lucky 7s with a Pair of Gambling Bills," *Atlanta Journal*, Jan. 14, 1991.

17. Quoted in Miller, *A National Party No More*, 47.

18. Bill Shipp, "Lottery Who's Who: Reputations, Big $$ Riding on Lottery," *Bill Shipp's Georgia*, Feb. 4, 1991.

19. Mark Sherman, "Miller Spells Out Education Lottery Plan," *Atlanta Journal and Constitution*, Nov. 15, 2001; Charles Walston, "Voters to Decide Lottery in 2002," *Atlanta Journal and Constitution*, Feb. 9, 1991; Walston, "Lottery Fight Ready to Proceed," *Atlanta Constitution*, May 7, 1992.

20. Bill Shipp, "Hold Still Little Bill, All I'm Gonna Do Is Gut You," *Bill Shipp's Georgia*, Feb. 17, 1992.

21 Andy Sher, "Florida Key to Miller's Lottery Push," *Chattanooga Times*, Oct. 27, 1992; Charles Walston, "Election '92: The Lottery," *Atlanta Journal and Constitution*, Oct. 27, 1992.

22. Walston, "Election '92: The Lottery"; Charles Walston, "Miller: Preschool Needs Lottery," *Atlanta Journal and Constitution*, Sept. 9, 1992.

23. David C. Garrett, III, "Election '92: Debating the Amendments, Amendment 1: Should the State Operate a Lottery? Yes," *Atlanta Journal and Constitution*, Nov. 1, 1992.

24. Walston, "Election '92: The Lottery"; Bill Shipp, "The Georgia Lottery: Will Georgia Become First State to Reject Lottery?" *Bill Shipp's Georgia*, Nov. 2, 1992; Charles Walston, "Action's Heavy on Gambling Bills During Assembly," *Atlanta Journal*, Feb. 25, 1991.

25. Interview with William T. Neal, editor, *Christian Index*, July 12, 1999; David Beasley and Gayle White, "Urban Vote May Have Boost State Lottery to Close Win," *Atlanta Journal and Constitution*, Nov. 4, 1992.

26. Charles Walston, "Taking Chances? Push to Meet Lottery Startup Date Raises Concerns," *Atlanta Journal and Constitution*, Apr. 25, 1993.

27. Bill Shipp, "If Money Won't Work, What Will?" *Atlanta Journal and Constitution*, Sept. 11, 1993; Betsy White, "The Georgia Lottery: Let the Games Begin," *Atlanta Journal and Constitution*, June 27, 1993.

28. Ken Foskett, "What'll Give Miller a Win? Lotto Votes," *Atlanta Journal and Constitution*, Nov. 5, 1994.

29. Peter Mantius, "The Georgia Lottery," *Atlanta Journal and Constitution*, June 28, 1998; Joseph McCrary and Thomas J. Pavlak, *Who Plays the Georgia Lottery?* (Athens: Carl Vinson Institute of Government, University of Georgia, 2000), 1; "Lottery's Success Silencing Critics," *Macon Telegraph*, May 24, 1998.

30. Tony Hefferman, "House OKs Limits on Lottery Funds," *Macon Telegraph*, Feb. 27, 1998; Andy Peters, "GOP Candidate Says He Will Seek Amendment to Protect Money," *Macon Telegraph*, Oct. 10, 2002.

31. Doug Cummings, "Clinton Goal: National HOPE," *Atlanta Constitution*, Feb. 5, 1997; Mantius, "The Georgia Lottery."

32. James Salzer and Andrea Jones, "Tightened HOPE Grading Expected," *Atlanta Journal and Constitution*, Nov. 12, 2003; James Salzer, "Holding on to HOPE," *Atlanta Journal and Constitution*, Nov. 11, 2003.

33. James Salzer, "Schools Win from Lottery," *Atlanta Journal and Constitution*, Aug. 13, 2000.

34. Joseph McCrary and Stephen E. Condrey, "The Georgia Lottery: Assessing Its Administrative, Economic, and Political Effects," *Review of Policy Research* 20 (Dec. 2003): 691–712; Joseph McCrary et al., *The Georgia Lottery: Participation, Revenue Generation, and Benefit Distribution* (Athens: Carl Vinson Institute of Government, University of Georgia, 2001), 3; Andy Peters, "Where Has All the HOPE Gone?" *Macon Telegraph*, Dec. 14, 2003.

35. Jay Croft, "Keeping HOPE Tougher Than Qualifying for It," *Atlanta Journal and Constitution*, Dec. 30, 1999; James Salzer, "Board Takes HOPE Rules Off the Table," *Atlanta Constitution*, Dec. 14, 2000.

36. James Salzer, "When HOPE Is Not Enough," *Atlanta Constitution*, Feb. 13, 2001.

37. McCrary and Condrey, "The Georgia Lottery"; David Firestone, "Free-Tuition Program Transforms a University," *New York Times*, Feb. 1, 2001.

38. Will Potter, "Georgia Program May Run Out of Cash," *Chronicle of Higher Education*, Sept. 12, 2003; Jeffrey Selingo, "Hope Wanes for Georgia's Merit-Based Scholarships," *Chronicle of Higher Education*, Nov. 21, 2003; James Salzer, "Democrats to Fight HOPE Link to SAT," *Atlanta Journal and Constitution*, Sept. 29, 2003; and Andy Peters, "Panel Suggests Changes to HOPE," *Macon Telegraph*, Nov. 14, 2003.

39. James Salzer, "HOPE Won't Include SAT Plan," *Atlanta Journal and Constitution*, Jan. 13, 2004; Salzer, "HOPE Book, Fee Payments Likely Saved—For Now," *Atlanta Journal and Constitution*, Mar. 5, 2004.

40. James Salzer, "HOPE Fee, Book Funds Look Secure," *Atlanta Journal and Constitution*, Feb. 26, 2004; Nancy Badertscher, "HOPE Scholarships: Rescue Plan Worked Out," *Atlanta Journal-Constitution*, Apr. 8, 2004.

41. The Senate voted 35 to 20 to approve Perdue's amendment on February 2, 2006, and the House for the amendment by 102 to 68 on March 13, with both chambers voting largely along party lines. James Salzer, "Perdue Offers Amendment to Shield HOPE," *Atlanta Journal and Constitution*, June 24, 2005; Doug Gross, "Taylor: Require Public Vote before Cutting HOPE," Associated Press State and Local Wire, LexisNexis, Jan. 30, 2006; Brandon Larrabee, "Senate Slows Plan for 'HOPE Chest,'" *Augusta Chronicle*, Feb. 3, 2006; Brandon Larrabee and Vicky Eckenrode, "Governor's Initiatives Fall Short," *Augusta Chronicle*, Mar. 14, 2006.

42. Lucy Soto, "Video Gambling May Soon Hit Georgia Jackpot," *Atlanta Constitution*, Oct. 9, 2000; Don Schanche Jr., "Critics: State Law Protects Billion-Dollar Industry," *Macon Telegraph*, May 13, 2001.

43. Don Schanche Jr., "Video Poker Machines Flourishing All Around State," *Macon Telegraph*, May 14, 2001; and Don Schanche Jr., "Senate OKs Barnes' Ban on Video Gambling," *Macon Telegraph*, Aug. 29, 2001.

44. Jim Wooten, "'Law Has Loopholes," *Atlanta Journal*, June 13, 2001; and Don Schanche Jr., "A Web War on Gambling," *Macon Telegraph*, Sept. 2, 2001; Soto, "Video Gambling May Soon Hit Ga. Jackpot."

45. Rhonda Cook, "House Folds Hand on Video Poker Law," *Atlanta Constitution*, Mar. 23, 2001.

46. James Salzer, "Christian Coalition Wants Poker Bill in Special Session," *Atlanta Constitution*, July 27, 2001.

47. Don Schanche Jr., "Barnes Calls for Ban on Video Gambling," *Macon Telegraph*, Aug. 22, 2001; "State Businesses Differ on Effects of a Video Gambling Ban," *Macon Telegraph*, Aug. 26, 2001; "Barnes Pressures House to Approve Video Gambling Ban," *Macon Telegraph*, Aug. 30, 2001.

48. Wayne C. Wehunt, "House Bans Video Poker," *Columbus Ledger-Enquirer*, Sept. 7, 2001; Don Schanche Jr., "House Lawmakers Vote to Ban Video Gambling," *Macon Telegraph*, Sept. 7, 2001; Don Schanche Jr. and Andy Peters, "Court: Gambling Ban OK," *Macon Telegraph*, May 29, 2002.

49. Brian Basinger, "Leaders Urged to Bet on Casinos," *Augusta Chronicle*, Nov. 9, 2003.

## Chapter 3

1. The prohibition was carried forward in the 1895 constitution, which governs the state today.

2. A second exception, for casino gambling on ships cruising at least three miles offshore, was made through inaction. Congress voted in 1992 to allow such gambling but gave each coastal state permission to ban the so-called cruises to nowhere from its waters. Despite repeated efforts by Republicans in South Carolina's House of Representatives to enact such a ban, influential senators from the port city of Charleston have blocked the state from acting. A compromise measure was enacted in 2005 to allow each county to decide the matter for itself.

3. Interview with John Scott, June 8, 2001.

4. Glen T. Broach and Lee Bandy, "South Carolina: A Decade of Rapid Republican Ascent," in *Southern Politics in the 1990s*, ed. Alexander P. Lamis (Baton Rouge: Louisiana State University Press, 1999), 50–80.

5. Ibid.

6. Pinball gambling machines that were illegal under state law were so widespread around South Carolina in the early 1970s that the state ranked third behind Nevada and Tennessee in the number of federal gambling stamps, which are issued to machines that can make cash payoffs. R. Randall Bridwell and Frank L. Quinn, "From Mad Joy to Misfortune: The Merger of Law and Politics in the World of Gambling," *Mississippi Law Journal* 72:573.

7. Bridwell and Quinn, "From Mad Joy to Misfortune," 575–79.

8. Reluctantly, the state supreme court agreed that what the machine operators were doing was consistent with the Lindsay amendment; see *State v. Blackmon* (1991).

9. David Palermo, "The Secret Slot Market," *International Gaming and Wagering Business* (Dec. 1998), 1, 18–22.

10. Bridwell and Quinn, "From Mad Joy to Misfortune," 583.

11. John Monk, "Ban Gets Credit for Steep Drop in Gambling Addicts," *State*, May 20, 2003.

12. "Odds not in favor of SC Lottery," *Rock Hill Herald*, Feb. 1, 1996.

13. Interview with Kevin Geddings, June 7, 2001.

14. Schuyler Kropf, "Poll Brings Bad News on Bridge," *Charleston Post and Courier*, Dec. 19, 1997.

15. Broach and Bandy, "South Carolina."

16. Jim Drinkard and William M. Welch, "Gambling Industry Ups the Ante in Politics," *USA Today*, Jan. 8, 1999.

17. Associated Press State and Local Wire, "Beasley, Hodges Square Off on Lottery, Gambling," LexisNexis, Oct. 27, 1998.

18. Tim Smith, "Collins Says He Hasn't Played," *Greenville News*, June 5, 2003.

19. Video of political ads compiled and supplied by Kevin Geddings, June 7, 2001.

20. Sid Gaulden, "Beasley Won't Fight Lottery Vote," *Charleston Post and Courier*, Sept. 29, 1998.

21. Michael Sponhour, "South Carolina Republicans Back Lottery Vote," *State*, Jan. 21, 1999.

22. Associated Press State and Local Wire, "Federal Study Points to South Carolina as Example of Video Gambling Gone Wrong," LexisNexis, June 18, 1999.

23. "Churches Enlist a Christian Army Against Video Poker," *Charleston Post and Courier*, Aug. 8, 1999; "New Foes for Video Poker," *Charleston Post and Courier*, Sept. 24, 1999.

24. Associated Press State and Local Wire, "Reverend Says Video Gambling Needs to be Fought on Many Levels," LexisNexus, Aug. 14, 1999.

25. Sarah O'Donnell, "Chamber Money to Back 'No' Vote," *Rock Hill Herald*, Oct. 3, 1999.

26. Sarah O'Donnell, "S.C. Poll: Ban Video Poker," *Rock Hill Herald*, Sept. 26, 1999.

27. Schuyler Kropf, "Video Poker Ruling Spotlights Voter's Limited Voice," *Charleston Post and Courier*, Oct. 25, 1999.

28. Essentially, but not entirely. For example, in 1993 the South of the Border entertainment complex that spans the North Carolina–South Carolina border along Interstate 95 was found guilty of letting gamblers play video poker on the North Carolina side and cash their winning

tickets on the South Carolina side. "Pedroland Pleads Guilty to Illegal Gambling," *State*, June 20, 2000.

29. Interview with Kevin Geddings, June 7, 2001.

30. Ibid.

31. "Governor Builds Lottery War Chest," *Rock Hill Herald*, Apr. 12, 2000.

32. Aaron Sheinin, "Lottery: Caucus Still Split; 'Bubba' is Back," *State*, Oct. 13, 2000.

33. "Lottery Ads Feature Bush Impersonator," *State*, Oct. 31, 2000.

34. Schuyler Kropf, "Bush Avoids S.C. Issues on Stump in Low Country," *Charleston Post and Courier*, Aug. 26, 1999.

35. Bill Swindell, "Hodges' Lottery Plan Sits in Committee," *Charleston Post and Courier*, Apr. 4, 2000; Seanna Adcox, "Lottery Stirring Controversy Already," *Rock Hill Herald*, May 30, 2000.

36. Gene Crider, "Lottery Groups Gear up for Vote," *Rock Hill Herald*, July 17, 2000.

37. Kevin Geddings, memo to himself, supplied to authors, June 7, 2001.

38. Video of political ads compiled and supplied by Kevin Geddings, June 7, 2001.

39. Memo supplied by Kevin Geddings, June 7, 2001.

40. Seanna Adcox, "Lottery a High-Stakes Numbers Game," *Rock Hill Herald*, July 30, 2000.

41. Clif LeBlanc, "Lottery Foes Question Hodges' Fund Raising," *State*, Oct. 27, 2000.

42. Aaron Sheinin, "Voting 'yes' for lottery turns next decisions to legislature," *State*, Sept. 3, 2000; interview with Kathy Bigham, June 7, 2001.

43. Interview with Jim Ritchie, June 7, 2001.

44. Conforming to the Administrative Procedures Act and Procurement Code means that the lottery commission, like all other state agencies, must report to the legislature about its decisions, policies, finances, staffing, and so on.

45. Interview with Scott Richardson, June 7, 2001.

46. Paul Alongi, "Law Prohibits Multistate Lottery Game," *Greenville News*, Aug. 22, 2001; Aaron Sheinen, "Senator Can Vie for Lottery Post," *State*, July 25, 2001.

47. Jason Zacher, "Peeler Suggests Using Lottery for New Buses," *Greenville News*, Oct. 25, 2001; Mary-Kathryn Craft, "S.C. Students Have More Scholarships Available," *Myrtle Beach Sun*, Oct. 12, 2001; Anna Simon, "Lottery Money May Help Research," *Greenville News*, Oct. 9, 2001; "Jackson: Use Lottery to Aid Black Colleges," *State*, Feb. 24, 2002.

48. James T. Hammond, "Scholarships Benefit from Lottery Plan," *Greenville News*, Mar. 1, 2002.

49. James T. Hammond, "House OKs More Lottery Cash for K-12," *Greenville News*, Mar. 15, 2002.

50. Jeff Stensland, "Lottery Fuels Scholarship Debate," *State*, July 28, 2002. In November 2002, a study by the state lottery commission found that the typical lottery player was a middle-aged black man with a high school education and an annual income of $10,000 to $39,000. Aaron Sheinin, "Portrait of Lottery Player: Black, Male, Under 55," *State*, Nov. 27, 2002.

51. "Lawmakers Raiding Lottery," *Rock Hill Herald*, May 3, 2004; Allison L. Bruce, "Lottery Funds Stir Concerns," *Charleston Post and Courier*, July 27, 2004; Jeff Stensland, "N.C. Senate Approves Lottery," *State*, Aug. 31, 2005; John O'Connor, "Lottery Sales Remain Robust," *State*, July 16, 2006.

52. Andrew Dys, "Does State Law Trump Catawba Settlement?" *Rock Hill Herald,* Sept. 26, 2003.

53. Andrew Dys, "Catawba Indian Nation Eyes Santee Bingo Hall," *Rock Hill Herald,* Sept. 25, 2003.

54. John Monk, "Catawbas Play Video Poker Card," *State,* Sept. 24, 2003; Brian Hicks, "Catawba Indian Nation vs. State of South Carolina," *Charleston Post and Courier,* Dec. 14, 2003.

55. Clif LeBlanc, "Catawba Tribe Sues for Right to Offer Video Poker in South Carolina," *State,* May 6, 2004; Meg Kinnard, "Judge Upholds Order Allowing Catawbas to Operate Video Poker," Associated Press State and Local Wire, LexisNexis, Jan. 6, 2006; Seanna Adcox, "Bill Would Let Catawbas Operate More Bingo," Associated Press State and Local Wire, LexisNexis, Feb. 16, 2006.

56. This is one of several factors that help explain why South Carolina has not given serious consideration to legalizing commercial casinos.

57. John Lyman Mason and Michael Nelson, *Governing Gambling: Politics and Policy in State, Tribe, and Nation* (Washington, D.C.: Brookings Institution, 2000), chap. 2.

## Chapter 4

1. Michael Barone, *Almanac of American Politics* (Washington, D.C.: National Journal, 1994); J. David Woodard, *The New Southern Politics* (Boulder, Colo.: Lynne Rienner, 2006), 341.

2. The Birmingham facility originally was authorized to open as a horse track in 1984. After failing to operate profitably, it was converted to dog racing in 1992.

3. The second was Virginia in 1987.

4. Interview with Rick Dent, Nov. 20, 2001. The more prevalent interpretation is plausible: Don Siegelman had won three previous statewide elections.

5. Michael Wilson, "Tracks Cited Revenue Decline in Push for Video Poker," Associated Press State and Local Wire, LexisNexis, Mar. 16, 1999.

6. Interview with Milo Dakin, Nov. 8, 2001.

7. Ibid.

8. Denise von Herrmann, *The Big Gamble: The Politics of Lottery and Casino Expansion* (Westport, Conn.: Praeger, 2002), 50, 54.

9. Interview with Rep. John Rogers, Nov. 9, 2001.

10. *National Gaming Summary,* Mar. 30, 1998.

11. Von Herrmann, *The Big Gamble,* 54–55; interview with Rick Dent, Nov. 20, 2001.

12. Interview with Rick Dent, Nov. 20, 2001.

13. Ibid.

14. "James' latest scholarship plan draws criticism," *Anniston Star,* Aug. 13, 1998.

15. Buster Kantrow and Sean Reilly, "Exit Polls Showed Siegelman Won Vast Majority of Black Vote," *Mobile Register,* Nov. 4, 1998; Tim Pryor, "Siegelman, James travel state on last hurrah before vote," *Anniston Star,* Nov. 3, 1998; Richard Coe, "Voters Cool Off the Vocal Right, Move to Center," *Anniston Star,* Nov. 4, 1998.

16. "Black Caucus Begins Making Demands on Siegelman after Helping to Deliver Victory," *Anniston Star,* Nov. 5, 1998.

17. Michael Barone, *Almanac of American Politics* (Washington, D.C.: National Journal, 2000), 70; Tim Pryor, "It's Gov. Siegelman," *Anniston Star,* Nov. 4, 1998.

18. Bill Poovey, "Former Georgia Governor Not Planning to Advise Siegelman on Lottery," Associated Press State and Local Wire, LexisNexis, Jan. 19, 1999; Phillip Rawls, "Jimmy Buffet, Zell Miller to Participate in Siegelman's Inauguration," Associated Press State and Local Wire, LexisNexis, Jan. 9, 1999; Tim Pryor, "Siegelman: Lottery Needed to Improve Schools, Pay Tuition," *Anniston Star,* Jan. 19, 1999.

19. John Lyman Mason and Michael Nelson, *Governing Gambling* (Washington, D.C.: Brookings Institution Press, 2001).

20. Phillip Rawls, "College Presidents Supporting Lottery in Legislature," Associated Press State and Local Wire, LexisNexis, Feb. 24, 1999; Charles T. Clotfelter and Philip J. Cook, *Selling Hope: State Lotteries in America* (Cambridge, Mass.: Harvard University Press, 1989).

21. "Poll: More than 75 Percent in State Want Vote on Lottery," *Anniston Star,* Feb. 8, 1999; David White, "Lottery Dominates Siegelman's Address," *Birmingham News,* Mar. 3, 1999; "House to Let Public Vote on Lottery Amendment," *Anniston Star,* Mar. 10, 1999.

22. Bill Poovey, "Gambling Opponents Counting on Alabama Senate to Block Lottery, Video Poker," Associated Press State and Local Wire, LexisNexis, Mar. 24, 1999.

23. The dispute pitted Lt. Gov. Steve Windom, twelve Republican senators, and five Democratic senators against Governor Siegelman and eighteen Democratic senators. What had to be resolved was how much power the state's lieutenant governor has in determining committee assignments and chairmanships. The arguments concerning such powers were all the more complicated given that the majority of the Senate was Democratic and Windom is a Republican. Phillip Rawls, "Lt. Gov. Gets Restroom Break as Senate Talks Compromise," Associated Press State and Local Wire, LexisNexis, Mar. 29, 1999.

24. Democrats voted 47 to 18 *aye;* Republicans voted 2 to 30 *nay.* Associated Press State and Local Wire, "House Roll Call—Video Poker," LexisNexis, Mar. 24, 1999.

25. Bill Poovey, "Video Poker Bill May Affect Odds on Passage of Proposed Lottery," Associated Press State and Local Wire, Mar. 22, 1999; Poovey, "Pryor: Bill Would Not Restrict Video Poker Machines to Dog Tracks," Associated Press State and Local Wire, LexisNexis, Apr. 9, 1999.

26. Mike Williams, "Despite Loud Protests, Alabamians to Vote on Lottery," *Atlanta Constitution,* Apr. 15, 1999; Tim Pryor, "Senators Have Their Say about the Lottery," *Anniston Star,* Apr. 14, 1999.

27. Interview with Rick Dent, Nov. 20, 2001.

28. David White, "Senate Approves Lottery Voters Will Give Final Verdict on Plan in Special Election," *Birmingham News,* Apr. 15, 1999.

29. U.S. Senate, Committee on Indian Affairs, *"Gimme Five"—Investigation of Tribal Lobbying Matters: Final Report* (June 22, 2006), part 1, chap. 1.

30. "Video Gaming Bill Stumbles at Senate Gate," *Anniston Star,* Apr. 16, 1999; Bill Poovey, "Demise of Video Poker Could Be Bad News for Lottery," Associated Press State and Local, LexisNexis, Apr. 17, 1999.

31. Interview with Rick Dent, Nov. 20, 2001.

32. Sean Reilly, "Panel Votes to Let Siegelman Set Up Standards for Lottery Scholarships," *Mobile Register,* May 13, 1999; Tim Pryor, "Piece of the Pie: Convenience Stores Want Larger Share of Lottery Money," *Anniston Star,* Apr. 23, 1999.

33. Paul M. Johnson, "Education, Gambling and the Churches: Religious Denominationalism and Voter Mobilization Patterns in the 1999 Alabama Lottery Referendum," paper presented at the Citadel Conference on Southern Politics, Charleston, S.C., Mar. 3, 2000.

34. Interview with Rick Dent, Nov. 20, 2001.

35. "Poll Shows Statewide Lottery Support," *Anniston Star,* Aug. 30, 1999; Brett J. Blackridge and Kim Chandler, "Lottery Effort Haunts Siegelman Grand Jury," *Birmingham News,* June 27, 2004; Kim Chandler, "Siegelman, Scrushy Guilty of Bribery," *Birmingham News,* June 30, 2006.

36. "State AG Says Anti-lottery Videos OK," *Anniston Star,* Oct. 24, 1999; "State's Economy Becoming Part of Lottery Debate," *Anniston Star,* Oct. 28, 1999.

37. Interview with Joe Bob Mizzell, Nov. 8, 2001.

38. Phillip Rawls, "Could Lottery Become Political Powerhouse? Windom Says Yes; Siegelman No," Associated Press State and Local Wire, LexisNexis, Oct. 4, 1999.

39. Interview with John Rogers, Nov. 9, 2001; Robin DeMonie, "Rogers: Lottery Plan Not Fair," *Birmingham News,* Aug. 13, 1999.

40. Interview with Joe Bob Mizzell, Nov. 8, 2001.

41. Bob Johnson, "Anti-Tax Group President Says He Gave Indian Money to Christian Coalition," Associated Press, LexisNexis, May 13, 2005. According to Grover Norquist, the head of Americans for Tax Reform, CALL did not know that the money came from the tribe. See also U.S. Senate, *"Gimme Five."*

42. Interview with Jim Cooper, Nov. 15, 2001.

43. John Anderson, "Lottery Support Starting to Shrink," *Huntsville Times,* Oct. 3, 1999.

44. John Peck, "Anti-lottery Group Pounces on Scandal, but Fallout Unknown," *Huntsville Times,* Oct. 3, 1999; Rawls, "Could Lottery Become Political Powerhouse?"; Johnson, "Education, Gambling and the Churches"; interview with Rick Dent, Nov. 20, 2001.

45. Johnson, "Education, Gambling and the Churches"; William Rabb, "Siegelman Faces Other Important Issues," *Mobile Register,* Oct. 13, 1999.

46. Phillip Rawls, "Video Gambling at Dog Tracks Has Strong Opposition," Associated Press State and Local Wire, LexisNexis, Jan. 31, 2000; Associated Press State and Local Wire, "Poll: Alabama Voters Oppose Video Gambling," LexisNexis, Mar. 21, 2000; Associated Press State and Local Wire, "Anti-gambling Group Reloads to Block Video Poker," LexisNexis, Jan. 23, 2000; Kim Chandler, "Anti-Lottery Groups Got Tribe Money," *Birmingham News,* May 14, 2005; Kim Chandler and Mary Orndorff, "Choctaw, Lobbyist Figure in Cash Trail," *Birmingham News,* June 24, 2005.

47. The Indian Gaming Regulatory Act of 1988 allows tribes to operate bingo-style gambling halls on their lands without regard for the state's policy toward gambling.

48. Mike Cason, "Bill May OK Cash Payments," *Montgomery Advertiser,* Mar. 12, 2003.

49. Phillip Rawls, "Senate Begins Debate on Gambling Bill," Associated Press State and Local Wire, LexisNexis, May 1, 2001; Rawls, "Supreme Court Says Many Video Gambling Machines Unconstitutional," Associated Press State and Local Wire, LexisNexis, Apr. 24, 2001.

50. Phillip Rawls, "Appeals Court Deals Blow to Adult Arcades," Associated Press State and Local Wire, LexisNexis, Dec. 13, 2002.

51. Thanks to Professor Susan Pace Hamill of the University of Alabama Law School for directing our attention to the county amendment procedure, which is outlined in Amendments 425 and 555 of the Alabama constitution. See Hamill, "Constitutional Reform in Alabama: A Necessary Step Toward Achieving a Fair and Efficient Tax Structure," *Cumberland Law Review* 33 (2002–2003): 437–62.

52. "B-Gone Bingo Has No Place in Current Special Session," *Birmingham News,* May 30, 2003.

53. Phillip Rawls, "Legislature's Final Day Could Mix Money, God, Sex, Gambling," Associated Press State and Local Wire, LexisNexis, May 15, 2004.

54. William C. Singleton III, "Race Course Brings New Games to Birmingham," *Birmingham News,* Dec. 15, 2005; Thomas Spencer, "McGregor Betting on His Acumen and Political Wits," *Birmingham News,* June 11, 2006; Eric Velasco, "Judge Rules Race Course Games Legal but a 'Sham,'" *Birmingham News,* Feb. 1, 2006.

55. Bob Johnson, "Siegelman's Performance Top Issue in Democratic Governor's Race," Associated Press State and Local Wire, LexisNexis, May 30, 2002; Associated Press State and Local Wire, "Gambling History Becomes Issue Among Republicans," LexisNexis, May 24, 2002; Phillip Rawls, "Vote Battles Include Celebrities, Nonstop Appearances," Associated Press State and Local Wire, LexisNexis, Nov. 3, 2002. Once again, the Mississippi Choctaws were covertly active in trying to influence Alabama politics in an antigambling direction. They channeled $350,000 to the Riley campaign and an additional $150 million to the Alabama Republican Party through the Republican Governors Association. Mary Orndorff, "Casino Consultant Donated to PAC That Helped Riley," *Birmingham News,* May 5, 2004.

56. Kim Chandler, "Siegelman Stumps on Lottery, Auto Plants," *Birmingham News,* June 5, 2006. Siegelman's campaign was clouded by his simultaneous trial for bribery, fraud, and obstructing justice in connection with funds illegally obtained to support the 1999 lottery referendum. He was found guilty on seven counts by a jury on June 29, 2006, three weeks after the primary.

57. Mike Cason, "Cash Payouts for Gaming Closer," *Montgomery Advertiser,* Mar. 13, 2003; Garry Mitchell, "Creeks, Happy with Bingo Defeat, Seek Compact with Alabama," Associated Press State and Local Wire, LexisNexis, May 20, 2004.

58. Thomas Spencer, "Once Scorned as Indians, Mowa Now Seek Official Status," *Birmingham News,* Jan. 28, 2006.

59. Kent Faulk, "Alabama Pumps Up Tennessee Lottery," *Birmingham News,* Jan. 21, 2005; Bob Johnson, "Siegelman Departs with 'No Regrets' and Says Lottery Not Dead," Associated Press State and Local Wire, LexisNexis, Jan. 10, 2003.

60. Poovey, "Former Georgia Governor."

61. Interview with Rick Dent, Nov. 20, 2001.

62. Larry Powell, "End of the Road," *Birmingham News,* July 9, 2006.

63. Johnson, "Education, Gambling and the Churches."

64. Ibid.

## Chapter 5

1. Interview with Ned McWherter, Jan. 7, 2000.

2. Lewis L. Laska, "The Life and Death of the Lottery in Tennessee, 1787–1836," *Tennessee Historical Quarterly* 45 (1986): 95–118.

3. "Pinball Gambling," *Tennessee Journal,* May 7, 1979; "Pinball Gambling," *Tennessee Journal,* Mar. 14, 1977.

4. Interview with Lamar Alexander, Mar. 1, 2000.

5. Ibid.

6. "Gambling," *Tennessee Journal,* Apr. 30, 1984. In Tennessee, an attorney general's opinion on a constitutional matter carries unusual weight because the attorney general is appointed for a lengthy term by the state supreme court rather than elected by the voters or appointed by the governor.

7. William Lyons, John M. Scheb II, and Billy Stair, *Government and Politics in Tennessee* (Knoxville: University of Tennessee Press, 2001), 51; Philip Ashford, "Alexander Wishes That He Could Veto Lottery, Pay Plan," *Memphis Commercial Appeal,* June 9, 1984.

8. Interview with Lamar Alexander, Mar. 1, 2000.

9. *Secretary of State v. St. Augustine Church / St. Augustine School,* 766 S. W. 2d. 499 (Tennessee 1989).

10. Interview with Roy Herron, Jan. 7, 2000.

11. Interview with Ned McWherter, Jan. 7, 2000.

12. "Horse, Dog Racing," *Tennessee Journal,* Dec. 7, 1981.

13. Interview with Lamar Alexander, Mar. 1, 2000; "Racing," *Tennessee Journal,* Oct. 12, 1987.

14. The Senate deadlocked fifteen to fifteen on a lottery proposal by Cohen in 1989, but the House did not consider the lottery in this period.

15. "Fools Gold / Lottery Is Excuse For Politicians," *Memphis Commercial Appeal,* Oct. 25, 1990; Richard Locker, "Lottery Taxes Heat Up Tepid Governor's Race," *Memphis Commercial Appeal,* Oct. 24, 1990.

16. Richard Locker, "Support Grows For Income Tax Plan," *Memphis Commercial Appeal,* Nov. 3, 1991. The Tennessee Poll is administered by the University of Tennessee.

17. Lyons, Scheb, and Stair, *Government and Politics in Tennessee,* chap. 2.

18. Patti Patterson, "Crime Feared, Tourism Favored, City Poll Finds," *Memphis Commercial Appeal,* Mar. 25, 1993.

19. Philip Ashford and Richard Locker, "Tennessee: A Partisan Bang Amid Quiet Accommodation," in *Southern Politics in the 1990s,* ed. Alexander P. Lamis (Baton Rouge: Louisiana State University Press, 1999), 206–7.

20. Richard Locker, "Some Gambling Is Legal In Tennessee: Games of Pure Chance, However, Need Constitutional Amendment," *Memphis Commercial Appeal,* May 5, 1992; Steve Cohen, "Reforms Would Give Voters Voice, Power On Taxes, and Revive Trust In Government," *Memphis Commercial Appeal,* Feb. 20, 1992.

21. Interview with Steve Cohen, Dec. 16, 1999.

22. M. Lee Smith, "Capitol Commentary," syndicated column, Feb. 21, 1993; copy given to authors by Smith.

23. David Waters, "Moral Ministry Starts Drive Against Lottery," *Memphis Commercial Appeal,* July 2, 1993.

24. Paula Wade, "Most In Tennessee Support Having State-Run Lottery," *Memphis Commercial Appeal,* Nov. 7, 1993.

25. "Methodists Girding To Fight Move To Legalize Lotteries," *Memphis Commercial Appeal,* Dec. 28, 1993.

26. Technically, this modification narrowed rather than broadened the scope of the amendment the General Assembly had voted to approve in 1991 and so was not regarded as a new amendment. The narrowing effect was to assure that after the constitution's lottery ban was lifted, casinos would be constitutionally prohibited everywhere but Memphis.

27. Ironically, Memphis ended up getting the NBA team sought by Nashville after Nashville got the National Football League team sought by Memphis.

28. Video of legislation debates on Apr. 14, 1994, supplied by Steve Cohen.

29. In 2003 Herenton revived his campaign for a constitutional amendment to authorize casino gambling in downtown Memphis. This time Cohen refused to help the mayor pursue what he thought was a politically hopeless cause. "I think it would be more difficult than it would be for me to beat Tiger Woods in a one-on-one golf match" Cohen said. "I foresee the University of Memphis playing in the Rose Bowl sooner," he said on another occasion. Michael Erskine, "Casino in Pyramid 'Far-Fetched,'" *Memphis Commercial Appeal,* Apr. 13, 2003; Blake Fontenay, "Herenton Rolls the Dice for Casinos," *Memphis Commercial Appeal,* Aug. 21, 2003. In 2004 the General Assembly spurned the idea with barely a hearing. "Casino Dreams Cloud Pyramid Future," *Memphis Commercial Appeal,* Feb. 27, 2004.

30. Two economists, Charles Clotfelter and Philip Cook, wrote a book about lotteries which contained a chapter on the spread of lotteries. They identified diffusion as a significant explanatory factor in the increased number of state-operated lotteries between 1964 and 1989. Clotfelter and Cook, *Selling Hope: State Lotteries in America* (Cambridge, Mass.: Harvard University Press, 1989).

31. "Lottery? Governor Keeps His Distance," *Memphis Commercial Appeal,* Sept. 19, 1993; interview with Ned McWherter, Jan. 7, 2000.

32. From 1991 to 1994, support for a lottery in the Tennessee Poll never fell below 70 percent. Lyons, Scheb, and Stair, *Government and Politics in Tennessee,* 214.

33. Interview with Tom Humphrey, Jan. 6, 2000. See also Bill Lewis, "Rocky Bingo History Casts Shadow on Lottery Chance," *Nashville Business Journal,* July 12–16, 1993. Interview with Ned McWherter, Jan. 7, 2000.

34. Calculated from data in Harold W. Stanley and Richard G. Niemi, *Vital Statistics on American Politics 1997–1998* (Washington, D.C.: Congressional Quarterly Press, 1999), 288–89. See also Lyons, Scheb, and Stair, *Government and Politics in Tennessee,* 32–34.

35. John J. Dinan, *The American State Constitutional Tradition* (Lawrence: University Press of Kansas, 2006), chap. 2.

36. Ibid.

37. Interview with Matt Kisber, Jan. 5, 2000.

38. Poll results provided by William Lyons of the University of Tennessee.

39. *State Tax Notes,* Oct. 4, 1999.

40. Interview with Tom Humphrey, Jan. 6, 2000; interview with Bobbie Patray, Jan. 6, 2000; Bill Carey, "Lottery Firms Keep Close Eye on Debate," *Nashville Tennessean,* Jan. 28, 1998.

41. Interview with Roy Herron, Jan. 7, 2000.

42. "Sundquist May Gamble on State Lottery For Scholarships," *Tennessee Journal,* Nov. 3, 1997.

43. Richard Locker, "House Approves Lottery Convention Vote/Senate Success Linked To Annexation Issue," *Memphis Commercial Appeal,* Apr. 16, 1998.

44. Under the Tennessee constitution, six years must intervene between constitutional conventions.

45. Richard Locker, "Action on Lottery Stalled, But Supporters Hopeful," *Memphis Commercial Appeal,* Feb. 25, 1998. Cohen's argument had historical roots. The 1834 constitutional convention, ignoring its mandate to focus on taxation and judicial competence, wrote an entirely new constitution. Lyons, Scheb, and Stair, *Government and Politics in Tennessee,* 30–31.

46. Paula Wade, "Lawmakers to 'Put Up or Shut Up' on Taxes," *Memphis Commercial Appeal,* Jan. 23, 2000.

47. Jack L. Walker, "The Diffusion of Innovation Among the American States," *American Political Science Review* 63 (Sept. 1969): 880–99.

48. Interview with Matt Kisber, Jan. 5, 2000.

49. Ibid.

50. Bonna de la Cruz, "Casinos Favored, As Well As Lottery," *Nashville Tennessean,* Jan. 8, 2001; John Commins, "Lottery Backers Betting on Support for Referendum Issue," *Chattanooga Times Free Press,* Feb. 4, 2001.

51. Richard Locker, "In New Senate Membership, Lottery Stands Its Best Chance," *Memphis Commercial Appeal,* Jan. 14, 2001.

52. Tom Humphrey, "Senate Panel OKs Lottery Proposal," *Knoxville News-Sentinel,* Jan. 31, 2001.

53. Bonna de la Cruz, "Lottery Would Bring Casinos, Bingo, Foes Say," *Nashville Tennessean,* Feb. 6, 2001; Commins, "Lottery Backers"; Bonna de la Cruz, "Would Casinos Follow a Lottery?" *Nashville Tennessean,* Feb. 11, 2001.

54. David Firestone, "Free-Tuition Program Transforms a University," *New York Times,* Feb. 4, 2001.

55. Rebecca Ferrar, "Tennessee Leaps Lottery Hurdle," *Knoxville News-Sentinel,* Feb. 8, 2001.

56. Richard Locker, "House Vote on State Lottery Referendum Scheduled for Wednesday," *Memphis Commercial Appeal,* Feb. 9, 2001; Rebecca Ferrar, "House Gets Lottery Bill Rolling," *Knoxville News-Sentinel,* Feb. 9, 2001.

57. Jane DuBose, "Tennessee Lottery Vote Likely," *Atlanta Journal-Constitution,* Feb. 14, 2001; Tom Sharp, "Lottery Gets 15 Votes in Senate," *Chattanooga Times Free Press,* Feb. 6, 2001.

58. Bonna de la Cruz, "Georgian Cites Scholarships' Advantages," *Nashville Tennessean,* Dec. 14, 2001. See, e.g., Gary Tanner and Dorie Turner, "Odds Favor Heated Lottery Battle," *Chattanooga Times Free Press,* Feb. 3, 2002.

59. Jim Balloch, "Lottery Just Ducky with Boys, Girls Clubs," *Knoxville News-Sentinel,* Oct. 29, 2002.

60. Rebecca Ferrar, "Lottery Vote Won't Open Door for Casinos," *Knoxville News-Sentinel,* Apr. 27, 2001. So sensitive were legislators to their constituents' fears about casino gambling that they also enacted a bill declaring that casino gambling is against the public policy in Tennessee. Duren Cheek, "House and Senate Pass Gambling Bill to Prohibit Casinos," *Nashville Tennessean,* June 30, 2001.

61. Richard Locker, "Lottery Proposal Splits Anti-Tax Forces," *Memphis Commercial Appeal,* Sept. 11, 2001; John Shiffman, "Lottery Money Is No Jackpot for Budget Woes," *Nashville Tennessean,* Jan. 26, 2002.

62. Bill Poovey, "Battle Lines Drawn Over Lottery Referendum," *Memphis Commercial Appeal,* May 26, 2002.

63. Rebecca Ferrar, "Proponents of State Lottery Form Coalition to Organize Campaign for Passage," *Knoxville News-Sentinel,* Feb. 16, 2001; Ferrar, "55% Say They Will Vote for Lottery," *Knoxville News-Sentinel,* Nov. 11, 2001.

64. "Fears of Another Rocky Top Scandal Shroud Lottery Issue," *Memphis Commercial Appeal,* Feb. 23, 2002; Mickie Anderson, "Provision for Charity Causes Lottery Worries," *Memphis Commercial Appeal,* Nov. 3, 2002; Michael Cass, "'Legal Jargon' Concerns Lottery Supporters," *Nashville Tennessean,* Nov. 5, 2002.

65. Rebecca Ferrar, "Anti-Lottery Campaign Circling Its Wagons," *Knoxville News-Sentinel,* Nov. 15, 2001; Tom Humphrey, "Lottery Vote Could Sway Governor Race," *Knoxville News-Sentinel,* Nov. 3, 2002.

66. Paula Wade, "Lottery Foes to Wage Costly Battle," *Memphis Commercial Appeal,* Feb. 16, 2001; Rebecca Ferrar, "Betting on Education," *Knoxville News-Sentinel,* Nov. 11, 2001; Bonna de la Cruz, "Bredesen Wants Lottery Proceeds to Support Would-Be Teachers," *Nashville Tennessean,* Oct. 15, 2002.

67. Rebecca Ferrar, "Lottery Foes Hope to Ride on Coattails of Hilleary," *Knoxville News-Sentinel,* Apr. 13, 2002; Larry Daughtrey, "As Bad as a Lottery May Be, Campaign Against It Is Out of Control," *Nashville Tennessean,* Apr. 21, 2002; Bonna de la Cruz, "Analysts Doubt Lottery Affecting Governor's Race," *Nashville Tennessean,* Oct. 5, 2002; Lela Garlington, "Senator, Pastor Debate Lottery," *Memphis Commercial Appeal,* Apr. 15, 2002; Georgiana Vines, "Lottery Foes Differ on Rhetoric, Not Goals, Tyree Says," *Knoxville News-Sentinel,* Apr. 20, 2002; Rebecca Ferrar, "Lottery Foes Hope to Ride on Coattails of Hilleary," *Knoxville News-Sentinel,* Apr. 13, 2002.

68. Jay Hamburg, "Poll Finds Support for Lottery," *Nashville Tennessean,* July 9, 2002; Mickie Anderson, "Lottery Rivals Go Tit for Tat in Debate," *Memphis Commercial Appeal,* Oct. 15, 2002; Anderson, "Lottery Foes Ante Up 4½ Times More Cash Than Backers," *Memphis Commercial Appeal,* Oct. 30, 2002.

69. Ashley M. Heher, "Lottery Opponent Says Effort 'Not in Good Shape,'" *Chattanooga Times Free Press,* Sept. 20, 2002; Tom Humphrey, "Poll Shows Lottery's Support Slipping," *Knoxville News-Sentinel,* Oct. 22, 2002; Michael Cass, "Lottery Opponents Gain in Poll," *Nashville Tennessean,* Oct. 29, 2002; Tom Humphrey, "Lottery Vote Could Sway Governor Race," *Knoxville*

*News-Sentinel,* Nov. 3, 2002; Mickie Anderson, "Lottery Turns Hot Page at Library," *Memphis Commercial Appeal,* Oct. 23, 2002.

70. Duren Cheek, "Lottery Easily Approved as Voter Results Verified," *Nashville Tennessean,* Dec. 3, 2002; Mickie Anderson and Richard Locker, "Details Left to Lawmakers with Voters' OK of Lottery," *Memphis Commercial Appeal,* Nov. 7, 2002; Michael Cass, "Several Factors Propelled Lottery Proposal at Polls," *Nashville Tennessean,* Nov. 7, 2002.

71. Jacinthia Jones, "New Baptist Leader Plans to Continue Fight on Lottery," *Memphis Commercial Appeal,* Nov. 14, 2002.

72. Georgiana Vines, "Lawmakers Going Down to Georgia for Lottery Lessons," *Knoxville News-Sentinel,* Dec. 16, 2002.

73. Duren Cheek, "Bills for Gambling Events in Limbo," *Nashville Tennessean,* Feb. 24, 2003; Richard Locker, "House OK's Bill Setting Up Lottery," *Memphis Commercial Appeal,* May 8, 2003; Steve Cohen, "Keep HOPE Alive," *Memphis Flyer,* Mar. 14, 2003.

74. Richard Locker, "Plan Outlines State Lottery Scholarships," *Memphis Commercial Appeal,* Feb. 19, 2003.

75. "Lottery Scholarship Bill Goes to Governor for Signature," *Nashville Tennessean,* May 22, 2003.

76. Bonna de la Cruz, "Harper Calls Cohen a Liar in Debate on Lottery Delay," *Nashville Tennessean,* Mar. 7, 2003; Bonna de la Cruz and Duren Cheek, "Cohen Fights Lottery 'Pork,'" *Nashville Tennessean,* Mar. 26, 2003; Bonna de la Cruz, "Lottery Forces, Governor Agree on Equal Awards," *Nashville Tennessean,* Mar. 28, 2003; Larry Daughtrey, "Bigger Issue for Lawmakers Ought to Be Keeping the Lottery Clean," *Nashville Tennessean,* Mar. 30, 2003; Tom Humphrey, "No Dice Yet for Bill on Lottery," *Knoxville News-Sentinel,* May 26, 2003; Sam Youngman and Richard Locker, "Cohen 'Read the Tea Leaves,'" *Memphis Commercial Appeal,* June 1, 2003.

77. Bonna de la Cruz, "Big Games Enter Lottery's Big Picture," *Nashville Tennessean,* Aug. 12, 2003.

78. Richard Locker, "Lottery Board Rejects Georgia Offer," *Memphis Commercial Appeal,* Sept. 4, 2003; Duren Cheek, "Legality of Tennessee-Georgia Lottery Partnership Questioned," *Nashville Tennessean,* Aug. 14, 2003.

79. Larry Daughtry, "Bredesen May Be Putting Brakes on Runaway Gambling Train," *Nashville Tennessean,* Mar. 7, 2004; Tom Humphrey, "Can State Become Gambling Capital?" *Knoxville News-Sentinel,* Mar. 7, 2004; Duren Cheek, "Charity Fund-raising Bill Approved, Sent to Governor," *Nashville Tennessean,* Apr. 6, 2004.

80. Richard Locker, "Lottery = $863 Million," *Memphis Commercial Appeal,* Jan. 21, 2005; Jody Callahan, "Bredesen Talks Up Using Lottery Funds for Pre-K," *Memphis Commercial Appeal,* Feb. 17, 2005; Richard Locker, "Cohen Lashes Out at Bredesen Over Lottery," *Memphis Commercial Appeal,* Feb. 4, 2005; Richard Locker, "Legislation Ends Session," *Memphis Commercial Appeal,* May 29, 2005. Another potential issue concerns the distribution of lottery-funded scholarships, which early research indicates "benefits . . . disproportionately wealthy and better-educated" families (Katie Frink, "The Tennessee Lottery Education Scholarship and Its Effect on Income Distribution," *Rhodes Journal of Regional Studies* 4 [2007]).

81. Dorie Tenner, "Many Students Lose Scholarships," *Chattanooga Times Free Press*, Feb. 28, 2006.

82. The scholarships increased from $3,300 to $3,800 at four-year colleges, from $1,650 to $1,900 at community colleges, and from $1,300 to $1,500 at state technical schools. Richard Locker, "Bredesen Hails Budget's Passage," *Memphis Commercial Appeal*, May 27, 2006.

## Chapter 6

1. The ban appears in Article 19, section 13. For court decisions, see *Longstreth v. Cook*, 215 Ark. 72, 220 S.W.2d 433 (1949); and *Scott v. Dunaway*, 228 Ark. 943, 311 S.W.2d 305 (1958).

2. Rodney Bowers, "Gambling Has Rocky Record in Arkansas," *Arkansas Democrat-Gazette*, Aug. 2, 2004; John Ward, *The Arkansas Rockefeller* (Baton Rouge: Louisiana State University Press, 1978), 35.

3. Ed Reid and Ovid Demaris, *The Greenfelt Jungle* (New York: Pocket Books, 1964).

4. Cathy Kenzinger Urwin, *Agenda for Reform: Winthrop Rockefeller as Governor of Arkansas, 1967–71* (Fayetteville: University of Arkansas Press, 1991), 71–72, 106-8.

5. John Dombrink and William N. Thompson, *The Last Resort: Success and Failure in Campaigns for Casinos* (Reno: University of Nevada Press, 1990), 149.

6. Ibid.; Diane D. Blair and Jay Barth, *Arkansas Politics and Government: Do the People Decide?* 2d ed. (Lincoln: University of Nebraska Press, 2005), chap. 13.

7. "Letter to Bugie Hastings" Sept. 18, 1984; and "Letter to Mrs. Harry O. Dunn," Sept. 13, 1985, unprocessed materials, Bill Clinton State Government Project, Central Arkansas Library System, Little Rock, Arkansas; "State Representative Lottery Initiative," *Arkansas Democrat-Gazette*, Feb. 2, 1986; Bob Wells, "Lottery is Easy Money," *Arkansas Democrat-Gazette*, May 21, 1986.

8. "He'd Favor Lottery Vote, Clinton Says," *Arkansas Democrat-Gazette*, Apr. 25, 1989; Scott Morris, "Hybrid Amendment Deemed Too Chancy," *Arkansas Democrat-Gazette*, Mar. 8, 1989.

9. "Betting on a Lottery Amendment," *Arkansas Democrat-Gazette*, June 26, 1988.

10. "Voters Favor State Lottery, Poll Indicates," *Arkansas Democrat-Gazette*, Mar. 30, 1990; Susan Traylor, "South Takes a Chance on Profit from Gambling: Economics a Big Factor in Push for Lotteries," *Arkansas Democrat-Gazette*, Aug. 19, 1990.

11. Interview with Eric Jackson, Mar. 8, 2001; "Official: Ark. Can't Be 'Island' in Gaming," *Memphis Commercial Appeal*, Oct. 28, 1993.

12. Interview with Larry Page, Mar. 9, 2001.

13. Noel Oman, "Odds Against Casinos, Poll Shows But Charitable Bingo Looks Like Even Bet," *Arkansas Democrat-Gazette*, Oct. 14, 1994.

14. Southland stayed out, partly because of the cost of another campaign and partly because the legislature in 1995 reduced the state's tax on the handle from 7 to 3 percent (Grant Tennille, "Tax Break Greases Way for Southland Gamblers," *Arkansas Democrat-Gazette*, Feb. 19, 1995).

15. Robert Yates, "Status Whoa or Status Go? Amendment 4 Plan Better than Even-Money Favorite among Oaklawn Horsemen," *Arkansas Democrat-Gazette*, Nov. 3, 1996; Michelle Hillier, *Arkansas Democrat-Gazette*, Jan. 24, 1996.

16. Elizabeth Caldwell, *Arkansas Democrat-Gazette*, Jan. 19, 1996; interview with Larry Page, Mar. 9, 2001.

17. Interview with Larry Page, Mar. 9, 2001; Elizabeth Caldwell, "Common Cause Outlines Objections to 2 Proposed Gambling Amendments," *Arkansas Democrat-Gazette,* Mar. 30, 1996.

18. Joan I. Duffy, "Huckabee Opposes Ark.-Run Lottery; Coulter Replies Issue Worth Vote," *Memphis Commercial Appeal,* July 15, 1993.

19. Michelle Hillier, "Lack of Theme Parks, Casinos Hurting Tourism, State Panel Told," *Arkansas Democrat-Gazette,* May 17, 1996; Elizabeth Caldwell, "Two Months Before Election, Gambling Interests Are Spending Big," *Arkansas Democrat-Gazette,* Aug. 24, 1996; Michelle Hillier, "Firm with Ties to Mississippi Casinos Behind Arkansas Anti-Gambling Ads," *Arkansas Democrat-Gazette,* Oct. 3, 1996; interview with Eric Jackson, Mar. 8, 2001.

20. Rodney Bowers, "Casino Amendment Foe Reports Money from Gambling Interests," *Arkansas Democrat-Gazette,* Nov. 5, 1996.

21. Rodney Bowers, "Poll: Gambling Measures' Odds Pretty Even," *Arkansas Democrat-Gazette,* Oct. 19, 1996; interview with Eric Jackson, Mar. 8, 2001.

22. Act 877, a new state law enacted in 1999, had streamlined the initiative review process to prevent a recurrence of last-minute removals of initiatives from the ballot.

23. Interview with Larry Page, Mar. 9, 2001; interview with Scott Trotter, Mar. 9, 2001.

24. Bartholomew Sullivan, "Arkansas Voters Face Divisive Gambling Initiative," *Memphis Commercial Appeal,* Oct. 30, 2000.

25. David Flaum, "Experts Betting Lottery Won't Rattle Tunica—But Dog Track in Ark. Will Feel Tenn. Bite," *Memphis Commercial Appeal,* Nov. 7, 2002; Laura Kellams, "Racetrack Video-Poker Bill Turns Up in House," *Arkansas Democrat-Gazette,* Apr. 3, 2003.

26. Michael R. Wickline, "State Chamber of Commerce Favors Gambling Bill," *Arkansas Democrat-Gazette,* Mar. 19, 2003; Laura Kellams, "Lottery Advocate Seeks Ballot Title," *Arkansas Democrat-Gazette,* June 11, 2003; Laura Kellams, "Push Against Gambling in State Tied to Casinos," *Arkansas Democrat-Gazette,* Aug. 1, 2003; Michael Rowett and Michael R. Wickline, "Video Poker Loses in House," *Arkansas Democrat-Gazette,* Apr. 4, 2003; "Gambling Initiatives Seem Unlikely to Pass," Associated Press (Little Rock), Mar. 31, 2003; Kellams, "Push Against Gambling."

27. Michael R. Wickline, "Anti-Gambling Calls Tie Up Senate Lines," *Arkansas Democrat-Gazette,* Dec. 11, 2003; Laura Kellams, "Video Poker Is a Bad Bet, Officials Told," *Arkansas Democrat-Gazette,* Jan. 20, 2005.

28. James Jefferson, "Senate Sends House Bill Expanding Video Gambling at Two Arkansas Tracks," Associated Press State and Local Wire, LexisNexis, Mar. 10, 2005; Laura Kellams, "Huckabee to Let Bill on Gambling Ride," *Arkansas Democrat-Gazette,* Mar. 17, 2005; interview with Larry Page, Nov. 18, 2005.

29. Huckabee's explanation for not fighting the bill was disingenuous. While declaring that he opposed it, he said that to veto the bill would be "futile" because, constitutionally, the Arkansas legislature can override a governor's veto by a simple majority vote. See Laura Kellams, "Huckabee to Let Bill on Gambling Ride," *Arkansas Democrat-Gazette,* Mar. 17, 2005. But the vote for passage had been close enough in the Senate that a fight by the governor might have made a difference.

30. Michael R. Wickline, "Tracks Slow to Propose Gambling Votes," *Arkansas Democrat-Gazette,* May 9, 2005; Rodney Bowers and Kenneth Heard, "Racetracks Putting Money on Machines," *Arkansas Democrat-Gazette,* Nov. 6, 2005; Pamela Ferkins, "Gambling Votes Down to Wire," *Memphis Commercial Appeal,* Nov. 7, 2005.

31. Page explains that his organization does not get heavily involved in local referenda, in part because its resources are insufficient and in part because such referenda "are driven by turnout and local churches can get their people out better than we can." Interview with Page, Nov. 18, 2005.

32. Rodney Bowers, "Group: Law Allowing Gambling Votes Suspect," *Arkansas Democrat-Gazette,* Nov. 10, 2005; Bowers, "Lawsuits Challenge Racetrack Elections," *Arkansas Democrat-Gazette,* Dec. 6, 2005; Associated Press State and Local Wire, "Group Appealing Ark. Gambling Decision," LexisNexis, July 10, 2006; Associated Press State and Local Wire, "Ark. Board Fails to Give Final OK to Electronic Games at Track," LexisNexis, July 7, 2006.

33. Page says that he and others would be inclined to fight the Racing Commission in court on that basis. Interview with Page, Nov. 18, 2005.

34. Rodney Bowers, "With Betting Rules Set, Tracks Keen to Get Gear," *Arkansas Democrat-Gazette,* Aug. 2, 2006.

35. "Gambling Opponents Say Their Predictions Are Coming True," Associated Press State and Local Wire, Mar. 9, 2006; Traci Dungan, "Developer to Seek City's Blessing for Casino," *Arkansas Democrat-Gazette,* Apr. 10, 2006; Dungan, "Fort Smith Mayor Rallies 600 against Casino," *Arkansas Democrat-Gazette,* July 7, 2006.

36. Seth Blomeley, "Huckabee, Rival Leery of Lotteries," *Arkansas Democrat-Gazette,* Aug. 8, 2002.

37. Peggy Harris, "Family Group Argues Against Ark. Lottery," *Memphis Commercial Appeal,* Dec. 13, 2002; Kelly Wiese, "Let People Decide on Lottery, Legislator Urges," Associated Press (Little Rock), Feb. 20, 2003.

38. Quoted in Chris Hathorn, "Explaining the Enigma: Understanding the Failure of Further Legalized Gambling in Arkansas," *Rhodes Journal of Regional Studies* 1 (2004): 61–95.

39. Seth Blomeley, "51.9 % in Poll See State Lottery as the Ticket to Fund Programs," *Arkansas Democrat-Gazette,* Aug. 21, 2002.

40. Rainer Sabin, "Bill to Legalize Bingo Awaiting More Sponsors," Associated Press State and Local Wire, Jan. 13, 2005; Seth Blomeley, "Bingo on Ballot Closer for State," *Arkansas Democrat-Gazette,* Apr. 6, 2005.

41. Andrew DeMillo, "Gambling Foes Mum on Charitable Bingo Proposal," Associated Press State and Local Wire, LexisNexis, July 31, 2006.

42. Interview with Larry Page, Mar. 9, 2001.

43. Interview with Eric Jackson, Mar. 8, 2001; interview with Scott Trotter, Mar. 8, 2001.

44. Abbey Begun, *Gambling* (Wylie, Tex.: Information Plus, 2000).

45. "Poll Shows Voters Split on Allowing Casinos," *Arkansas Democrat-Gazette,* Sept. 19, 1996.

46. Michael R. Wickline, "AFL-CIO Backs Gambling Proposal," *Arkansas Democrat-Gazette,* Apr. 11, 2006; Warwick Sabin, "Casino Amendment Proposal Pulled Until 2008," *Arkansas Times,* June 22, 2006.

47. Harold W. Stanley and Richard G. Niemi. *Vital Statistics on American Politics: 1997–1998* (Washington, D.C.: Congressional Quarterly Press, 1998), 288–90; interview with Scott Trotter, Mar. 8, 2001; Associated Press, "Gambling Initiatives Seem Unlikely to Pass," LexisNexis, Mar. 31, 2003.

## Chapter 7

1. John Samuel Ezell, *Fortune's Merry Wheel: The Lottery in America* (Cambridge, Mass.: Harvard University Press, 1960), 253.

2. T. Harry Williams, *Huey Long: A Biography* (New York: Knopf, 1970), 341-44.

3. Richard D. White, *Kingfish: The Reign of Huey P. Long* (New York: Random House, 2006), 221-22.

4. Tyler Bridges, *Bad Bet on the Bayou: The Rise of Gambling in Louisiana and the Fall of Governor Edwin Edwards* (New York: Farrar, Strauss, and Giroux, 2001), 16.

5. Grevemberg's account of his efforts may be found in Francis C. Grevemberg, *My Wars: Mobsters, Gambling and Corruption* (Lafayette, La.: Beau Bayou Pub. Co., 2006).

6. Ibid., 26.

7. Wayne Parent, *Inside the Carnival: Unmasking Louisiana Politics* (Baton Rouge: Louisiana State University Press, 2004), 23.

8. Royal Brightbill, "Legislature Can Balance Budget Without Governor's Help," United Press International, LexisNexis, May 3, 1986.

9. United Press International, "Edwards to Stump State for Gambling Proposals," LexisNexis, Jan. 31, 1986.

10. Interview with Charles E. "Buddy" Roemer III, May 2, 2002.

11. Interview with Raymond "LaLa" LaLonde, May 2, 2002.

12. Ibid.

13. Ibid.

14. Ibid.

15. David Landry and Joseph Parker, "The Louisiana Political Culture," in *Louisiana Politics: Festival in a Labyrinth,* ed. James Bolner (Baton Rouge: Louisiana State University Press, 1982), 2.

16. Interview with Ken Ward, May 2, 2002.

17. Bridges, *Bad Bet on the Bayou,* 41.

18. Interview with Ward, May 2, 2002.

19. Interview with Roemer, May 2, 2002.

20. Ibid.

21. "Roemer: Don't Repeal Riverboat Gambling," Associated Press State and Local Wire, LexisNexis, Nov. 23, 1998.

22. Bridges, *Bad Bet on the Bayou,* 47.

23. Ibid., 44.

24. Ibid., 45 .

25. Interview with LaLonde, May 2, 2002.

26. Interview with Roemer, May 2, 2002.

27. Bridges, *Bad Bet on the Bayou,* 39.

28. Ibid., 54.

29. Ibid., 58–59.

30. Ibid., 64.

31. Ibid., 66–69.

32. Interview with Roemer, May 2, 2002.

33. Greg Garland, "Majority in Poll Feel State Has Too Much Gambling," *Baton Rouge Advocate*, Jan. 14, 1994.

34. Bridges, *Bad Bet on the Bayou*, 267; and James Gill, "Gambling Foes Alter Their Views," *New Orleans Times-Picayune*, Feb. 19, 2000.

35. Bridges, *Bad Bet on the Bayou*, 304–7.

36. Ibid., 129.

37. Susan Finch, "Ex-Governor, Others Lose Latest Appeal," *New Orleans Times-Picayune*, Mar. 2, 2006.

38. "Riverboats, New Orleans Casino Off List for Possible Tax Hikes," Associated Press State and Local Wire, Mar. 24, 2005.

39. Alan Sayre, "Louisiana Casinos Make Something of an October Rebound," Associated Press State and Local Wire, LexisNexis, Nov. 15, 2005; Sayre, "Storms or Not, Gambling Take Keeps Rolling," Associated Press State and Local Wire, LexisNexis, Dec. 25, 2005; "Louisiana's Gaming Revenue Run Continues in May," *New Orleans City Business*, June 26, 2006.

40. Bridges, *Bad Bet on the Bayou*, 94–95.

41. Ibid., 100.

42. Caesars was dropped from the deal and so, eventually, was Hemmeter.

43. James Gill, "Can Anyone Learn from Our Mistakes in Casino Mess?" *New Orleans Times-Picayune*, Jan. 12, 1997.

44. Richard Slawsky, "New Orleans Ads New Chapter to Long History of Gambling," *New Orleans City Business*, Apr. 25, 2005.

45. Calculated from data in "Louisiana's Gaming Revenue Run Continues in May," *New Orleans City Business*, June 26, 2006.

46. Rebecca Dana, "Full House: In 10 Years Video Poker Has Changed the Face of Louisiana," *New Orleans Times-Picayune*, June 30, 2002.

47. Frank Donze, "Gambling Issue's Meaning Debated," *New Orleans Times-Picayune*, Sept. 10, 1996.

48. Christopher Cooper, "Foster, Morial Signals Mixed," *New Orleans Times-Picayune*, Oct. 27, 1996.

49. Natalie Gott, "Video Poker Machines Shut Down," Associated Press State and Local Wire, LexisNexis, July 2, 1999.

50. Alan Sayre, "Video Poker Take Up Along Truck Stops," Associated Press State and Local Wire, LexisNexis, July 20, 2005.

51. "La. Gets $110.6 Million from Lottery in 1994," *Baton Rouge Advocate*, Dec. 30, 1993; Chris Frink, "Lottery a Jackpot for State," *Baton Rouge Morning Advocate*, July 24, 2004.

52. Scott Dyer, "Lottery Officials See Sales Slump Ending," *Baton Rouge Advocate*, Sept. 6, 1994.

53. *Seminole Tribe v. Florida* 517 U.S. 44 (1996).

54. Peter Whoriskey, "A Tribe Takes Grim Satisfaction in Abramoff's Fall," *Washington Post,* Jan. 7, 2006; U.S. Senate, Committee on Indian Affairs, *"Gimme Five"—Investigation of Tribal Lobbying Matters: Final Report* (June 26, 2006), part 1, chap. 2. The amount paid by the Coushattas for these services was universally regarded as wildly excessive, and its revelation in the news media set in motion the events that led to the Abramoff scandals in 2005 and 2006. See Matthew Continetti, *The K Street Gang: The Rise and Fall of the Republican Machine* (New York: Doubleday, 2006), chap. 9.

55. James Gill, "Foster Has One More Bet Before He Folds," *New Orleans Times-Picayune,* Nov. 21, 2003; John Solomon and Sharon Theimer, "Lawmakers Pressured Interior While Getting Donations from Tribes," Associated Press State and Local Wire, LexisNexis, Nov. 17, 2005.

56. "Jena Band Proposes Grant Parish Casino to Blanco," *Casino Magazine,* Apr. 22, 2004.

57. U.S. Senate, *"Gimme Five"—Investigation of Tribal Lobbying Matters: Final Report,* part 1, chaps. 2 and 5. See also Continetti, *The K Street Gang,* chap. 7; and Michael Isikoff, Holly Bailey, and Evan Thomas, "A Washington Tidal Wave," *Newsweek,* Jan. 16, 2006, 40–43.

58. Suzanne Gamboa, "Texas Tribe Names Abramoff, Reed in Civil Suit," Associated Press State and Local Wire, July 12, 2006. Abramoff was also a defendant in the lawsuit.

59. Christopher Cooper, "Bill Eliminating La. Gambling Faces Tough Odds," *New Orleans Times-Picayune,* Apr. 16, 1997.

## Conclusion

1. For purposes of this study, the District of Columbia, which has a lottery, is counted as a state.

2. Republican gains continued to mount through the 1990s and early 2000s. By 2004, eighteen of twenty-two southern senators, seven of eleven southern governors, and 63 percent of all southern House members were Republicans.

3. Earlier campaigns for lotteries in Florida and Virginia were not led by the governors of those states. See Charles T. Clotfelter and Philip J. Cook, *Selling Hope: State Lotteries in America* (Cambridge, Mass.: Harvard University Press, 1989), 154-58.

4. The four southern states not covered in this book—Florida, North Carolina, Texas, and Virginia—all have lotteries but not casinos.

5. An obvious second question is: What should happen in the area of legalized gambling? We began our research without strong opinions on the rightness or wrongness of various forms of gambling but with a vague sense that casinos were a more dubious proposition than lotteries. In popular culture, casinos have sketchy associations (gangsters, desperate people losing all their savings) that lotteries (play the lottery!) do not. Our growing familiarity with the subject, however, reversed this initial impression. As state-operated institutions, lotteries place the government in the business of encouraging people to gamble and profiting from their losses. The 20 percent of the population who account for more than 80 percent of lottery ticket sales tend to be poor and uneducated, the last people the state should be exploiting (Charles T. Clotfelter, et al., *State Lotteries at the Turn of the Century: Report to the National Gambling Impact Study Commission,* 1999.

This study is now available online at www.pubpol.duke.edu/people/faculty/clotfelter/lottrep.pdf.) To the extent that the benefits of southern lotteries have been linked to college scholarships (a worthy purpose, but one that could be funded by taxes), they have gone disproportionately to the children of the middle- and upper-middle classes. A policy in which poor people pay the college tuition of prosperous people seems almost self-evidently bad to us. What's more, with lottery tickets available at every gas station and convenience store, kids find it all too easy to gamble in lottery states.

In contrast, the state doesn't lend its moral authority to casinos by owning them; it merely allows them to operate. Unlike lotteries, casinos represent capital investments, generate jobs, may promote tourism, and effectively screen out underage gamblers. To be sure, casinos, with their charged atmospheres, free drinks, high-stakes table games, and "comps" for people who bet a lot, are a dangerous setting for anyone with a tendency to gamble excessively. The economic benefits of casinos tend to be concentrated where they are located, while the economic and social costs tend to be exported diffusely into the towns and cities to which gamblers return when they go home. But as a tool for economic development, casinos offer opportunities that lotteries do not.

For a fuller statement of our opinions about gambling, see John Lyman Mason and Michael Nelson, *Governing Gambling* (New York: Century Foundation Press / Brookings Institution, 2001).

# INDEX